FUNDAMENTALISM
in
American Religion
1880 - 1950

A forty-five-volume facsimile series
reproducing often extremely rare material
documenting the development of one of the
major religious movements of our time

■ *Edited by*
Joel A. Carpenter
Billy Graham Center, Wheaton College
■ *Advisory Editors*
Donald W. Dayton,
Northern Baptist Theological Seminary
George M. Marsden,
Duke University
Mark A. Noll,
Wheaton College
Grant Wacker,
University of North Carolina

A GARLAND SERIES

■ Inside History of First Baptist Church, Fort Worth, and Temple Baptist Church, Detroit

Life Story of Dr. J. Frank Norris

Garland Publishing, Inc.
New York & London 1988

For a list of the titles in this series see the final pages of this volume. This facsimile has been made from a copy in the Billy Graham Center of Wheaton College.

Library of Congress Cataloging-in-Publication Data

Inside history of First Baptist Church, Fort Worth, and Temple
  Baptist Church, Detroit : life story of Dr. J. Frank Norris.
      p. cm. -- (Fundamentalism in American religion, 1880-1950)
      ISBN 0-8240-5035-5 (alk. paper)
   1. Norris, J. Frank (John Frank), 1877-1952. 2. First Baptist
Church (Fort Worth, Tex.)--History. 3. Temple Baptist Church
(Detroit, Mich.)--History. 4. Baptists--United States--Clergy--
Biography. 5. Fort Worth (Tex.)--Church history. 6. Detroit
(Mich.)--Church history. I. Series
BX6495.N59I57 1988
286'.5--dc19   88-9781
   [B]   CIP

Design by Valerie Mergentime
Printed on acid-free, 250-year-life paper
Manufactured in the United States of America

EDITOR'S NOTE

■ No assessment of American fundamentalism can avoid J. Frank Norris (1877-1952) who personified the movement's more extreme wing. This sensational Texas Baptist preacher held simultaneous pastorates in Fort Worth and Detroit, and fostered an internally divided but vigorous movement of independent Baptist churches. Today those churches boast several million members and some of the largest congregations in the nation. Fervently separatist in ecclesiology, and ultraconservative in theology and politics, the heirs of Norris form a large portion of the new religious right's base of support. This volume is a compendium of stenographically recorded sermons by Norris, accounts and testimonials by his associates, and a variety of other documents. It is a valuable introduction to this magnetic and disturbing preacher.

J.A.C.

DR. J. FRANK NORRIS

Rev. Gilbert Wilson, Associate Pastor, First Baptist Church, Fort Worth.

THE VICTORY AT THE END OF A LONG WAR

Dr. R. C. Buckner was president of the Baptist General Convention of Texas for twenty-two years. He built up the greatest orphanage in America.

BUCKNER'S ORPHANS HOME

Dallas, Texas, Dec. 19, 1918.

Pastor J. Frank Norris:

I rejoice in the triumph in the late Tarrant County election, Fort Worth and all. I believe the late victory should be attributed to you more than any one else. Truly you laid the foundation and others have builded on it, and more attention may be directed to the rattle in nailing on the last shingle over the structure, but J. Frank Norris did more work and the most effectual work as a wise master builder, heroic and untiring in everything from the bed rock all the way up till the Hall of Fame was completed. Honor to whom honor is due, and with me J. Frank Norris stock is not tamely at par but scores a very high premium.

Accept my congratulation. You fought and bled, and instead of having died, you are today recognized as mightily alive—you are a "live wire."

Your friend all the way through,

(Signed) R. C. Buckner.

Regular Sunday Congregation of the First Baptist Church, Fort Worth

REPORT FOR THE 3 YEARS WITH JOINT PASTORATE OF DR. NORRIS OF FIRST BAPTIST AND TEMPLE BAPTIST CHURCHES

There were 6,193 additions during this period.

There was raised for all purposes $421,333.62.

There was issued 6,376,500 copies of the Fundamentalist.

The pastor travelled 119,000 miles during this period.

There was a total of over 18,000 attendance in the special Bible Schools during this period.

The combined membership at both churches is over 15,000.

SINCLAIR LEWIS ATTENDS FIRST BAPTIST CHURCH

Says: "I Satisfied a Desire of a Great Many Years Standing." "I Never Before Have Seen So Many People at Church at Once."

The Monday morning paper of the Fort Worth Star-Telegram has a large article occupying about one-quarter of the page, containing the report of an interview with Sinclair Lewis who is visiting Fort Worth to lecture. Upon being asked by the Star-Telegram reporter where he spent Sunday morning he replied:

"What did I do this morning? I satisfied a desire of a great many years standing—I went to hear Dr. J. Frank Norris preach. I admire the eloquence and vigor of Dr. Norris and have wanted to hear him. I have never seen before so many people at church at once."

Audience in New Auditorium, Temple Baptist Church.

INSIDE HISTORY OF THE TWO CHURCHES, FIRST BAPTIST CHURCH, FORT WORTH, TEXAS, TEMPLE BAPTIST CHURCH, DETROIT, MICHIGAN

The two largest congregations in the South and North, respectively, largest in membership, largest in Sunday School, greater attendance upon their regular services, and most important of all, people being saved in large numbers "daily" in New Testament fashion—These brief chapters on the inside history are given with the hope that some discouraged pastor or defeated layman may "Thank God and take courage."

If the reader thinks the language is often too plain and blunt let him remember that David did not go against Goliath with a bottle of perfume or did John the Baptist answer the Sadducees and Pharisees with a pearl handled pen knife, "But wisdom is justified of all her children." And remember "That a notable miracle hath been done . . . is manifest . . . we cannot deny."

With churches as with individuals, do men gather grapes of thorns or figs of thistles?

In this day of defeatism, downgradism, modernism, communism, and atheism, there is but one need, and that need is to come back to the God of our fathers.

This book is composed of chapters and addresses given without regard to sequence or chronological order. In the main the addresses as published were given when the fires were hot, and in times of great crises, and the pointed arrows are left as first delivered.

Dr. T. T. Shields of Toronto, Ontario, Canada, Writes as Follows on the First Baptist Church, Fort Worth

"It is always a tonic for jaded spirits to come into the presence of Dr. Norris. He is always bubbling over like a mountain torrent, and radiates energy like the summer sun. We do not know much about the constitution of radium, but when it was discovered years ago by the Curies it was hailed as new element. We understand, however, that one of the characteristics of radium is that it never diminishes, it never burns itself out. We have seen many human dynamos, many men of abounding energy, but almost invariably after a while their energy diminished, their pace slackened, they reached the crest of the hill and descended; and by and by they passed from public memory.

"Dr. Norris is, of course, still a young man. It would therefore scarcely be appropriate to quote what is said of Moses in relation to him, that 'his natural force was not abated.' We have a suspicion that, were it possible chemically to analyze Dr. Norris' constitution it would be found to contain a large proportion of radium. At all events, we found it most refreshing to meet him again. It was like getting a new atmosphere, electrically charged.

"We were last in Fort Worth in 1926, when the old auditorium of the First Baptist Church was still standing. Dr. Norris and his people have seen strenuous times since then. Their building was destroyed by fire, and through failure of the insurance companies they received little insurance. For more than a year now they have been in their new auditorium. It has an enormous area. We shall not say what it will seat, although we know within fifty. The average estimate of a building's seating capacity is so far from being accurate that to give exact numbers would have the effect of misrepresenting things as they are to the popular mind. It is enough to say that from our count the First Baptist Church auditorium seats approximately the same as the Metropolitan Tabernacle, London. There is, however, this difference, Spurgeon's Tabernacle has two galleries, the Fort Worth auditorium has none; the people are seated on one ascending floor.

"We have heard Dr. Norris many times, and in many places, under varying circumstances, but we were never more thrilled by his messages than we were when we heard him from his own platform in Fort Worth. Evidently he is a larger figure in Fort Worth than ever before. He enjoys a larger measure of public esteem, and is therefore more popular than ever before. In this, we greatly rejoice. There never was but one Dr. J. Frank Norris, and the passage of time serves only to endear him to the multitude, and more firmly to establish him in public confidence. May his bow long abide in strength."

The World's Work of New York in Its Two Issues, September and October, 1923, Published the Following: "The Fundamentalist War Among the Churches"

"I hear the Fundamental Movement 'lacks a leader,' and so it does—at present. Fundamentalism has only started. No one man started it. It is a result of simultaneous uprising all over the country. Organization, with accredited leadership, will come later. Potential leaders abound, and among the strongest, shrewdest, and most romantically adventurous is J. Frank Norris, of Fort Worth, Texas. But he denies he is a leader.

"In Fort Worth opinion regarding Norris is divided. Several years ago his enemies got him tried 'for burning up his church.' He was acquitted. Later on, a mass-meeting ordered him out of town. Legend recounts that he and his merry men prepared to defend themselves with a machine-gun. I asked him about that. 'No,' he replied, 'I had nothing—that gun business is just newspaper headlines. Never carried one since I entered the ministry.'

"Many of 'Frank's' former foes adore him, as does half the community. Buildings covering a block and more attest his success, and his auditorium, when alterations are complete, will hold five thousand applausive adherents, with a choir of seven hundred.

"Recently his paper—circulation 55,000 (I saw the affidavit)—proclaimed in red headlines, 'WAR IS DECLARED—SECOND COMING OF CHRIST ISSUE!' Nailed to the door of his church, meanwhile, was a huge poster announcing his 'World Convention of Fundamentalists.' The array of celebrated speakers included William Jennings Bryan.

"Prince of crowd-gatherers, paragon of advertisers, Norris has created a new profession, that of the church-efficiency expert, and is its most brilliant practitioner. Heralded as 'the Texas Cyclone,' he will enter any city you choose to name, lay hold of some doddering, dead-an-alive downtown church, draw crowds into it, galvanize them, get the gloriously revivified institution financed, and erect a living, lasting monument to his abilities. After witnessing his performance in Cleveland, Dr. W. W. Bustard declared that in the service of a business corporation Norris' genius would be worth $50,000 a year. He understated the case.

"It is true that Norris' belief in 'the literal, personal, bodily, visible, imminent return of the Lord to this earth as King' somewhat limits his leadership.

"It was Norris who said to me at the very start of the first talk I had with him, 'There is going to be a new denomination.' He named the three distinguished Fundamentalists who are about to organize it.

"The champion college-baiter, so far, is Rev. J. Frank Norris, who has transformed his church bulletin into a weekly newspaper, the Searchlight (now The Fundamentalist). In an upper corner of its front page, we behold Norris grasping a Bible in one hand, while the other directs the glare of a searchlight. In the corner opposite, revealed by the glare, cowers Satan. Red headlines complete the effect. Week by week Norris flays the evolutionists in this adventurous journal, and mails it far and wide.

"A year or so ago, hearing that evolution was tolerated at Wake Forest University, near Raleigh, he raged against Wake Forest and mailed Searchlights to all the North Carolina ministers. Uproar followed. A local religious paper attacked President Wm. L. Poteat, and all over North Carolina anti-evolutionists demanded his resignation.

"In his warfare upon his Alma-Mater—Baylor University at Waco, Texas—Norris is succeeding. Professor G. Samuel Dow, author of 'Society and Its Problems,' and an 'Introduction to the Principles of Sociology,' stood his ground until flesh and blood could endure no more, then resigned. Professor O. C. Bradbury has done the same. Encouraged by these triumphs, Norris is not only assailing Professor Pace, a lady, but insisting that President Samuel Palmer Brooks must go.

"Of late, Rev. J. Frank Norris has invented a new instrument of torture for colleges—the trial. At his recent 'world convention' of Fundamentalists, he turned his church into a courtroom and tried three Methodist institutions, the accused being Southern Methodist University at Dallas, Southwestern University at Georgetown, and the Texas Woman's College at Fort Worth. Dr. W. B. Riley, eminent Fundamentalist, presided. Armed with college notebooks, six young folks, graduates or undergraduates of the accused, appeared as witnesses. Before a vast congregation, Rev. W. E. Hawkins, Jr., as prosecuting attorney, examined the witnesses for two and a half hours. Defense there was none. All the accused were convicted."

THE FATE OF THE CONSPIRATORS

"So, they hanged Haman on the gallows that he had prepared for Mordecai."

It is with no small hesitation that reference is made to the unfortunate fate of the men who conspired to destroy the pastor of the First Baptist Church. It is no small ground for gratitude that many of them have not only ceased to be his enemies, but are very warm personal friends.

A large number have been saved and been baptized and are now the most active members of the First Baptist Church, and it is a regular occurrence to hear the testimony in both churches of hardened sinners saved, and who declare to the whole world, "I once hated Dr. Norris, but through his preaching I have been saved."

As an example of how things have changed in Fort Worth, during the dark days of 1912 and 1913, the pastor of the First Baptist Church went into one of the leading clothing stores of Fort Worth and not one clerk would even approach him to wait on him. He stood there and waited and then walked out while the clerks cast suspicious glances at him. But today when he goes into that same store, the same proprietor and same employees, it is like holding a family reunion, proprietor, clerks and the pastor all join in happy, cordial good humor.

During those same dark days, there was not a business house in Fort Worth that would give credit to the pastor of the First Baptist Church and, today he does not need their credit and his name is not on the books of any business concern for credit, "Behold what God hath wrought."

It is true that he had no credit and worse than that he was broke and still worse he was an absolute bankrupt and owed $12,500.00, and had a wife and three little children. This was in the dark days of 1913, but every cent was paid and today in both Detroit and Fort Worth he can borrow on his own note $10,000.00 and has borrowed as much as $25,000.00 to go into the building program of the two churches.

Reference is made to the Detroit Bank which declined to loan Temple Baptist Church any money on the grounds that the churches of Detroit were in default over $7,000,000.00 to the banks, but the bank did loan $25,000.00 upon the name of the pastor. To God be all the glory! (For full information, ask the bank or the finance committee.)

"Vengeance is mine; I will repay, saith the Lord." What has been the fate of the conspirators? No names will be called, but Old Timers will readily recognize the characters.

The District Attorney, who was the tool of the liquor interests, and who framed and forged the indictment in 1912, met with a horrible death, driving in an eight cylinder Cadillac over North Main Street Viaduct, with his lady companion, and his automobile full of liquor, a head on crash with a street car and both were hurled into eternity and their blood, brains, and the broken bottles covered the pavement.

A half broken quart bottle of liquor was picked up from the pavement near the wreck, that was filled with liquor and brains, and was carried to the pastor of the First Baptist Church and he took this broken bottle of brains and liquor to the pulpit and preached on the text: "Thou art weighed in the balances, and art found wanting."

Of course, there were many who criticized but more than fifty people were saved as they were brought face to face with judgment.

One of Fort Worth's richest citizens was the "expert witness" on hand writing in the framed testimony and later, he walked out on the railroad track, near his house, and laid down and a long line of freight cars cut his body half in two.

The president of a bank swore that he would spend every dollar he had or "send Frank Norris to the penitentiary." He proclaimed these words to every customer and to all his acquaintances. This bank went broke and when he died, his relatives had to buy his shroud and casket.

Another capitalist, who was deep in the conspiracy and made large contributions, his bank went broke and, at that time he lived in the costliest home in Fort Worth, one morning before breakfast, he blew his brains out in his garage with a 38 Smith & Wesson.

The president of another bank where the brewery and liquor interests deposited their money and where the funds were raised to "prosecute" the pastor of the First Baptist Church, this bank also went broke and one afternoon when the president and his wife started for a drive, he went back into the house and she heard the crack of a shotgun and found him with the top of his head blown off by his own hand.

Another prominent citizen, who helped to raise the funds by personal solicitation to "prosecute" the pastor of the First Baptist Church, went broke and he has joined the others, waiting the hour when the leaves of the Judgment Book unfold.

The mayor of the city, at that time, called his crowd, some 3,000 or more, together and delivered such a bitter vindictive address on the pastor of the First Baptist Church, and closed with these words, "If there are enough red-blooded men left in Fort Worth, a preacher will be hanging to a telephone post before daylight." (The church was burned the next night.) That mayor was relegated to private life and is now the warm personal friend of the pastor of the First Baptist Church.

Another man, a wholesaler, who had spent large sums of money in the "prosecution" of the pastor—he died suddenly under circumstances that charity would forbid to be published.

Another lawyer who was in the Grand Jury, a member of the District Attorney's office force, that framed the indictment— he has long since become a pitiful spectacle, all that is left of a drunkard's life. The Deputy Sheriff who came to the pastor's home to serve the indictment and who brought along a crowd of hoodlums to stand outside and look on, and who invited the newspapers that they could take flashlights of the scene, in six days afterwards was driving across the railroad on South Hemphill and ran head on into a fast north bound train and never knew what hit him.

The chairman of the board of deacons, a good man, but was influenced and became very bitter, as is the case of good men when they go wrong, and who did the pastor much injury because of his high standing, it took him a year of long lingering suffering to leave this world, and before he passed away called for the man he had persecuted and wept and said "The saddest tragedy that ever happened was when I and others who ought to have stood by you forsook you."

A number of pastors, especially Baptist pastors, were used by the ex-members of the First Baptist Church, who had money to do harm to the pastor of the First Baptist Church. They passed many resolutions and gave these resolutions to enemy papers and Associated Press, but they have all gone.

For example, the leader, the man who was brought to Fort Worth with the avowed purpose of fighting Norris, he was fired out of his pulpit and was given a denominational pallet for some time and is out somewhere in the mesquite flats of West Texas.

During the meeting conducted by Mordecai F. Ham in 1916 the police commissioner joined with the underworld, of which he was the representative, and undertook to harass the meeting by having a large number of automobiles to circle the tabernacle with horns wide open. In vain we begged for police protection but this police commissioner met with a horrible fate too gruesome to describe.

The most powerful firm of criminal lawyers in the state who received big money to act as the hired prosecution—that firm of lawyers is no more and the remnants are scattered.

The famous brewery investigation by the Attorney General of Texas, the correspondence was unearthed showing where the Anheuser Busch Brewing Company, through its president, August Busch, wrote letters to the Texas Brewing Company in Fort Worth, giving instructions on how to stop Norris, and also the letter said, "spare no expense." The interesting thing about the Texas Brewing Company, the president of this brewing company was one of the main directors of the bank where several deacons of the First Baptist Church were also officials and directors, and which caused the pastor so much trouble.

But August Busch, the big St. Louis brewer, blew his own brains out with his own gun.

A young preacher who lived in Norris' home and was sent to school by him, was promised promotion if he would turn against Norris and he accepted the 30 pieces of silver. The ecclesiastical power in alliance with the powers of darkness promoted him to a prominent pastorate, but soon thereafter he became involved, his wife divorced him and he was driven from the ministry and in later years walked into the offices of the pastor of the First Baptist Church and begged forgiveness, which was readily granted.

A capitalist with a string of banks, he and three of the other above referred to bankers were members of the First Baptist Church. His entire fortune was swept away, he moved West, and died under circumstances that are well known to the Old Timers.

156 men, including the Chief of Police, Sheriff, Constabulary, City and County Officials, met in the Metropolitan dining room and voted a demand that the pastor of the First Baptist Church leave Fort Worth in 30 days and so notified him. The man that presided over that meeting—in six days, a fast interurban limited struck his car and not a bone was broken of one of the more than 40 odd people on the two cars, the negro chauffeur was unscathed, the motorman was unhurt, but the brains and blood of this man who presided over this meeting were scattered for more than 30 feet on the tracks.

Immediately after the fire of the First Baptist Church in 1912, there was a hurried meeting called in the Chamber of Commerce and $11,000.00 was raised for the "prosecution" and the man who presided over that meeting lived only a short time and died a horrible death.

The foreman of the Grand Jury that returned the indictment in 1912 was the editor of Fort Worth's leading paper and was one of the most popular political figures and the most influential editor of the State. He was also a member of the First Baptist Church. His paper went broke, and he was driven from public life, and while he still lives, he is long since forgotten.

One of the richest property owners in Fort Worth went to one of the closest friends of the pastor and threatened the shotgun route, he has long since gone—peace to his ashes.

Another editor of a daily paper in Fort Worth wrote very bitter editorials and his paper misrepresented day after day, issuing as many as ten extras on the pastor of the First Baptist Church and sent out, also, many false representations and reports to the various news agencies—he went to his long home after more than a year of lingering illness.

Another very influential man, attorney, newspaper proprietor, came to the First Baptist Church one night with his crowd to reply to the pastor and caused no small disturbance and commotion. It was the beginning of his end and after a long, lingering illness, mind gone, he passed to the long eternity.

Another capitalist, also member of the First Baptist Church, played double. He, too, went broke and after a long seige, he went over the river.

Another capitalist, who was chairman of the Board of Deacons of the church when the first row broke between the pastor and the ungodly element—this deacon owned buildings rented to the wholesale liquor houses—he, too, waits the hour of judgment.

The Fort Worth Record issued extra after extra on the pastor and would send them by the bundle all over the country for free distribution—that paper went broke three times and even the name is no longer seen, except when referred to as past history.

Fort Worth Baptist Pastors' Association, controlled by the rich, unGodly element of their churches, in the absence of the pastor of the First Baptist Church, excluded him from the Pastors' Conference and not a single one of those dear brethren reside in Fort Worth and haven't for some time. The minister who led the conspiracy left his church financially bankrupt and as a reward for his hatred and attack on the pastor of the First Baptist Church, he was put on a pension by the denominational machine. And long since the machine said to him "See thou to that."

Another mayor, who was known for his hatred of preachers and churches, took his special spite out on the First Baptist Church and pastor and sent a would-be assassin to the study of the pastor of the First Baptist Church—this mayor was driven from office, lost his fortune, and the once magnificent store that ran from street to street and blocks of valuable property are all gone and he admitted under oath these words:

"I sent D. E. Chipps to the office of J. Frank Norris to kill him" and he did this while he was mayor and after he was put out of the mayorship and lost his fortune, he soon went the way of the earth.

There was a cause for the anger of the mayor. As the head of the city his conduct was exposed before a great crowd and over the radio, and closed with these words: "He is not fit to be mayor of a hog pen."

The mayor was at a ball game, and he left his box in the middle of the game, thirty minutes before the fateful hour, and immediately was in his car with two of his appointees in front of the pastor's office across the street when the would-be assassin reached the steps to come to the pastor's office. A few seconds after the tragedy two of these officers rushed into the pastor's office, locked the door, and they were never permitted to testify. What took place in that office after the pastor left, only the leaves of the judgment book will reveal. But the Grand Jury testimony shows that two guns were found.

The testimony, which is a matter of record, showed that the would-be assassin had a long police record, and that he was considered a dangerous man, and he told a number of people on his way to the First Baptist Church: "Tomorrow morning's Star-Telegram front page headline will read, 'D. E. Chipps Killed J. Frank Norris.' "

The mayor's testimony on ex parte hearing that "I'd give $100,000 to send J. Frank Norris to the penitentiary, and I have agreed to pay $50,000 for the prosecution and expenses."

Why the First Baptist Church Turned Out of Convention

The First Baptist Church was turned out of the Association and Convention and among the nearly seven pages of printed "charges," the two principal "charges" were that the pastor of the First Baptist Church,

First, "opposed the 75 Million Campaign." And on this charge, the minutes of the Convention show the following on page 22 of the Galveston Convention: "Second, concerning the charge of opposition to the 75 Million Campaign, your committee believes that the charge is true, and that the challenge should, therefore, be sustained, and it submits the following proof: 1. That the pastor and church did not co-operate in putting over the 75 Million Campaign. 2. The pastor has misrepresented the campaign by declaring it to be an ecclesiastical machine which made assessments on the churches. Proof: In the Searchlight of September 29, 1922, page 2, we quote, 'They sent me an assessment of $100,000, and I said, Thank you, then they said, 'Do it this way, or you are not co-operating.' The tragedy of the hour is that preacher after preacher has been crushed by this ecclesiastical machine. . . . This ecclesiastical machine wants money, money, money.' "

The 75 Million Campaign was the most disastrous campaign that ever happened to Southern Baptists, and the whole denominational machinery has completely collapsed and wrecked itself and the First Baptist Church, which refused to bow to the ecclesiastical machine, is today as glorious as the sun, as fair as the moon, and as terrible as an army with banners.

Another "charge" was that the First Baptist Church refused further to use the denominational literature and took the Bible as its only textbook. This is found also on page 22 of the same minutes of the same convention.

Eighteen of the signers of the "charges" against the First Baptist Church, including laymen and ministers, have either gone into bankruptcy or been driven from the ministry, or passed to their rewards.

It is interesting that only a short time ago the pastor who was the chairman of the committee that brought in the false charges against the First Baptist Church to the Convention—he was forced to resign from his church in Houston under circumstances about which the least said is best.

And the high priest which forced young ministers to sign false charges, the two Baptist institutions located in Fort Worth are facing bankruptcy to the tune of nearly three-quarters of a million dollars' indebtedness.

The list of casualties is multiplying very rapidly in Detroit and Isaiah 54:17 is true in the twentieth century and in the north as well as the south, east as well as west.

"No weapon that is formed against thee shall prosper; and every tongue that shall rise against thee in judgment thou shalt condemn. This is the heritage of the servants of the Lord, and their righteousness is of me, saith the Lord."

The chairman of the board of trustees for Temple Baptist Church for many years, a man with a small clique, ran the church. He led a very vicious fight against Norris and it has now been brought out that he sold $20,000.00 of very valuable property belonging to the church and for which the church only received $4,000.00, but judgment has come to him.

Another former and prominent official of the Temple Baptist Church, the head of the Detroit Baptist machine, the minutes of the church show that in 1922 as chairman of the committee he spent "$31,005.00 on improvements" made on the church but now a check by competent and reputable architects show that $7,000.00 is a maximum price for the "improvements." He was excluded from the Temple Baptist Church after the present pastor began.

The Executive Secretary of the Detroit Baptist Union was very active in opposing the call to Temple Church of Dr. Norris and constantly hindered the work of the church even during the great revival on Oakman Boulevard, but he has ceased his interference and opposition to the church after he made a signed, sweeping and public retraction and apology of the things he said against Dr. Norris and made this retraction and apology on February 13, 1936.

Why add to the list? It is with great hesitation that these matters are referred to. This is inside the cup. The outside world has not known these things. But what has been the effect on the growth of the church?

"And great fear came upon all the church, and upon as many as heard these things."—Acts 5:11.

But there is another and glorious side. Multitudes of the bitterest enemies have been converted and baptized by the very man they fought. For example, the founder and head of the Retail Liquor Dealers' Association of Texas, a saloon keeper for 40 years, was gloriously saved and baptized in the First Baptist Church and sits on the front seat at every service.

His name is William Blevins. A stenographic report of his testimony is as follows:

"I was in the liquor business for 40 years. I organized the Malt and Retail Liquor Dealers' Association of Texas and was its only head until it went out of business. When J. Frank Norris came to Fort Worth it wasn't long until I recognized that he was going to put us out of business unless we put him out of business. I called our gang together and we got in touch with the leading business men and they in turn called the representative churchmen together of the various denominations, and it wasn't long until we had all the preachers silenced except this young fellow Norris. I went out to hear him and I was convinced that we had a dangerous foe. He would never let up. We thought we had him down and out when we got him indicted and tried, but he was vindicated so overwhelmingly and then his church grew as never before and we were in worse fix than ever. Then he did begin his war on us in dead earnest.

"He went and brought that fellow Mordecai Ham here and he was as bad or worse than Norris. So something had to be done. We thought we had Ham put out of business when a fellow jumped on him and knocked him in the head one night and we were soon through with Ham and Ramsey, but Norris was still fighting away and we called a representative group of 150 or more of the leading business men of the city together at the Metropolitan Hotel dining room and Paul Waples presided. We lifted our glasses at the close of the fireworks when we decided to finish Norris, and gave a toast to his exit or finish.

"A few nights afterwards we called a huge mass meeting in the auditorium of the Chamber of Commerce, one block from the First Baptist Church, and Mr. George Armstrong presided and called for fifteen men to go and take Norris out. I was heartily in favor of taking him out and so was everybody else, but we could not get the 15 men.

"And ladies and gentlemen, I believe the hand of God interfered that night and I am so glad that we didn't deprive his wife and children of their husband and father, and this church of its pastor, and since I could not put him out of business, I decided to join him. I came to the church, walked down to the front and got down on my knees and he got down with me on his knees and put his arms around my shoulders while I prayed, and I prayed the prayer 'God be merciful to me, a sinner' and He heard me and this man that I so hated and tried with others at every foot of ground at my command to put out of business, baptized me and I am now past my 80th milestone and in the course of nature will precede him to the other shore, and when I get there I am going to hunt up the Superintendent of that fair land and make two requests of him.

"First, I want him to let me know the day that Frank comes, and second, I want him to let me off that day that I may be standing down at the beautiful gate and be the first to put my arms around him as the man who led me to Christ, by whose grace I am saved."

William (Bill) Blevins who organized the Retail Liquor Dealers Association of Texas, and one of the crowd that called a mass meeting to get rid of Dr. Norris, but who later was saved and baptized in the First Baptist Church, and now sits on the front seat every Sunday.

Tent Hall and crowd at Glasgow, Scotland, where Dr. Norris spoke three times.

A CALL TO THE FIRST BAPTIST CHURCH, FORT WORTH, JUST ANOTHER CHAPTER OF "INSIDE THE CUP"

The preceding three years at Dallas as pastor of McKinney Avenue Baptist Church and editor of the Baptist Standard furnished the background to the call to Fort Worth.

Not sparing myself, I am giving this testimony, with the hope and prayer that it may help some young preachers to avoid my mistakes.

I graduated from Southern Baptist Theological Seminary, Louisville, Ky., in May, 1906, having finished all the courses required for the Master's Degree in Theology. I finished the three-year course in two years' time. I had a wife and one-year-old baby. And that was the cause of the shortening of the sentence from three to two years.

When I finished at Baylor, I had a call to the First Baptist Church at Rockdale, and the Pulpit Committee of the First Baptist Church, Corsicana, also wanted me.

My wife's father, Jim Gaddy, and Dr. B. H. Carroll, wanted me to take one of these important pulpits, and I wished afterwards I had. But it would have been a mistake.

It is a doubtful question as to whether a man should marry before he finishes his education. I wondered about it before I married, and my wife wondered more after we married.

Because of my record at the Seminary, I was appointed by the faculty to deliver one of the graduating addresses. And no question about my address; it was a "hum dinger." I had a great subject—"International Justification of Japan in Its War With Russia."

The Louisville Courier-Journal thought this address was states-manlike and had international merit, for they published it in full.

I was broke but I bought an armful of this great paper and sent a marked copy to all my kinfolks and acquaintances.

It was a gala occasion the night of the graduation, and, of course, the most important event of that occasion was not the address by Dr. Mullins or the giving of the diplomas, but my address in defense of Japan. Ever since I was a boy on the farm I was a close student of international affairs, in fact I became an "expert" before I left the farm—I mean on international affairs.

When I graduated the McKinney Avenue Church at Dallas called me; they called me sight unseen before I graduated—and I accepted sight unseen. Talk about marrying by correspondence, that is nothing. They thought I was some pumpkin, and I thought they were some pumpkins, because they were in Dallas. No young Roman Catholic priest ever looked with stronger devotion towards St. Peter's at Rome than I looked on the denominational headquarters at Dallas. What disillusionment was awaiting me!

I landed in Dallas the first Sunday in June, 1906. And the thermometer was—well, I think it set the record for all that summer. I went to the St. George Hotel, sent my double breasted, long tail Prince Albert coat and striped trousers down to the pressing shop—I delivered the address on Japan in this same outfit.

The coat was a heavy winter coat, and came down almost like the skirts of the robe of Aaron, had satin lapels, and the pants —the trousers, breeches—whichever called—had stripes as big as a lead pencil. I had a white vest also. And with it a heavy black satin tie. But the most important part about the regalia was the stove pipe collar. I was long and slender, wore a 14 collar—now 16½. I was as tall as I am now—think I was taller—and weighed about 130 pounds—some 50 or 60 pounds lighter than at present. And that coat was made to fit me tight.

All the distinguished city pastors wore long tailed coats— they carried their theology in their coat tails. That is where I carried mine.

Incidentally I wore this same suit when I preached the annual sermon at the Baptist General Convention of Texas the next year.

I had some "standing" in those days. I remember after preaching the sermon, Dr. George W. Truett came up to me and put his arm around me and said, "My lad, the world will hear from you." Of course, he has forgotten the prophecy, but I haven't. That may be the reason why I have done some things that I perhaps ought not to have done. Great preachers should be very careful how they put their hands on young ministerial sprouts.

I went to the church at McKinney and Ruth. It was a flat topped tabernacle—looked like a hay barn. And I could stand on the platform and touch the ceiling with my hands. There were thirteen present—the thirteen original colonies.

I had a prepared sermon for that occasion, all written out. For had I not just finished a course in Homiletics? And I was an expert Homiletician, too. Dr. E. C. Dargin, the professor, said so. He called me in one day and said, "My young brother, the world will hear from you."

Dr. E. Y. Mullins called me in his office one day, showed me my grades in theology—I had perfect grades in all my subjects. He also made a very extravagant prophecy.

I believed all these great preachers said. And still have some of it left.

But I didn't preach that prepared sermon that day. I don't know whether it was the heat—for my stove pipe collar melted down as soon as I got in—or whether it was the vacant wood yard, or whether it was a deacon that leaned up against one of the posts and went sound asleep. I didn't mind his going to sleep, but he snored. The rest of the crowd were used to it and didn't pay any attention to it, but it got on my nerves.

There I was, a highly distinguished preacher, valedictorian of my class, having delivered a great "statesmanlike" address on Japan. And Theodore Roosevelt who settled the war between Russia and Japan—why his coat wouldn't have made me a neck tie.

I had that manuscript, the prepared sermon in the inside of that long tailed coat. And it stayed there, too.

I shall never forget my first message. It was impromptu. It was spoken out of a heart of distress. And I meant every word of it. It was from the text, Mark 11:22, "Have faith in God."

There wasn't anything else around there to have faith in then. I was on four flats—worse than that, I was wilted.

The first month I got $12.50. The next month I got $22.50, and I owed over $800.00 and had my wife and baby girl on my hands.

I couldn't get away to hold meetings to supplement with, because if I had gone, there wouldn't have been anything there when I got back, so I had to stay.

But we got along fine. Somehow they gave me enough to live on, and no finer, nobler set of people ever drew the breath of life. They built a magnificent building at McKinney Avenue. And the church grew to a thousand membership. And they are a great church today. I love them very tenderly.

Right in the midst of the rapid growth of this church, Judge T. B. Butler, former business manager of the Baptist Standard and a director at that time of the Standard, called me before a group of men to take over the management of the Baptist Standard.

I was not thirty years old. I had never written an article in my life for a paper. Didn't know what a printing press looked like. I didn't know what a Mergenthaler linotype machine was. But it wasn't long until I knew—bills, bills! And I was fool enough to take it, or rather let it take me. Talk about a fellow getting a bear by the tail!

But the brethren wanted me to take it. Dr. J. B. Cranfill and Dr. S. A. Hayden were still on the scene. Dr. Hayden published the "Texas Baptist Herald," and Dr. J. B. Cranfill was coming rapidly back in power with his paper, "The Advance."

And right here I want to say that the greatest injustice ever done any man was the way the Texas Baptist machine treated Dr. J. B. Cranfill. It was his pen that fought their battles. And he is the greatest religious editor of this age.

I bought the whole outfit of the "Texas Baptist Herald" for $30,000, including its machinery. And that was $29,999.90 more than it was worth—I am just telling of my fool mistakes.

I bought out Dr. Cranfill's, "The Advance," and the condition of sale was he signed a contract he would not go back into the Baptist paper business for ten years—and that was another mistake I made.

But I bought out both Drs. Hayden and Cranfill because the brethren wanted me to do it. That is what they got me for.

I did only one smart thing in the whole business, and I don't know why I did that. I got the stockholders to transfer to me in fee simple 54 per cent of the active voting stock. There was

$7,000 "preferred stock" which Mr. George W. Carroll, a noble man, who had given large sums to the denomination, in his financial embarrassment had put up for collateral. And I didn't know anything about this $7,000. But I heard about it later to my great sorrow. No man was ever talked about or misrepresented so much as I was on the whole transaction.

I had a perfectly corking good time while running the Standard. And I ran it, too!

I decided the thing needed some new life in it, something to stir up its dead bones. So I put a lot of news in there, and the circulation increased from 16,000 to 38,000.

I made one advertising contract with Jacobs and Company for $40,000.00.

So I was flying high.

I believed all the prophecies that had been said concerning me. If I had consulted the Sybillian Books of ancient Rome I am sure I would have found something in there concerning my destiny.

My First Big Fight

One day I got a letter from a country mother, twelve pages, from a little town in Southeast Texas, telling of the suicide of her only son. He was cashier in the bank, and he played the races and lost. He embezzled the funds of the bank. He wrote his mother and said, "I am sorry, Mother, but this is the only way out. I would rather be dead than in the penitentiary."

I laid the letter aside after writing her a word of sympathy. What could I do? But the thing got on my mind, and I took Deacon H. Z. Duke, as fine a man as ever lived, and went out to the Dallas fair with him. And we counted forty-eight bookmaking stands, and saw five thousand men and women in a drunken gambling debauch, women's hair disheveled, hanging over their shoulders—it was in the days before bobbed hair.

I found the city of Dallas got $125,000 annually out of this gambling. I went and had the whole thing photographed, and wrote it up in the Baptist Standard, front page, this title, "Racing at the Dallas Fair Gambling Hell."

Hon. T. M. Campbell was governor at that time. A Baptist deacon by the name of Greer from East Texas was in the Senate, and Judge Robinson, a Methodist, in the House of Representatives. They introduced the bill to stop race track gambling. The first thing I knew I was called before the Judiciary Committee. The greatest and most famous criminal lawyer, Hon. William Crawford, was there to defend the gambling. All the members of the legislature read my exposure and it stirred things up.

Colonel Crawford, through long experience at criminal law, made an attack on me, evading the issue of gambling. That was the first public cussing that I ever received. I wasn't used to it then.

He denied all that I had published, and the committee asked me for the proof. I went back to Dallas and brought it down. Dr. W. D. Bradfield, now of Southern Methodist University, joined with me, and things were stirred up. They were red hot.

We spent seven weeks in Austin. And the brethren everywhere would write us wonderful letters, but didn't enclose any checks. They always said, "God bless you." I learned then for the first time the meaning of the song, "Jesus Paid It All." My friends, don't think that I am irreverent. I am simply telling some of my fool mistakes.

The General Ministerial Association of Dallas was called in special session. All the big preachers were there. Dr. J. Frank Smith of Central Presbyterian Church, Dr. Thornton Whaling, Dr. George W. Truett, Dr. J. W. Hill of the First Methodist. There were about a hundred in all. I was there.

I remember Dr. Jeff D. Ray was a visitor, and he had some things to say.

A committee of seven was appointed—I thought to help me in the gambling fight, but I found out differently afterwards.

The first thing I knew there was a called meeting in the Dallas News editorial office. I was not invited to this meeting.

Present at that meeting was the editorial staff of the Dallas News, Messrs. Tooney, Clark and Lombardy, and President of the National Exchange Bank, President of Chamber of Commerce, and several other representative business men. Among the distinguished Divines, Drs. Thornton Whaling, J. Frank Smith, George W. Truett, G. C. Rankin, and J. B. Gambrell. The meeting was called to put a "kibash" on me, and when Dr. Gambrell found it out he would not go any further until they phoned me to come.

I went.

I arrived, not knowing that my execution had been arranged,

like the two noted former associates of Stalin who were shot this week.

Dr. Gambrell got up and said, "Gentlemen, this institution is on one corner of hell. The gambling at the fair is a disgrace and ought to be stopped. That is all I have to say."

He reached down and picked up his hat and walked out. I followed him. And the meeting adjourned sine die. Dr. Truett condemned gambling in principle and also condemned my "methods."

One night in the Driscoll Hotel at Austin adjoining my room I hard my name used. I never heard so much cussing in my life, before or since. They didn't know I was in the adjoining room. It scared me. They told what they were going to do to me. For the first time since I was grown I felt a challenge to become religious. I saw I was into it. What could I do with all that crowd? Two whole train loads came down from Dallas to defend the gamblers. And they were all present at a joint session of the Legislature, House and Senate, Supreme Court and the governor were present.

And I shall never forget what a knock-down, drag-out fight we had. I closed the argument about two o'clock in the morning.

The bill was passed and race track gambling stopped in Texas for twenty-five years.

I was not strong physically, and when this fight was over I was over. My health was gone. I had a good friend, Dr. J. H. Wayland, who wanted me to come out there and take charge of Plainview College, and that would have been a sure enough mistake. But I went and wife and I stayed with him a while. He had a fine herd of thoroughbred cows grazing on the rich alfalfa, and I got myself together.

During this time things went awry with the printing business.

But we got out the paper.

Concerning the fight against race track gambling in Texas the Literary Digest published, "Two ministers, Drs. J. Frank Norris and W. D. Bradfield, fought the combined forces of book makers, and what former governor, Charles E. Hughes, did for New York in 1905 these two Texas ministers did for the Lone Star State four years later."

There are some who see no humor in anything. They never laugh—neither do the people in the lower world—and some married people. But everybody is in a good humor in heaven. Even the Lord Himself laughs—"He that sitteth in the heavens shall laugh."

Therefore it is a free country and every man can take his choice. In hades they remind one of candidates for the divorce bill—chewing on each other and gnashing with their teeth. But in heaven they rejoice always. And if you expect to enjoy heaven, or even go there, better get in a good humor here.

I read a very able discussion by one of the world's outstanding psychologists, a very wonderful book, recently, on the effect of good humor and bad humor on the physical condition, and how the humor of the soul affects a man's features. A lot of women throw away their money going to beauty parlors, when if they would get in love with their husbands and enjoy life—in other words if they work at it from within—a woman who is ugly as home made sin could be as beautiful as Raphael's Madonna.

In giving the background to the call at Fort Worth I left out an important chapter, and I give it because of its effect on my inner life.

As I said, I didn't want the Baptist Standard, but was persuaded to take it, and knew nothing in the world about the publishing business. I was thrown in the midst of the Atlantic Ocean without any life preservers and with a hundred pounds of lead on both feet and a ton around my neck.

I found several thousand dollars of debts. And well has someone said, "The three greatest enemies of man are dirt, debt, and the devil."

Talk about a ninety-nine year sentence. I have served ten times ninety-nine year sentences paying debts—and still at it. I have been at it through this, the hottest summer in America, both in Fort Worth and Detroit. However, I am glad to say that through the fine business management here in Detroit we are caught up, and have a balance.

And, we are out of the woods at Fort Worth.

Since I had the majority of stock in the Baptist Standard, I was prepared for the inevitable conflict of an "irresistible force meeting an immovable object."

The long, bitter fight from the race track conflict stirred up all the underworld, and some of the prominent big rich Baptist laymen in Dallas whose names I will not call, for they have gone on to their long rest. ·

Before I knew it, there was a meeting of the directors of the Baptist Standard called, and for the purpose of firing me. There have been several efforts to fire me since, and up to this time the cap failed to go off—or the powder was wet—I am not bragging, because I may get fired yet. The life of a minister is a very precarious career.

I went to my attorney, Honorable A. B. Flannery, and he said, "You need not worry since you own a majority of the stock. Send out a notice to all the stockholders and call a stockholders' meeting at the time of the Directors' meeting."

I did as he advised, and when the Directors met—and the distinguished pastor of the First Baptist Church, Dallas, was back of it as it developed—and I suspected as much, and it was all brought out in the specially called meeting of the directors.

Therefore, when the joint meeting of the Board of Directors and stockholders was called, as president I announced:

"Gentlemen, as president of the Baptist Standard Publishing Company, I have called a meeting of the stockholders, and the following minutes are made a record:

"1. The resignation of all the present directors (naming them) has been accepted.

"2. The following new directors have been elected by the stockholders (giving names).

"3. The meeting of the stockholders is now adjourned."

That ended the meeting of the directors to fire me.

My good friend, Dr. I. E. Gates, who was then pastor of the Ervay Street Baptist Church, came to me and said:

"Frank, you have ruined everything. The denominational leaders will not support you."

I replied, "I am ruined already, and it makes little difference what else they do. All that remains is my epitaph, and I don't know of anything that will be more fitting when you conduct my funeral than to inscribe, "The saddest words of tongue or pen are these, 'It might have been'."

I don't think that is an exact quotation, but that is what I learned when I was a freshman in Baylor, but the readers get the idea.

Dr. Truett informed me that he would not write any more for the Standard.

And I told him that I needed the space anyhow. And I told him two things:

First, if it was an honor to be in the Standard each week, it should be passed around, and

Second, if it was a burden, it was a shame to overwork him.

But the Standard grew.

It wasn't long until Dr. Truett wrote a wonderful letter to the membership of the First Baptist Church, urging them to take the Baptist Standard. And I was paying for a shorthand reporter to take down his sermons. And everywhere he went, he would always send me the daily papers giving wonderful accounts of his great crowds and meetings, and I published them. I thought that was what he sent them to me for. I knew he never sent me these clippings before I was editor, and he hasn't sent them to me since. And I remember his meeting at Atlanta and Brooklyn, and other places, greater or lesser.

There would be no comment, just a large envelope of clippings from the daily papers. And the boys in the forks of the creek wondered how I got hold of these papers. Of course, Dr. Truett "detested the publicity."

Another thing I found out while editor of the Standard, namely, that all denominational bishops were just humans—they had feet of clay and lips of clay, just old East Texas red clay. That was a great shock to my young faith, for no young Israelite ever looked upon Aaron on the day of atonement with priestly garments down to his feet, going into the Holy of Holies, with greater reverence than I, as I stood at a safe distance, and eyed the denominational leaders. It took me several years before I felt comfortable in their presence—I was such a sinner. They filled me with awe.

I had heard somewhere George Elliott's expression, that there were three orders of creation—men, women, and preachers. But here was a fourth order, a sort of annex to the heavenly world, let down by a sheet like the animals to Peter on the house top in Joppa.

Take this instance:

One time, before the Convention, the leaders called the brethren —the rank and file—to a special prayer meeting. There was a great crisis on. Deep anxiety prevailed. And the main High Priest got up before the prayer meeting and said:

"My dearly belov-ed brethren, we must keep step; we must have one mind; we must have heavenly guidance. The issue that is before the Convention presents the greatest cris-es—it is indeed an epoch-al hour. We are at the cross roads of Texas Baptist history."

And I believed every word of it.

Why shouldn't I?

The brethren prayed, and then prayed some more, and prayed until everybody had his handkerchief out—I had mine out too— and we pulled our noses until they were as red as a turkey gobler's snout on the day before Thanksgiving.

Now the thing that they were praying for was already set up in type in the Baptist Standard office!

The prayer meeting adjourned about midnight. I went to my room, but I couldn't sleep. I was still in my twenties, and I wondered what it was all about. My disillusionment was on, and I felt something going on inside of me that I wasn't expecting.

Praying for what?

I soon found out that the leaders were not praying for objective of results, but for subjective of effects; that is, getting the brethren in notion to follow the leadership, not from above, but at the headquarters.

I tried my best to adjust myself, but it was like fitting a square stick in a round hole. I was as unreconstructible—this is a new word—as my granddaddy was at the close of the Civil War when he refused to be reconstructed to the Union. Both of us were wrong, my granddad and I. I know it—and I knew it then.

Praying for a matter that was already fixed!

But I am glad I found this out, because it has helped me a great deal to understand a lot of things since.

Incidentally that is one reason why I have never been afraid of the Sanhedrin. I soon found out that the little tin gods were like Dagon when the priests went in and found him on his face one morning, and took the old man and set him back on his pedestal. The next morning they came in and found him not only down on the floor, but his legs, arms, and head were off, and nothing but his trunk was left, and the Scripture says, "And they left and haven't been back until this day."

They didn't have much suspicion as to his impotency the first time they found Dagon on his face, but when they went back and saw his whole anatomy dismembered, their suspicions were aroused, and hopelessly so.

In all seriousness it was a terrible shock to me. There was a San Francisco earthquake inside. And it nearly destroyed my faith—I didn't have much to destroy.

How I Helped to Establish the Southwestern Baptist Theological Seminary

This is one thing that I have never been accused of. But in order that the record might be complete I want to make another confession. I should not say, confession, because that is a great institution. And in this day of world wide sweep of atheism and communism, even though we may not agree with all of its teachings, yet on the whole, we rejoice that the Gospel of salvation goes out from this great institution, the Southwestern Seminary.

While I was editor of the Standard, Dr. B. H. Carroll came to Dallas and called me to room 303, Oriental Hotel—the site is now occupied by the Baker Hotel. I went to his room and was happy to do so. What a giant figure he was, standing way above six feet and with long venerable white beard—and I thought I was standing in the presence of Samuel. And he was indeed a prophet for his day and generation.

He ordered refreshments—two bottles of Apollinaris water, one for each of us. It was the first time I had ever tasted any. I liked it, and it is good for what ails you. It will blow the top of your head off.

He said, "Frank, how much of the stock of the Baptist Standard do you own? And what is your legal relation to it?"

I said, "Dr. Carroll, I own the majority of the stock, and can control its policies."

"What do you think of the establishment of a seminary here in the Southwest? You were my student for four years, and you took my English Bible course. There is a great crisis coming, and it may not come in my day, but it will in your day. I see a dark cloud on the horizon, it is German Rationalism. It has already struck our Northern schools and seminaries, and it will soon come South, and the only way to meet it is to establish a Gibraltar of Orthodoxy in the Southwest."

I was for it and told him so.

Then he told me that the other denominational leaders were opposed to it, and he named Drs. A. J. Barton, S. P. Brooks, and George W. Truett.

But this family row among the denominational leaders didn't concern me any more than an ancient Athenian was concerned about the war among the gods of Olympus.

I was for him, and told him so.

He said, "All I want is plenty of space in the Standard—not much to begin with, but more later on. And if you will stand by me I will go afield and raise $55,000.00 to endow the chair of the English Bible.

"What I want you to do at present is to print the telegrams that I will send each week, giving full report of my work and of money raised."

I told him he could have the space, and soon the telegrams signed, "B. H. Carroll," appeared on the front page of the Standard.

Immediately the other denominational leaders got their heads together and called me into a conference and told me what would happen to me if I didn't stop it.

It was all funny to me.

But the telegrams kept coming from Dr. Carroll.

Then Dr. Carroll would get various brethren to write articles advocating the establishment of the seminary. And the first argument that was published was from the able pen of W. K. Penrod, the pastor of the First Baptist Church of Cleburne, Texas. He is now in glory with Dr. Carroll.

The opposition to the establishment of the seminary began to pour in arguments, and I poured everyone of them into the waste basket.

They said I was partisan, that I was running the Standard with an iron hand, and I was accused even of being a dictator. That was a long time before Mussolini and Hitler got on the scene.

It didn't make any difference with me. I told Dr. Carroll what was going on, and he told me just to stand pat and publish what he sent in and what he got his supporters to send in, and to continue to throw the opposition in the waste basket.

However, he said once, "Frank, perhaps you had better let some of the articles opposing the seminary be published, but send them to me before you publish them, and I will write a reply, and you can run it as an 'editorial.' "

I picked out a typical article of the opposition and forwarded it to Dr. Carroll, and he annihilated it.

I ran it as an "editorial," and my, how many comments I got! There were quite a number who wrote and one brother said,

"You are the most brilliant editor in the religious world!"

And I believed it—this was another one of my fool mistakes, to believe it.

I did feel a little mean about it, but it is now thirty-three years ago, and I am glad the Lord says, "I will remember your sins against you no more forever."

But I did a good deed. And so I have some part in the Southwestern Baptist Theological seminary, even though some of the members of the faculty may not appreciate it.

They have had a little hard time getting their salary and per diem and I wish I could get old man Henry Ford or somebody to send them a million dollars. And if he knows what is good for him he will do it, because if you destroy these seminaries and churches, the reds will hang Henry Ford and Sloan higher than Haman.

Incidentally I had some "standing" among my denominational leaders in my youth.

Oh, I forgot to say, Dr. Carroll had me as his assistant before I became editor of the Standard while I was in the seminary at Louisville. He also like the other leaders made most flattering prophecies concerning my future. He said one day, "Frank, you have in you the making of a great preacher."

I believed it then. And this was another mistake of foolish youth.

Of course, the other denominational leaders never did forgive me for siding with Dr. Carroll. But some of them are dead, and all the rest of us will go to our reward. And in the ages upon ages we will rejoice together.

Call to Fort Worth—1909

When Mr. G. H. Connell called me to come to Fort Worth to to supply, I accepted, and they gave me $25.00 for that Sunday.

Evidently they liked the sample and asked me to come back the next Sunday.

But I had made all arrangements to leave Dallas and go to the far West to regain my health. But the pulpit committee asked me to supply again, which I did. And there was some time required to wind up my affairs with the Standard, and they asked me if I would supply during this time.

There was a pulpit committee of thirty, and the committee had voted unanimously to call Dr. Samuel J. Porter, than whom there was never a nobler, finer man, preacher, scholar, and he was a great orator. He had been pastor of the First Baptist Church, San Antonio, then he went to the Roger Williams church, Washington, from which place he went on to glory.

One morning the chairman of the pulpit committee got up before the church and said,

"The pulpit committee is ready to report on the call of pastor next Wednesday night, and everybody should be present. I thought, of course that Dr. Porter would be called. And I know we preachers do like the old maid when proposed to—"This is so sudden and unexpected, and I am surprised." But certainly this was true when near midnight Judge R. H. Buck called me in Dallas and said,

"As chairman of the notification committee I am happy to tell you that you have been called to the pastorate of the First Baptist Church, Fort Worth."

Judge Buck was a great lawyer, occupying the high position of Judge of the forty-eighth district court, and then went to the court of civil appeals, from which honored place he went to his reward.

The committee went before the church and said, "We have no

recommendation to make concerning any man, and recommend that the church proceed by ballot."

There were 334 votes cast by ballot.

There was opposition to the call, and only one whole family, and that was J. T. Pemberton and his family.

Mr. Pemberton said, "I am not opposed to J. Frank Norris; I am for him, but this church is not in condition for his type of ministry. If he comes there will be the all-firedest explosion ever witnessed in any church. We are at peace with the world, the flesh, and the devil, and with one another. And this fellow carries a broad axe and not a pearl handle pen knife. I just want to warn you. But now since you have called him, I am going to stay by him."

And he stayed by me. He is the best friend I ever had. At a later time I will give his whole connection and loyalty.

Not sparing myself, I had very little faith. My experiences above related with the denominational leaders shattered my soul to its deepest depths. I wanted to quit the ministry. My dad always told me that I would make a great lawyer, and so did everybody else. That was my boyhood ambition. And now what was I going to do?

I was utterly disgusted with churches, the ministry, and the whole machinery.

But I went back the next Sunday, and to the great surprise of the First Church I didn't accept it. I only referred to the call and said, "I thank you." And they were amazed that I didn't jump in head over heels. It was the richest church in the city, or the state, or the South. Millionaires hung in bunches. It was the church known as "The Home of the Cattle Kings."

I shall never forget my first text:—Job. 19:25-26, "For I know that my redeemer liveth, and that he shall stand at the latter day upon the earth: And though after my skin worms destroy this body, yet in my flesh shall I see God."

Job was in the deepest, darkest depths of despair when he uttered these words, which I consider the heighest height of Old Testament revelation. The only difference between me and Job was he came up from the bottom to the heighest heights, but I stayed down there. Every time I would start to climb up I was like the proverbial frog which crawled up out of the well two feet every day and fell back three feet every night. How long did it take the frog to get out?

I was pale, wan, worn, and weary. I had a terrible cough. And because of my condition I was greatly surprised at the call.

A large group of men, among them three bank presidents, quite a number of capitalists and cattle kings met with me for a conference. They told me what a wonderful church they had—and it was all true. They did the talking. They had no idea what was going on in my soul. My faith—what little I had left—was fast ebbing away; my unbelief changed into contempt. The darkness of Gethsemane was fast settling over my soul.

When they finished the long conference of eulogizing the great church, its wealth, its prestige, its standing, et certera, ad infinitum, ad nauseam, I rose and said just one sentence:

"Gentlemen, if I come to you I don't know what will happen. All I know is we won't look like we do now when we get through with each other."

I had forgotten the expression, but many years afterwards Mr. J. W. Spencer who went out with the exodus and later became my good friend before his death, and we often laughed about it afterwards—he reminded me of what I said.

It was a typical church with the B. Y. P. U's, Ladies Aid, W. M. U's, Boards, Gee-whiz "high falutin" choir, pipe organ, ushers, and twenty some odd committees.

I had a literal contempt for the whole machinery.

But I went on with it, and for two years did my best to fit into the program. They were exceedingly lovely to me and my family. They showered their gifts, they gave the largest salary of any church in the state or South. And if they heard of anybody giving one larger they would raise mine—and I never objected—They furnished me a home, paid all the bills, I never bought a suit of clothes, overcoat, hat, necktie, or even a pair of socks. They remembered my family on Thanksgiving Day, Christmas, birthdays, and between times. The chairman of the board of trustees drove up one day with a handful of twenty dollar gold pieces and gave everybody one, including the cook and the yard man. My rich officials had one of the finest cars ever made driven up to my door, and the fellow told me to get in—and I did. And that was the first time I had ever sat in an automobile. He dove me around, and asked me "How do you like it?"

Well, I told him what Mark Twain said concerning Niagara Falls—"It's a success."

"He said, "It is yours." And then he explained to me how it

came, and then the best part, explained to me how he was to keep it up.

It was customary for the pastor to take a whole summer vacation, not one month, but the entire summer. At the time for the first vacation the chairman of the finance committee gave me a moroco bound book of travelers checks, $20.00 each. I had never seen one of them before, never even heard of them while I was down there in the black lands of West Texas pulling the bell chord over the gray backs of Beck and Jude from the break of day until dark.

When I got home I counted these twenty dollar travelers checks, and it was just even $1000. I took a trip, but I couldn't spend the amount, and they would have been insulted if I had given any change back. And I never liked to insult people deliberately.

The next summer my wife and children and myself all went up into Colorado and they paid all expenses.

No danger of anything happening to the church while I was gone—no more than there would to a corpse.

I was a typical city pastor. I was the chief after dinner speaker. I had tuxedoes, swallow tail coats, a selection of "biled" shirts, several of them, and I would give $10.00 for the latest joke. I was, as I said, the main attraction at all the gatherings of the Rotarians, Lions, Kiwanis, Eagles. I was Will Rogers and Mark Twain both combined; they thought so, so did I.

It made little difference to me what the church did. Thus I spent my first two years.

I went home one Sunday night and told my wife, "I am going to quit the ministry."

She said, "When did you ever begin?"

Such unkindness!

I agreed with her and said, "I am going to quit before I begin. I didn't want to come here, I have no faith. I don't even know whether I am a Christian. I thought I was once—fact is I don't know whether there is a God. I am going to leave it all."

My good friend Charlie Carroll, son of Dr. B. H. Carroll, was then pastor in Owensboro, Kentucky, and wanted me to come for a meeting, and I wired him I would come. I didn't go for the meeting, just went to get away from things, and meet myself coming, or find out which way I was going.

I was in the same fix I was up here not long ago in Detroit when I made the wrong turn, didn't know the traffic rules. I saw the policeman and thought I would beat him to it, and called out to him, "Mr. Officer, do you know where I am going?"

He said, "Yes, you are going with me down to the City Hall."

I pulled out a letter from Colonel Heinrich Pickert, the Police Commissioner in which he told me he would do everything he could to help me. The officer relented and stood on the running board to the next corner.

I thanked him.

Incidentally I used that letter several times afterwards until Entzminger borrowed it, and then he lost it.

Before I went to the Owensboro engagement I was in a very bad state of mind. I didn't care what happened—mark you there was perfect peace in the church—just as there is in a grave yard. The only difference between that church and the grave yard was the people in the grave yard were buried and everybody knew it, but in the church they were dead and unburied and didn't know it.

The Ladies Aid—and don't anybody get the idea that I have it in for the Ladies Aid—I just haven't anything for them—They were very nice to cover the platform and pulpit with a lot of pot plants—ferns—geraniums—gladioli—palms—chrysanthemums—it was decorated the same way for weddings, funerals, and preaching. And there I stood straight up, all embalmed, and all that was needed was that peculiar scent of the mixture of roses and carbolic acid. I had on my long tail coat and striped breeches—I had several suits by that time.

I did a very mean thing, but I think the Lord forgave me, even before I did it. I went down in the poor section near the Trinity River and got a whole crowd of poor people with their children, and got them all up at the church one night and gave them free entertainment—ice cream was served, as well as some other things, and they got it all over that fine heavy carpet.

The next day when the diamond bedecked sisters of the Ladies Aid came and saw how their very rich, highly colored carpet was ruined—"It is terrible—It is terrible—It is terrible"—"He is going to ruin our church, going to make a regular Salvation Army out of it."

When I came back from Owensboro, after a month's meditation on the banks of the Ohio, I decided I would enter the ministry.

I began to preach the gospel after the fashion of John the Baptist in the wilderness of Judea. I didn't use a pearl handle pen knife; I did what J. T. Pemberton said, I had a broad axe and laid it at the tap root of the trees of dancing, gambling, saloons, houses of ill fame, ungodly conduct, high and low, far and near. And you talk about a bonfire—the whole woods was set on fire and it looked like the forest fire I saw in Northern Michigan once when it appeared that the infernal regions below had burst through the crust of the earth and painted the lurid flames of the inferno itself on the clouds above.

With all the intensity of my soul I waded into the thing, right and left, fore and aft, inside and outside. I asked no questions for conscience's sake or stomach's sake. I got me a Scotch tweed, salt and pepper suit of clothes and went in arm and hammer brand style.

The crowds came, large numbers were saved.

First thing I knew I got a call from the chairman of the board of trustees. He was in the wholesale grocery business, a very domineering type of man, and he had been one of my closest friends. He was the one who gave the twenty-dollar gold pieces on Thanksgiving. He called me up as if I had been a negro janitor and talked to me with less respect than I would speak to the janitor. He said in a few curt words:—"I want you to come down here right away. I want to see you."

I started to tell him to go where the fires don't go out, but fortunately I decided otherwise, and I went.

I knew then I had put my foot on the edge of a bottomless abyss covered with flowers.

I knew then I had entered the ministry.

I knew then that I was in the supreme fight of my life.

Before I got there he had told all his office force, and everybody on the outside heard him say it, "We are going to fire that blankety blank preacher, and I am going to tell him what I think of him."

I went into that office as a lamb led to the slaughter. Only afterwards did I find out what he said. When I went in he never even asked me to sit down, had his feet propped up on his desk, and he just rared back and they heard him all over the place as he began to tell me what a fool I was, and what a mistake they had made, and closed by saying, "Norris, when we called you we thought you had some sense, but you are a D.......... fool! And this is to notify you that you are fired!"

I walked up close to him, and if the Lord ever helped a poor preacher He helped me that noon. I was made over. There was something beyond human power and wisdom that shot through my soul. I looked him squarely in the eye, and I wasn't afraid of him. I had already come to the point where it mattered little what happened to me. All sense of fear was gone.

I said, "Mr. W.........., No. You have not made a mistake. I thought you made a mistake in the call, but you are the one that is fired!"

He had objected to the crowd of poor people I was bringing to the church, and even went on to say, "I noticed the other night where you baptized a notorious street walker in the very same baptistry where I was baptized."

I said, "You are mistaken. There was not one; there were two. And I don't know how you know who they are, but last Sunday night they came to the church and it was crowded and they couldn't get in, but stood on the outside and heard the message. And the next day they came to my house, and one of them had a little girl five years of age. And they both in the presence of my wife and me related the story of their sin and sorrow and wanted to be saved and start life over again. We prayed, and they were both saved. And I want to say to you, Sir, that I would rather have my church filled with publicans and sinners that come to hear the gospel, than to have it run by a worldly, ungodly crowd of officials that have their automobiles full of liquor and women and go out and spend all night on the lake and then come around the next Sunday and pass around the bread and wine at the Lord's table. You are fired! And next Sunday I am going to tell the whole world your threats!"

And I did, and the fight was on, and it has been on ever since.

The picture on the opposite page was taken in London 1920. Dr. E. Y. Mullins was president of the Southern Baptist Theological Seminary, Dr. J. B. Gambrell, President Southern Baptist Convention, and Dr. J. Frank Norris, Pastor of the First Baptist Church.

Drs. Mullins and Gambrell were touring Europe in behalf of the Baptists, and the day before the three met, through the courtesy of Sir Arthur I. Dureant, Commissioner of His Majesty Works, I was carried to 10 Downing Street and introduced to David Lloyd George, the Prime Minister. He gave me an autographed photograph which I still have.

Drs. Gambrell and Mullins had been waiting in London for three days seeking an interview with David Lloyd George, and they could hardly believe it when they were informed of my interview the day before.

I immediately called up Sir Arthur I. Dureant and he arranged for their meeting with Lloyd George the next morning. I was on my first visit to London on my way to Palestine. Through the courtesy of Mr. John Coutts I was brought in contact with Sir Arthur I. Dureant who in turn secured special permit through the war department which at that time was closed and no passports were issued in Palestine.

The three of us had many happy experiences in London. The following letter from Dr. Mullins has always been prized very highly:

"Louisville, Kentucky

May 9, 1912.

"My dear Dr. Norris:

"I have followed the newspaper accounts of your trial with keenest interest and will say that I am delighted at the outcome expresses it mildly.

"I have read Dr. Gambrell's review in the Standard and I quite concur in his judgment that it was a 'Colossal frameup.'

"May this sorrow turn to the deepening of your Spiritual life and thereby enlarge your ministry.

"Yours very cordially,

"E. Y. MULLINS."

Dr. E. Y. Mullins—Dr. J. B. Gambrell—Dr. J. Frank Norris

New Sunday School Building, First Baptist Church, Fort Worth.

"RAZOR BLADES THOUSAND FEET HIGH" —ANOTHER CHAPTER OF INSIDE THE CUP

To use a well known expression of my lifelong friend, I. E. Gates, "Razor blades were flying a thousand feet high."

The year 1911 arrived, and that was the reddest hot prohibition fight in the history of Texas, and I was pulled into the fight, and here is how it happened.

There was a statewide gathering of the saloon crowd held in the Coliseum in Fort Worth, and the papers reported over 10,000 in attendance. All the red-nosed saloon keepers, white-apron bartenders, and all their henchmen—they were all on hand.

On Sunday morning I picked up the Fort Worth Record, which has since gone out of business for reasons that will hereinafter be stated, and saw where there was a big "Committee of prominent citizens," for the arrangement, entertainment, and handling of this liquor convention.

And the first three names of the committee were three deacons in the First Baptist Church! I will not call their names for they have passed to their reward, and notwithstanding a very bitter fight that became intensely personal, I am happy to state that all three died my good friends.

I won't carry anger long. I don't want to carry it. I believe the Scripture that says, "Be ye angry, and sin not: Let not the sun go down upon your wrath." It has not always been easy for me to carry out this Scripture. I am just as human as the humanest. There are some "pious," superlatively pious, preachers who go around and yarn about it, but I am not going to commit two sins, have anger and wrath, then lie about it. One sin is enough.

I believe the Lord is gracious enough to forgive, yet I don't want to overdraw my bank account.

When I read that account where my three deacons headed this committee entertaining the liquor crowd, I went down the list showing several other members of the First Baptist Church. The chief spokesman, the editor of the Fort Worth Record, who at that time was a member of the First Baptist Church—he was publisher as well as editor, a very brilliant man, and a remarkably gifted man.

What surgings of soul! What conflicts I had. One voice said, "Now you are the pastor of a great city church, and don't stir up a row over this liquor question. These men are men of wealth and prestige, bankers and capitalists and you will make a fool of yourself to say anything about it—besides you can't do anything about it."

But another voice said, "You, the pastor of a great church— will you permit officials and deacons to remain on your official board who are personally responsible before the world for this liquor convention? Have you forgotten the rivers of tears that liquor caused your own sainted mother? Have you forgotten how it wrapped its slimy coil around one of the best, and one of the most brilliant men who ever drew the breath of life and wrecked him? Have you forgotten that liquor knows no race, no color, no wealth, no poverty?"

I was brought up when a small boy on the editorial writings of Henry W. Grady, and I recall how he said:

"My friends, don't trust it. It is powerful, aggressive and universal in its attacks. Tonight it enters an humble home to strike the roses from a woman's cheeks, and tomorrow it challenges this republic in the halls of Congress.

"Today it strikes the crust from the lips of a starving child, and tomorrow levies the tribute from the government itself. There is no cottage humble enough to escape it—no palace strong enough to shut it out. . . .

"It is the mortal enemy of peace and order. The despoiler of men, the terror of women, the cloud that shadows the face of children, the demon that has dug more graves and sent more souls unshriven to judgment than all the pestilences that have wasted life since God sent the plagues to Egypt, and all the wars since Joshua stood before Jericho. . . .

"It can profit no man by its return. It can uplift no industry, revive no interests, remedy no wrong. . . . It comes to destroy, and it shall profit mainly by the ruin of your sons and mine. It comes to mislead human souls and crush human hearts under its rumbling wheels.

"It comes to bring gray-haired mothers down in sorrow to their graves. It comes to turn the wife's love into despair, and her pride into shame. It comes to still the laughter on the lips of little children, and to stifle all the music of the home and fill it with silence and desolation. It comes to ruin your body and mind, to wreck your home."

My decision was made; I acted promptly. I called a meeting of the deacons in the old church—just had one small office in the corner—and that meeting was held just before the morning service. I held that paper in my hand, with their names on the Liquor Committee, and I never shall forget my experience, my feelings. I had come to the do-and-dare decision. It was life and death. God was good to a young preacher that morning.

I knew then for the first time, a little something of what Daniel must have felt when he stood before Belshazzar and read the handwriting on the wall. I knew then something of what Peter must have felt when he stood before the Sanhedrin at Jerusalem, and said, "We ought to obey God rather than men." I knew something of what the Apostle Paul must have felt as he stood before the Roman Courts, and even Caesar himself.

I was entering into a new world, but I didn't know one ten-thousandth part of the things that awaited me. How wonderful that a gracious God keeps the future from us! I am so glad I didn't know what was ahead.

I threw the issue right square on the table, before these men. Of course, they could not defend the liquor business.

But as usual on such occasions there was the counsel for "caution and conservatism."

I gave them the ultimatum of choosing between the church and the liquor crowd, and right now, and not tomorrow. I made a most dangerous decision as it proved afterwards.

I am happy to say they resigned from the Board of Deacons.

But you talk about that warm country, spelled with four letters that sometimes breaks loose over in Georgia—the whole region broke loose in the First Baptist Church.

They dared not say what the real issue was.

They attacked my "methods." They objected to my sermons. They accused me of being "sensational." They said I was a "disturber of peace," a "divider of the brethren," an "agitator," and even went so far as to say I was a "public nuisance."

And I didn't deny anything, and I am not denying now, all they said, for I recall how they said the same things about the men of the Old Testament and the New Testament.

That's why they called Elijah—"A troubler in Israel.

And Paul—they called him a "pestilent fellow."

If any body has any idea that I wanted to fight, they are just ten thousand times mistaken. I never had wanted to fight; never did start one, but I have been there when several have been finished.

Talk about the "Timid soul"—I had a copyright on it.

But something happened in the church besides the row. The Lord came around and paid us a visit.

And the folks came.

And salvation came.

And hundreds were saved.

Yes, I preached on sensational subjects.

I saw the ball parks, the barber shops, the theatres and every other place full, and I was preaching to an empty wood-yard on Sunday nights.

I wouldn't preach now on some of the subjects I did then, and I wouldn't advise any other young preacher to do it. I am just telling about some of my mistakes, hoping they may help some other young preacher.

The fact that I got by with it—well, I might not get by with it now; no, I should say I didn't get by with it, the Lord just pulled me through it. It was the same God who pulled old Jacob out of his trouble, and who delivered Simon Peter out of the hands of Herod and the Jews. On more than one ocasion He has pulled me through. I confess it and deny not; yes, more, I am happy to state that He did. I know He did, and I expect Him to do it again.

I don't know what close places I will be in during the rest of my earthly journey, but I am dead certain to be in several. And I still believe that "He is a very present help in time of trouble."

That's why I have a through ticket from the beginning of my

earthly journey clear through to the end of eternity. And I am very glad that ticket is all paid for; even meals provided for; even lodging, clothes, armor—everything from helmet to shoes on my feet. Even the wells of water of salvation are overflowing, and an abundance of honey is found in the dry carcasses of lions on the roadside.

Yes, I preached on sensational subjects. But always on salvation.

Oh, the "high-falutin," lorgnette-sisters were terrily shocked! They threw up their hands in holy terror. The General Pastors Association had many things to say about it, just like the Detroit Council of Churches put in much of their time discussing my ministry in Detroit. Newspaper editorials were very caustic in their criticism. I intended that it should be discussed, and my intentions were more than abundantly realized.

Everybody was talking about the First Baptist Church.

When I first came here I went down Main Street, and asked five business concerns—one a popcorn stand, another a news stand—where the First Baptist Church was, and there wasn't a one of the five could tell me. I made up my mind if I stayed in Fort Worth it wouldn't be long until they would all soon find out. And they did!

The same thing has already happened with the Temple Baptist Church in Detroit. But like the fellow who had delirium tremens, said to the globe trotter when he returned, "You ain't seen nothing yet."

My message was on the prodigal's return. That was the answer to critics of the new plan. My text was, "I will arise and go to my father."

Walking up Main Street, two blocks from the church, was a Lieutenant and recruiting officer of the Marine Service. He saw the crowd standing on the outside, couldn't get in, and he said afterward, he wondered whether it was a fire or fight, so he came over. It happened to be both a fire and a fight. He was a great big, strong, strapping fellow, 34 years of age, a native of Connecticut. I never shall forget the name, Charles G. Fain. He had on the full uniform, brass buttons, braid, and everything else that goes with it. He elbowed his way into the vestibule of the Sunday School annex, and stood there towering over everybody. When I gave the appeal for the prodigal to come to God for mercy and salvation, this strong, athletic, military figure, pushed his way through the crowd, down the aisle. Of course, he attracted everybodys attention. Standing before the crowd, erect, as fine a specimen of physical manhood as I ever laid my eyes on—I said to him, "Do you come accepting my proposition, taking Christ as your Saviour?"

He said in a clear voice, "I do."

I took him by the hand and said, "Get up here on the platform, and tell this crowd why you have come."

I didn't know what he was going to say. I remember, as if it were yesterday—he stood there and began to weep, and said:

"My friends, I was walking up Main Street, saw the crowd, wondered what was happening, whether it was a fight or a fire. I came over. I haven't been to church in many years. I left my home in Connecticut when eighteen years of age. The last night I was home, my mother, who is now in heaven, came into my room, and knelt by my bed. As she tucked the cover in and kissed me, she said, 'My boy, you are leaving home tomorrow, and I want you to know wherever you sail the wide seas, your mother's prayers will always follow you.' She put a little Bible in my trunk on top of my clothes. I went into the service. Time rolled on, one day while in the harbor of Osaka, Japan, on one of Uncle Sam's battleships, I received this cablegram, 'Your mother passed away.' I went into my room, fell on my knees, lifted my heart to God, but I was surrounded by evil associations. Time rolled on—I have been a prodigal. I have lived the life of a sinner, but tonight as I stood yonder in the corner it seemed just as real, as I am looking in your face, my mother stood by me saying, 'Remember, wherever you go Mother's prayers will follow you.' I am happy to tell you I am now ready to meet my mother in the home beyond the skies."

Of course, the effect was electric. You could have heard a pin fall—sinners were coming from the right and from the left— "Wisdom is justified of her ways."

Results? Oh, the results when souls are saved, all hell cannot gainsay. That should have been enough to convince the most unGodly gainsayer.

But it added to their hatred. Their opposition grew, and I knew for the first time, the spirit of hell that took Stephen outside the gate of Jerusalem and gnashed on him with their teeth and stoned him to death.

MY FIRST MEETING OF DR. NORRIS

By Rev. Louis Entzminger

In August 1913 I received the following telegram:

"Would you consider becoming superintendent First Baptist Sunday School at your present salary. If so come to Fort Worth our expense."

In two or three weeks I headed for Fort Worth. I had never been this far West before. On the train between Dallas and Fort Worth I purchased a Fort Worth paper, and in that paper I read a paragraph which stated that the Judge of the District Court, on motion of the state's attorney himself had dismissed charges against Dr. J. Frank Norris for burning his church.

When I arrived, and while talking with his secretary, in a few minutes, a slim, tall, boyish looking fellow came walking in. He looked very much like a bean pole dressed in a gray suit, and I could not believe it for some seconds when he shook hands with me and said, "This is Norris."

Although a youngster myself I had had considerable experience in dealing with people in business, in schools and in religious circles, and it did not take me long to observe the penetrating gray eyes that pierced me through.

I do not know what his first sight opinion of me was, but I am frank to say he presented a problem to me. It was not until I had left Fort Worth, after this first visit, that I observed the characteristic of Dr. Norris that my years of experience in association with him has justified—a sense of fairness in dealing with a man, and wanting him to get all the facts and come to his own conclusion.

I was anxious for a conference with an old friend, who was in the Seminary in Fort Worth. In a little while we were alone, and he proceeded to tell me the whole story, presenting both sides of the question as fairly as I believe it could possibly be done:

"Norris was a great preacher"—"Large crowds attended his services"—"multitudes were saved." Well, this certainly was encouraging, but the other side of the question:

Many of the preachers and pastors of the leading churches,

denominational leaders, newspaper editorials, the city government, the county government, were against him—many, many unfavorable things.

I rode on the train from Georgetown to Louisville with Dr. J. B. Gambrell, and we had a most interesting visit. He was kind enough to give me the names of some good men who would talk to me frankly about Norris and the church and the situation there. I had the names of these men in my notebook.

Two of them, especially, I discovered in my conference with this student friend that these two men were Norris's friends and supporters, active members of his church. Dr. Gambrell's talk had left a most favorable impression on me concerning Norris, yet there was a serious question in my mind.

This seminary friend said:

"Norris is accused by the preachers as being an opportunist, of putting over many shrewd schemes."

He then stated one which was about as follows:

The seminary, opened on Tuesday, but many students arrived in Fort Worth on Friday, and said some married students, with their families. And because of the great publicity given Norris in the daily papers, all over the state of Texas and the Southwest and in the Texas Baptist Standard, it seemed these students flocked to the First Baptist Church for Sunday night's service. Norris had several rows of seats down front reserved. During the opening part of his services that night with a packed house he had asked all the preachers and their wives to stand. There were a hundred or more—then he invited them from all over the building to these reserved seats, preached a great and impressive sermon that moved the audience to tears, concluding with an invitation to profess Christ, and to join the church on a profession of faith and baptism, or by letter, and some seventy-five of these ministerial students, some of them with their wives, united with the church It seems that the preachers at the seminary thought this was a crime.

Frankly it greatly impressed me. Any preacher who could preach to a packed house and have 20 or 30 people saved and was so powerful in his message, and in spite of all the unfavorable publicity about him, receive 75 young seminary students into his church membership, certainly must have the confidence of a great many people and know how to win people to Christ and to church membership.

Naturally I wanted to go to Fort Worth. Instead of this "scheme" reacting unfavorably, it greatly impressed me.

Other incidents related unfavorable to Norris were of similar nature.

Jealousy of Good Men

It did not take me long to feel that possibly because of the great crowds he preached to and the tremendous results from his ministry, he would naturally create more or less jealousy even with good men.

I had a visit with one of these laymen whose name Dr. Gambrell had given me. I accidently ran into him where the new church was being constructed. I gave no intimation to him I was making any inquiry about Dr. Norris, but in a few minutes he opened up, and although a very conservative man, he soon had me almost enthusiastic over Norris.

But still there were questions in my mind as to the character of a man against whom so many accusations had been made, who had been tried in the courts, and although cleared yet had a host of enemies among the leaders in every phase of life in the City of Fort Worth.

The newspapers were bitterly opposed to him, and took every occasion to publish unfavorable news. Certain leaders in the Baptist denomination, while very careful in what they would say were unfavorable to Norris. I found out later why, and so have others found out.

The one question in my mind was, what about this man's character?

I met Mrs. J. Frank Norris—a beautiful, smiling, charming, sparkling personality. I am frank to say she completely won me almost instantly. The opinion I formed of her at that time I have never had any occasion to change. She has grown on me through the years. I was convinced then that she was a most remarkable woman.

Saw Norris Perform First Major Operation

When I reached the tabernacle Sunday evening, had it not been for his aid I doubt if I could have gotten in hearing distance. It seemed to me everybody in Fort Worth was there. The tabernacle was packed and jammed; the seats all around filled. The preacher in a large stone church just across the street was preaching to a little handfull, while the steps of his church was packed with Norris's audience, and all around the wall of his church men and women stood to hear Norris.

It is true he was preaching on a sensational subject—"The Ten Biggest Devils in Fort Worth, Names Given," but I had never dreamed of anything like what appeared as I finally, with Norris, had gotten in the tabernacle and to the platform.

Language to describe my experience as I looked over that immense multitude, I could not possibly command.

Dr. Norris got up after a rousing gospel song service led by an attorney, it seemed that all of the eight or ten thousand people—it looked like twenty-five thousand—had joined in those old gospel songs. It was tremendously impressive. He stood there making some announcements, looking humility personified. I could but wonder if he were not embarrassed by the tremendous audience. What in the world had all this crowd come out for? Was this little slim bean pole, dressed up in gray, adequate to such an occasion? He was very cool and calm, and calculating, also, intensely human. I was really afraid for him, so defenseless.

It did not take long to thoroughly disillusion me. Quietly he proceded to discuss some local matters—and then I observed his fingers for the first time. They were long and keen as railroad spikes. I observed them as he pointed out certain facts with reference to outstanding men who it seems had been using their influence against him.

He proved that one of them had a room in a certain hotel, although a married man with a family, where he entertained the ladies with beer and champagne parties; that this outstanding business man had a speaking tube from this hotel to the saloon through which he conveyed his orders to the bartender, and then the man who built the speaking tube, a long tall rowbone carpenter stood up to testify to the truth of what Norris had stated. Names were called. It scared me out of my wits.

Well, I was stunned at the courage, the boldness and the gameness with which this explosion came.

I could hardly realize where I was or what was going on.

Another one of these outstanding men was figuratively put on the stand, name called, and his record as proven by a number of facts presented, certainly looked bad, and then another with the same results, and then another—remember these were the leading men of the city.

And finally the outstanding man, possibly of the whole city, owner of the great daily paper, head of the biggest firm of lawyers, not only in Fort Worth, but in the Southwest. It seems that his paper had been making vigorous attacks on Norris, and that the editor of this paper had been one of the leaders in the fight against Norris. I believe he was on the grand jury, possibly, foreman of the grand jury that framed the indictment against Norris, and Norris had charged that this paper was, at least in part, owned by the brewery interests, and that it was dominated by the liquor interests. This charge had been vigorously denied.

When Norris finished his address after an hour and half, although it seemed like only a few minutes to me, it seemed he had invited all these men to be present, and he invited them then and there to the platform to make any reply they wished to make, and to my utter surprise, a large handsomely dressed gentleman walked to the platform and started to speak. I discovered then for the first time that the audience was divided. He was cheered by some and hooted by others. Dr. Norris stepped forward and quieted the audience and pleaded with them for a respectful and attentive hearing.

The speaker had no trouble from then on until he asked Dr. Norris a question, "What business of this is yours?" he said with reference to the ownership of his paper. The tall, pale spindling preacher made a charge pointing his finger at the big attorney.

I shall never forget the words with which he replied, and very cooly, and in clarion voice that could be heard by all the thousands said:

"That's exactly the way with you fellows—you control the street car system and the newspapers and run the liquor business, and use the newspapers as an instrument to create sentiment, and then you ask what business of mine it is who runs the newspapers?"

Well, by this time this prominent lawyer was shaking like an aspen leaf and having asked a question, certainly had to be fair enough to be asked a question, and Norris was quick as lightning in attacking at this point.

He asked the big attorney and owner of the daily newspaper if it were not a fact that one of the brewing companies, calling the name of it, owned stock in his paper. It was one of the most tense moments I have ever seen in my life. The lawyer hesitated and tried to sidestep, but the preacher held him on the spot until he blustered out excitedly,

"Yes, they own"—this was as far as he got.

At this admission the greater part of that tremendous audience cheered for almost five minutes. This was the end of the meeting. The corporation attorney disappeared instantaneously. The great mass of humanity rushed up to Norris, who stood calm and victorious, as David over Goliath.

It was during and at the close of this service that the final question as to my going to Fort Worth was decided. No man would make such a bold and courageous attack upon these big business leaders, prove his case and win the applause of possibly ten thousand people, if there was the least soiled spot on his character. I was convinced absolutely beyond question and accepted the place with Dr. Norris and the First Baptist Church.

Many who were exceedingly anxious for me to come felt that it would have been much more impressive upon me had Norris preached a great sermon. But that would not have settled the question in my mind as it was decided that night. I have thought about it a great many times, and I am satisfied that the hand of God was in it all. It was a case of where Romans 8:28 fits exactly: "And we know that all things work together for good to them that love God, to them who are the called according to his purpose."

Second Chapter
Superintendent First Baptist Sunday School

I found that in the early spring of 1913 a large group of the most prominent and influential members of the church left the First Baptist Church and joined other Baptist churches in the city. This included the superintendent of the Sunday School and all the departmental superintendents except one, and most of the teaching staff.

This opposition to Dr. Norris in the early winter and spring of 1913, many of the wealthy were either excluded or secured letters and left the church at practically the same time.

Norris Won By Revival

The story I have upon good authority, of this division in the church was told me by a man who was opposed to Dr. Norris and who went out with the group. He said, we wanted Norris to resign, he was creating such a stir in Fort Worth fighting the liquor crowd, and as he put it, almost everything and everybody else in the city felt that way. "We desired to take our summer vacation and then come back and get rid of Norris. While we were away for the three or four summer months Norris was in a continuous revival meeting, and when we got back we found that he had had more than 500 additions to the church while we were away. Many of those joining knew nothing of us whatever. We had no power or influence with them, and before we knew it we were entirely out of the picture. Norris could take that crowd and could have turned us everyone out if he had wanted to. Where we made the mistake was in not putting him out before we went off on our summer vacations."

It was easy to see as I had begun the work that the most of the members of the church were new and inexperienced.

To secure a teaching staff of over 100 out of this group was no easy task. Twenty or more of those put on the teaching staff had just been received into the church, in fact some of them had not been baptized yet but were awaiting baptism.

It was in connection with this work that I came to know Mrs. J. Frank Norris. She was my "right hand man." She helped me to select everyone of the teachers and officers, and on Sunday morning, October 1st, there was a total attendance of 266 present. We entered into the new church building, although unfinished, and there I formed between 75 and 80 classes. Out of the 266, many of the teachers had no class at all, just a list of prospects out of which to build a class. In four weeks the attendance had gone from 266 to over 700.

The average attendance of the Sunday School the first twelve months, from the first Sunday in October 1913 to the first Sunday in October, 1914, was approximately 1000.

We received out of the Sunday school over 300 members, men, women, boys and girls.

I do not know when Norris prepared his sermons. We both went night and day, going "from house to house," winning souls, building up the congregation and the Bible School.

Naturally there were those who disagreed with Norris in his policy and methods. Immediately they began to pour their complaints in my ears. The first one was one of the main deacons in the church.

He took me in a big Cadillac and started telling me about Norris's handling of finances, offering all kinds of criticism. I told him I thought we ought to get Norris and have a conference and straighten matters up. When I told him that he threw up his hands and said, "I would not have Norris to know anything about this for anything." I told him immediately there were no secrets between me and any member of the church where Dr. Norris was involved, and when I had finished a few remarks from the platform the following Sunday morning, there was no further criticism of Dr. Norris during my association with him in Fort Worth from members of the church.

The financial conditions were bad and financing the work was an exceedingly difficult matter.

When my first month's salary was due, it was not paid. I had discovered the financial condition was serious and waited a day or two without saying anything about it. But finally being hard pressed I mentioned it to Dr. Norris on Saturday. I think up to that time he did not know I had not been paid. At any rate that afternoon about five o'clock we went to a department store and I received my salary in cash from Dr. Norris' own hand. I found out later that he had called a man in Dallas that morning and borrowed it personally and had this man to call this department store manager who was a personal friend of his and have him pay the money to Dr. Norris.

Norris Gives Offerings From Meetings To Church

It was amusing to me to hear enemies of Dr. Norris criticise him on financial matters in connection with the church when I knew of my own personal experience and observation that he had gone out and held meetings to get money to pay my salary with. I saw him a number of times, in fact was with him in several meetings when every penny of offerings given him for three or four weeks meetings was placed in the church treasury to pay the obligations of the church.

When I began personal visitation I had had no experience and without letting Dr. Norris know it I planned some visitation for us to do together. I never shall forget the first visit we made. I had secured the information in the census. We went to see a mother who claimed to have been a member of a church somewhere in the country whose husband was lost. We had two of their children in Sunday School.

When we knocked at the door she came, and she hesitated as she opened it. Norris looked at her and said,

"This is Mr. Norris."

She was wiping her hands on an old fashioned gingham apron. She looked at him with a vengeance. From her looks I would not have been surprised if she had knocked him out the door and slammed it in his face. She seemed to be indignant. He managed somehow, I do not know how, to get inside. She did not want to see us; did not want to have anything to do with us, but in his tactful, kindly way we got in, and before I realized it we were seated, and he was asking her if he might read a passage from the Word of God. Before she had time to reply he was reading. Before reading the Scripture he had put his hand tenderly and kindly on both of the children's heads and gotten both their names. When he finished reading the Scripture he asked if we might pray, but without waiting for an answer we were all on our knees. Incidentally, I do not know when I ever heard a prayer that affected me as this prayer did. He prayed for this dear mother in such kind and tender words. In his prayer he talked about his own dear mother who loved God and who taught him the Scriptures at her knee, and he prayed that this mother who had the same God his mother had and the same Bible his mother had might be guided and blessed and rear her children in the fear and love of God; that she might have wisdom and grace and strength for the task. Then he prayed for each one of the little children by name and then for her husband who was a railroad engineer. I felt the very presence of God in the room. When we got up I turned away from them to wipe the tears from my eyes, but as I turned to look at her, great tears were streaming down her cheeks. She had not been able to speak for the moment. God had done His work that had changed the whole atmosphere, and in a moment this woman who was indignant because Dr. Norris had called, was unburdening her heart to him.

She had married this young railroad man twelve years before and moved from the country community and the old country church to Fort Worth.

Her husband took to drinking and as soon as he dismounted from his engine in the railroad yards as he came off his run he went to the saloon. She would often see very little of him while he was in Fort Worth. He would sober up just long enough before leaving on the next run to be ready for the task. He spent his salary for drink. The house was poorly furnished, the children poorly clad. She finally confessed, however, as much as she might like to come to the Sunday School and church that she had no clothes—that she was not able to clothe them adequately for church and Sunday School attendance. I never will forget the result of this visit. The next Sunday morning this mother with two little children were in the First Baptist Sunday School when the invitation was given at the close of the eleven o'clock service she was on the front seat asking to be restored to fellowship.

It was four weeks later at the close of a day long to be remembered when this husband and railroad engineer fell at the front seat in the church, buried his hands in his face and wept tears of repentance, and was gloriously saved at the close of the Sunday evening service.

On that memorable day 76 people came into the membership of the First Baptist Church!

But in spite of the favor and blessing of God upon the church and pastor, a large number of people saved and great increase in the Sunday School attendance, the enemies continued to work, and before the close of the first year of my connection a new indictment was secured against Dr. Norris for the same offense of which he had been cleared by twelve jurors.

Personally I was stunned. I could not understand it at all. I had been in the most intimate and inner circle of the Norris family and the church. I could not possibly conceive of such a thing as guilt on his part.

He went to make bond and waive commitment trial, but the thing was all evidently fixed, a new campaign of publicity against Norris was to be put on and the most unusual thing I have ever heard of was done. The court did not waive the commitment trial, but demanded that the case be tried before a Justice of Peace before being passed on to the Superior Court. This was done, and the purpose in the mind of the conspirators prosecuting him was served.

A new witness testified—I heard his testimony—that at 3 o'clock in the morning of the burning of the church he was loading his milk wagon on Third Street near Throckmorton at the creamery ready for his morning delivery. Looking back toward the church on the corner of Third and Taylor Streets, the other end of the block he saw a man coming out of the church who had on a certain kind of hat, black overcoat, and he described the collar and tie, in fact the dress of the man, and said because of the bright arc light that was burning, as well as the light burning over the church door he distinctly and clearly saw the man and knew who it was. It was a tense moment in the court room. The attorney asked,

"Who was the man?"

And he said, "Dr. J. Frank Norris."

The witness finished loading his milk wagon and drove away. He had hardly gotten to the south side of the city when he noticed that there was a fire, and it was in the direction of the First Baptist Church to which everybody was hastening. The church was burned and Norris was seen by this witness coming out of the church and could be clearly distinguished a block away because of a light over the church door and the big arc light over the street in front.

The papers issued extras and headlined it in box car letters,

"NORRIS WAS GUILTY BEYOND QUESTION"—"and ere long he would be behind prison walls."

He made bond of course, and in spite of his urging immediate trial in the superior court everything was put off as long as possible. And every effort to embarrass, humiliate and disgrace a man and his family that could possibly be made was then furthered.

Norris had fought to clean up the red light district. He had done everything in the world to put the saloon out of business.

Numbers of drunkards were converted under his ministry and I saw him baptize hundreds of them myself.

The Testimony of the Light Company Exposes the Frame Up

The trial in the district court was finally forced by Norris, and if at any time there was any embarrassment or it in any way affected him, mentally, spiritually, or otherwise he concealed it perfectly from me. If anything, he seemed to preach with greater power and effectiveness while at the same time all the powers of darkness were moved against him and the church, and yet the work grew and multiplied and multitudes of hardened sinners came confessing Christ and were baptized.

When the trial came up this perjurer who swore in the commitment trial that he saw Dr. Norris more than a block away come out of the church under the arc light, when he got on the witness stand he was confronted with the records of the light and power company of Fort Worth. These records showed there was a full moon, and that the light of the streets were turned off that night at 8 o'clock, and the time of the fire was two o'clock in the morning.

Then this perjured witness changed his testimony and said that it was the moon and not the arc light.

And the most terrible tense moment I ever saw took place in that court room.

Norris' attorney asked, "Who told you to change your testimony?"

The witness looked over toward the hired prosecution and the district attorney, "The district attorney, Mr. John W. Baskin, told me to change it."

That ended the conspiracy.

And I was in for another experience unlike anything I have ever witnessed before or since. The court room was turned into a revival meeting. There were several preachers in the court room who had been against Norris. They broke down and wept. The whole court room was bathed in tears. "Old Time Religion" and other revival songs were sung. People were converted. It was a most remarkable manifestation of the power and presence of God.

This was on Saturday. The question in my mind was what the preacher would do on Sunday. Now would be his chance, and he would most assuredly make a drive against his enemies. That is what everybody thought. I did not know.

The crowd was there on Sunday night. "And he cut off the hem of his garment."

The house was packed and possibly as many people on the outside as were on the inside. It was one of the most tender and effective messages I ever listened to—how that David had an opportunity to slay his enemy and finish him up, but instead of doing it he clipped off a piece of the skirt of his garment and showed it to his enemy after he had gone some distance, to convince him that he could have slain him had he chosen to do so, but that the life of his enemy was in the hands of God. The climax to that message was how like the Christ who died for a world that hated him, and quoting, Romans 5:9, "But God commendeth his love toward us, in that while we were yet sinners, Christ died for us."

At the conclusion of the sermon a multitude of people were saved. It was one of the greatest services I ever witnessed.

After this victory in the court room the growth of the church, including the Sunday School was more remarkable if possible than formerly. There was a great turning to the First Baptist Church.

I am including here an editorial by Dr. J. B. Gambrell who was the editor of the Baptist Standard, published at Dallas, Texas, which gives his opinion and judgment in the Norris trials in Fort Worth, also an editorial by the Texas Christian Advocate, the Methodist paper for Texas:

"The Whole Business a Colossal Frame-Up of Wickedness in Which the Machinery of the Law Has Been Seized and Used to Ruin an Innocent Man in Order to Screen Guilty Men"—J. B. Gambrell

Dr. J. B. Gambrell was editor of the Baptist Standard at that time and May 2, 1912, on the front page of the Standard under title, "The Vindication of Pastor Norris," Dr. J. B. Gambrell wrote the following editorial:

"The remarkable trial in Fort Worth, which has held the attention of the State and country for weeks, came to an end in a most triumphant way for Pastor J. F. Norris of the First Baptist Church, Fort Worth. The indictment was for perjury, but the trial was for perjury and arson. The verdict was 'Not guilty.' The whole country had rendered the verdict on the evidence in advance of the jury.

"Not in the history of America, perhaps, was there ever an indictment brought in by a grand jury on as flimsy and shadowy pretense of evidence. Nor was ever an indictment framed under more questionable circumstances. But that a grand jury would bring in an indictment against one occupying a place so exalted as that of pastor of a great church, and following a series of such crimes as had been committed in Fort Worth gave the country pause. The trial revealed a condition in and around that grand jury reprehensible and regrettable to the last degree.

"Not doubting for a moment that the underworld was beneath the prosecution of the pastor, making the atmosphere for it and filling Fort Worth with its spirit; and not doubting that Pastor Norris was innocent of the charge laid against him, I nevertheless felt that prudence, a decent regard for even the forms of law, as well as the ends of justice, dictated an attitude of waiting. This was the attitude of the country at large and of ministers in particular. The comparative silence of the Standard was in deference to civic decorum. But, now in words as plain as can be written, I give my conviction that

"That indictment was an outrage.

"The situation in Fort Worth was unfriendly to a fair trial. Passion was deeply stirred. Prejudice was rife. The forces of evil in Fort Worth are very strong, with ramifications widespread, personal matters, no way related to the case, unhappily became involved. The long and persistent war of Brother Norris on the allied and shameful vices of the city lay in the background. Putting everything together, the situation did not promise well for the defendant. That a verdict of 'not guilty' could be had under the conditions obtaining is highly gratifying and honoring to the spirit of justice which rose superior to partisan prejudice, and pronounced a righteous judgment. Great credit is due the twelve men who measured up to a high trust and vindicated the right.

"The First Church, as a body, stood by the pastor, and were present in large numbers when the verdict was brought in. The Dallas News correspondents thus describe the scene that followed the announcement 'not guilty':

"Following the reading of this verdict there was a remarkable demonstration. Dr. Norris was not in the court room at the time, having gone to the home of a friend to rest, but scores of women and other friends crowded about Mrs. Norris, sobs shaking their voices as they extended congratulations. Others were more demonstrative and gave a shrill cheer. In a moment this had swelled to what might be called a storm of rejoicing. Almost hysterical laughter, cheers, handclapping, the stamping of feet, all contributed to the noise.

"Demonstration Renewed

"Finally order was restored sufficiently to permit of the formal discharge of the jury, with the thanks of the court. This done, the demonstration was renewed. Some one began to sing 'Old-Time Religion' and scores joined in until the swelling chorus reminded one of the singing at a revival meeting. That hymn was succeeded by 'We Shall Meet on the Beautiful Shore'; 'Nearer My God to Thee'; 'There Is a Great Day Coming,' and 'Are You Ready?'

"Dr. Norris Arrives

"It was at this juncture that Dr. Norris arrived at the court room. He had been notified by telephone of the result and had responded in great haste. As he came in the door he was greeted with the Chautauqua salute and cheered. After greeting Mrs. Norris very affectionately, he personally thanked the jury, while the crowd sang 'We Praise Thee, O Lord,' 'Revive Us Again' and 'How Firm a Foundation.' This last hymn was started by Hon. O. S. Lattimore. Mr. Norris was called upon to speak, and at last, replying to some utterance by Mr. Lattimore, said:

"Confident of Acquittal

" 'Yes, I will say something, and it will be the first time I have had anything to say publicly in this matter. I have been confident of the result all along, and this ending today simply confirms that confidence. I am only going to say a few words, but I will have something to say next Sunday night. I will have a few plain words to say, then, just a few.

"Victim of Prejudice

" 'My friends, when fifteen years ago I went down into the water as a symbol of Christianity, I never even imagined that I could ever by any possibility stand before any of my fellow citizens as one accused of crime. And now, the victim of passion and prejudice as I have been, I want publicly to express my appreciation of the friends who have stood by me. But first of all, I want to lay the crown of laurels on the head of my wife, whose sustaining cheer, comfort and strengthening can simply never be told.

"Thanks His Friends

" 'To my friends who have gone down in this valley of trial with me I also give thanks. I can not undertake to name them. There are too many. But to one and all of them go my heartfelt thanks.

" 'To my counsel—the fifteen lawyers who struggled for the right—there was much comment on the number, fifteen, but it could just as well have been five hundred as fifteen if I had taken them all—also go my grateful thanks.

" 'To the jurors who have so nobly done their duty to themselves, to justice, and to their State, a jury of the fair, honest, impartial citizenship of Tarrant County, who have given their aid in the vindication of my good name, that of my wife, that of my children, that of the pastor of the First Baptist Church and the membership of that church—to them are special thanks due.

"'As to the enemies—'

"Forgiveness for Enemies

"Here Mr. Lattimore and Mr. Doyle, of Mr. Norris' counsel, made some suggestions that could not be heard. Mr. Norris made a low-voiced reply to them and then said aloud: 'I know just what I am going to say, and I am not going to say too much. As to the enemies, I have none but the kindest feelings and not a harsh or unkind word to say. Some have been swept from their feet in this matter, influenced maybe by loud and continued talk, misrepresentations in newspapers or by other influences. Whatever the cause, I repeat I have only the kindest, charitable feelings.'

"Dr. Gambrell Pays Tribute to J. M. Gaddy

"Such a scene is not often witnessed in this world, and no heart can resist its pathos. I can but enter into this joyous scene to the full. The woman most conspicuous in it is the daughter of J. M. Gaddy, than whom Texas never had a more valiant soldier for the right. He was brother to my soul. I joined this woman in holy wedlock to the man by whose side she walked these days in the fiery furnace of trial and all the time in the dauntless spirit of her noble sire.

"The verdict might have been properly instructed by the Judge, for the prosecution stood at the end with not the decent shadow of a case. The defense not only destroyed the case of the prosecution, but on the arson part of the case, made out an affirmative case as impregnable as Gibraltar.

"This is an hour for forgiveness and forgetting. In the stress of the battle natural friends may have wounded each other. Vision was blurred. Mischief makers have been in their heyday. Pastor Norris' words of forgiveness suit a great hour. They were well and nobly spoken. Let all hearts respond and all live up to a high duty and privilege. There is no time for personal wars. The great church must go on with its work. The preacher must proclaim the divine message of peace and good will, living it as well as preaching it. The work of controlling evil is ever with us and must be pushed. Fort Worth has a duty to perform to herself. She ought to inaugurate a campaign for civic righteousness to redeem herself from her bad condition.

"A Colossal Frame-Up of Wickedness

"It has been given out that the arson indictment against Pastor Norris is to be prosecuted harder than the perjury indictment was. The country has come with great unanimity to the belief that the whole business is a colossal frame-up of wickedness in which the machine y of the law has been seized and used to ruin an innocent man in order to screen guilty men. The complete play-out of the perjury case, the utter inefficiency of the evidence, even total lack of any evidence in the case, has settled public opinion as to the grand jury, the legal adviser of the jury and the whole business. Hon. O. S. Lattimore did not put it too strong when he said it was a disgrace to the State."

Dr. Gambrell was editor of the Baptist Standard and the editorial above was published May 2, 1912.

"The Advocate" on the Trial

Leading editorial of the Texas Christian Advocate, official organ of the M. E. Church, South, says in the issue of May 2, 1912:

" 'The effect of the verdict was not simply a vindication of Dr. Norris from the charge of perjury, but it was a rebuke to the grand jury which found the indictment. It would seem to mean that the grand jury had little, if any ground for the indictment. The defense contended that it was personal ill-will toward the minister and a disposition to do him all the injury possible regardless of the evidence involved. That ill-will realized that the trial would give an opportunity to abuse and vilify Dr. Norris and present him before the community in the worst light possible, and that this would compensate for their failure to convict him. In proof of this a certain juryman, a venerable citizen of nearly sixty years' residence in the county and a member of the grand jury, but who voted against the indictment, testified that a juryman said to him, just before the indictment was voted, 'I do not believe myself that we have enough evidence to indict him,' but soon thereafter voted for the indictment."

Threats on Norris' Life

A number of times to my personal knowledge, Norris' life was threatened, sometimes by individuals and sometimes by groups.

In the midst of the hottest prohibition fight any city ever had, a group of the outstanding men of Fort Worth held a meeting at which they voted unanimously to run Norris out of town. They notified him that he was to never speak again or appear on the streets of Fort Worth, and they gave him 30 days, I think, to get out of the city, and so notified him.

The first I knew about it was late one afternoon I saw hand bills passed out as I passed along one of the streets announcing,

"J. FRANK NORRIS SPEAKS TONIGHT AT THE CORNER OF FIFTEENTH AND MAIN AT SEVEN O'CLOCK."

In that handbill the threat of these men was quoted, and he was speaking there directly in the face of the order for him never to do so any more. It developed that he had received this order and threat and since he could get no advertisement in the newspaper he had ordered 25,000 copies of this handbill distributed all over the city of Fort Worth.

The atmosphere was so tense I felt sure that there would be trouble at 15th and Main that night.

I debated the question as to whether I should go there or not. I thought my days of physical encounter with men had passed when I left the turpentine camp of Florida where often drunken and unruly labor had to be dealt with, and sometimes severe measures had to be taken.

However, I could not find Norris anywhere, and when speaking time came I found my way to the advertised place. And of all the mobs I ever saw—well, they were certainly there.

The streets were packed and jammed; half the city was there, and in great confusion. There were three saloons, if not four, one on each corner at this particular place.

He stood in a Ford roadster to speak. There certainly was a mob spirit there.

It developed soon that Norris had several thousand very warm rooters and supporters present. It could have developed into a very serious situation. Norris led that excited mob in singing "The Sweet By and By." It quieted the whole crowd and they listened attentively.

Another experience I shall not forget to my dying day—it was during this same prohibition fight, a friend of Norris' came walking up to the church one day just as he and I started out to go some place. The friend's face was almost white as a sheet, and he was trembling with great excitement, saying, "Dr. Norris, let me beg you not to go down the street, you stay right here"— I will not quote the man's name. He was one of the leading real estate men of Fort Worth, and is now one of the best friends Norris has—"he says that the first time he lays his eyes on you he is going to shoot your heart out," and he is right down there now at the corner of Sixth and Main, and he said, "I beg you not to go that way."

Norris looked at me and said, "Come on, Entz"—brushed by the man making some nonchalant response and off we went, and to my surprise and amazement, and I might add almost to my consternation, he proceeded forthwith to Sixth and Main Streets.

Between Fifth and Sixth on Main Street was the largest bank in the city. In front of this bank was an old time hitching rack. Standing there leaning upon that was this real estate man who was going to kill Norris on first sight, talking to another man.

Norris and I arm in arm, turned up the street directly to the place where these men were standing talking. He did the turning—I reluctantly—almost had to turn with him. I simply knew the fire works was going to come off. All my past life came up before me as I thought of every mean thing I had done and what my wife would do without me. I did not want to be buried in Fort Worth or be shipped back to Florida where most of my relatives were at that time; I wondered about my insurance. My mind was working like lightning, and my feet were not going in the direction of my heart's desire. But there was nothing else to do.

We walked to the entrance of the bank in ten feet of the place where this man who was going to kill Norris on first sight was standing talking. As we walked up to the bank Norris turned his back to the entrance where this man was standing, picked up a magazine off the display stand; we stood there just a moment, but there was no effort on the part of this man who was going to kill Norris on first sight to make any movement in that direction.

To my amazement and very great delight he and the man to whom he was talking, while we paused in ten feet of them, turned away and went angling across the street to the other side and off down the street somewhere. I was so relieved I paid very little attention to where they went except that they had left that immediate vicinity.

Norris looked at me with what seemed to me then as disdain and said,

"Entz, that's the only way to handle this crowd. If they had the least idea you are afraid of them they would kill you."

And I am sure now he was right.

I have been in all kinds of experiences with this man, and I say beyond all question he fears no one but God.

And yet I do not believe there is a man living—indeed this will surprise many people I am sure—that would avoid trouble, that would almost be imposed on rather than have difficulty.

His patience in dealing with difficult situations, his evident desire to avoid difficulty surprised me many times. While he will not run from it, I know of no man who would use greater endeavor to avoid difficulty with anybody. But I certainly am sorry for the other man when that patience comes to an end.

I would not be telling the truth to say that Norris does not like a fight, and yet as I look back over the history of the past 22 years, in almost every one of the major difficulties with denominational leadership, and the evolutionists and modernists, along with political office holders and others whom he has engaged in public discussion, either on moral or religious questions, taking into consideration his conviction, it would have been practically impossible to have avoided them.

In all of the trying experiences I have been through with J. Frank Norris there has always been a sense of humor, and in fact many humorous experiences. He has gotten off some good jokes on me, some of them made out of whole cloth, and they are good, I will confess.

I remember several that he enjoyed hugely. I, too, after it was over with. As an illustration, he had been making an attack on the indecent moving picture shows and fighting the opening of the moving picture shows on Sunday, had spoken before the Legislature on the matter, preached on it, and in fact had done everything possible to keep the shows from opening on Sunday in Fort Worth, and the moving picture people certainly had no use for him. One of the largest moving picture houses in the city of Fort Worth was owned by a Jew. (This man is now one of Norris' best friends.)

We were trying to find room for extra Sunday School classes. I suggested we might rent one of the moving picture buildings on Sunday. Norris seemed to thrill to the idea, carried me to this big theater and said, "You go in and see what you can do about getting it."

"Tell him you will be glad to pay him for it," etc.

I thought he was going to see somebody else next door. I went in and approached the owner of the moving picture show about the matter. He asked me like a flash,

"Aren't you associated with Norris?"

I said, "I am superintendent of the Sunday School up there."

Everything else I heard for the next two or three minutes was "blankety! blankety! blank! I quietly retired, somewhat confused and in fact fighting mad—not angry, just fighting mad. Norris pretended to be busy looking for somebody or something, but in a few minutes the whole situation dawned on me, he had been splitting his sides laughing at the way that theater owner was "cussing" me out.

I forgave him for it long ago. In fact did it then.

Yes, we had lots of fun together.

One of the most unusual experiences we have ever had was the story he told on me about pulling people out of bed at night to win them to Christ. We were both young and strong at the time and went night and day. When he prepared his sermons I don't know. The biggest part of the time for nearly four years we were going night and day after people. I have never kept any records much on anything I have done. I know lots of people who have kept files of advertisements in newspapers, articles about pictures, diaries and all kinds of things, the number of marriages performed, number of people baptized. I have no records whatever on these things; all I have is the record in my memory of the many wonderful experiences that J. Frank Norris and I had together in winning people to Christ—if all were written it would fill many volumes—night and day, summer and winter, hot and cold, sunshine and rain, morning, noon and night we have gone from house to house seeking to win people to Jesus Christ.

There was a railroad man and his wife, large, stout people, both of them. I had been to see them several times, could not find them at home. The woman had told me her husband would be there a certain night—they had been misinformed like multiplied thousands of others about Norris. I wanted to meet him, so Norris was visiting with me that evening. We went by the house early in the evening and again they were not at home. We came back that way after making a number of calls. It must have been around 10 o'clock at night. Norris insisted it was too late, but I rang the door bell anyway. A light went on—I called him from the car where he was seated in front of the house, as he got to the door the man opened it. He was dressed in an old fashioned all-over-everything night gown almost dragging the floor. He looked about like a bale of cotton rolling around. We apologized for disturbing them at that time of the night, but he insisted on us having a seat and said he would call his wife. As we were seated she came down the stairway, and to my amazement she was in her night gown, the same kind her husband wore. We took our seats and they rolled into a big armed chair. It was easy to see Norris and I were ill at ease. I made up my mind to make the best of the situation.

I pulled out my New Testament and started to talk with them; finally I said, "Let's get down here and pray about it. We all four knelt—Norris was kneeling so that he could see their feet, and see them both with his eyes open. I could not quite appreciate his predicament—I prayed, then called on him to pray. We arose from our knees and he almost abruptly left the house. I tarried, however, until they both gave me their hands accepting Christ, and I thank God for saving them. We went on home discussing the matter at some length. This was Saturday night. Sunday evening we were in our accustomed place at the main entrance of the church auditorium watching especially for those we had visited and won during the week. Presently two well dressed, fine looking people came walking up and in a moment I recognized them as the people we had visited the night before. Norris could hardly believe it when I presented them to him. I saw that the ushers seated them in a favorable place. Later, before the sermon, I had a chance to greet them again and say a word to them in their seats. When the invitation was given at the close of the service that evening these two friends went forward to make a public confession of Christ.

Norris has told this experience many times, and no doubt some people have doubted—two preachers actually pulling people out of the bed at ten or eleven o'clock at night to win them to Christ—and in their nightgowns!

But why not? If people are lost without Christ, and if there is a hell, and sinners are lost and will spend eternity in hell, why should not we be intensely in earnest and day and night seek to lead men and women to Christ?

Norris might have many faults; if people are looking for faults they are usually easy to find. But I know of no man who will work longer or harder in season and out of season and who will go forth and pay any kind of price to win men to Jesus Christ.

I have already said, I do not know when Norris prepares his sermons. He has gone with me six days in the week from morning till night and preached two or three great sermons on Sunday. I do not know when he prepared them. I have seen him go home with half dozen magazines under his arm at 6 o'clock or 7 o'clock in the evening, and go by his home at 10 or 11 o'clock at night and find them scattered around all over the floor or piled up in the waste basket. I can understand now after several years of association with him something of how and when he prepares his sermons.

In the first place, he has one of the keenest and most brilliant minds in the world today. He can spin historical facts, giving dates, persons, and places by the hour. He can read what there is in a newspaper or magazine while I am getting started, and he never forget anything he reads.

He is the best educated man I know anything about.

He knows the Bible from the first word in Genesis to the last amen in Revelation. He memorizes scripture all the time.

After three years with the First Baptist Church I resigned to accept a position as instructor in practical Sunday School work at the Southwestern Theological Seminary at the invitation of Dr. L. R. Scarborough. Dr. Scarborough was at that time a member of the First Baptist Church. The day I finally accepted the position with Dr. Scarborough he said to me his only regret was he was afraid the Sunday School would go to pieces at the First Baptist Church, and regretted the great loss my leaving would be to the church and the injury it would do to the work. I said to him then, "You evidently do not know J. Frank Norris—you needn't worry about anything he puts his hand to being a failure." I have often thought about this in the conflicts between these good men. It was years after this while I was in Fort Worth on a visit that Dr. Scarborough asked me if I had any letters from Norris similar to one I had received which had, without my knowledge, fallen into the hands of some of those who were against Norris.

In this letter he had written me he said he had a car load of dynamite he was going to turn loose on the machine, and a number of other things to that effect. I was surprised that Dr. Scarborough asked me the question, "Have you any more letters from Norris similar to the one I saw sometime ago?"

I said, "Yes, I receive letters from Norris constantly, and many of them along the same line."

He said, "Would you mind turning some of them over to me? We are going to dehorn Norris. We have got it to do."

I strongly advised Dr. Scarborough not to do it. I said Norris has been charged with practically everything a man could be charged with; has been cleared in every case, and nobody would believe anything he might be charged with now, and you are a good man. You do not enjoy a fight and you would be constantly in hot water and besides before it is over with you will be charged with doing everything from shooting craps to cattle stealing, and if I were you I would go right ahead with my work and waste no time attacking Norris.

Some of the things that were brought out in the now famous fight between the denominational leaders and Norris during the past several years have been rather amusing, and one particular with reference to cattle was certainly amusing.

One of the things that has always impressed me is Norris' continual reference to his mother, how she taught him the Scriptures, how she prayed for him. She must have been a most remarkable woman and his father undoubtedly a remarkable man; ruined by the awful curse of drink. No wonder J. Frank Norris has all his life made constant, vigorous warfare against the liquor traffic.

I could better understand it after I had heard him from the platform recite some of his boyhood experiences. No man in these modern times has ever more forcefully and effectively fought the liquor traffic than J. Frank Norris. I have heard him preach on it time after time, and I have seen him baptize multitudes of drunkards and saloon keepers.

Whatever else J. Frank Norris may preach on, in practically every message he reaches the heart of the lost sinner.

It seems to be like the Apostle Paul, "his heart's desire," and the great church in Fort Worth and now the one in Detroit in their remarkable soul winning work is a testimony to this passion.

MY TWENTY-ONE YEARS IN FORT WORTH
OR INSIDE THE CUP NO. 1

Sermon by Dr. J. Frank Norris, Sunday Night, September 14, 1930
(Stenographically Reported)

I want to call your attention to one verse of Scripture. Just take it and let it stick in your mind—Paul's second letter to Timothy, fourth chapter and seventh verse, "I have fought a good fight, I have finished my course, I have kept the faith." There are two great statements in that text, two of them I would like to notice: "I have fought a good fight. I have kept the faith."

I have a little motto that hangs on my wall that I often look at, and it is a wonderful motto, lots of good sense in it. I think much of what Kipling wrote, but this is, I think, his best. As I look back on these twenty-one years with all the shadows and all the sunshine—which I will go into a little tonight, I am reminded of this—(Dr. Norris repeats from memory):

"If you can keep your head when all about you
    Are losing theirs and blaming it on you;
If you can trust yourself when all men doubt you,
    But make allowance for their doubting too:
If you can wait and not be tired by waiting,
    Or being lied about, don't deal in lies;
Or being hated, don't give way to hating,
    And yet don't look too good, nor talk too wise;

If you can dream—and not make dreams your master;
    If you can think—and not make thoughts your aim,
If you can meet with Triumph and Disaster
    And treat those two impostors just the same:
If you can bear to hear the truth you've spoken
    Twisted by knaves to make a trap for fools,
Or watch the things you gave your life to, broken,
    And stoop and build 'em up with worn-out tools;

If you can make one heap of all your winnings
    And risk it on one turn of pitch-and-toss,
And lose, and start again at your beginnings
    And never breathe a word about your loss:
If you can force your heart and nerve and sinew
    To serve your turn long after they are gone,
And so hold on when there is nothing in you
    Except the Will which says to them: 'Hold on!'

If you can talk with crowds and keep your virtue
Or walk with Kings—nor lose the common touch,
If neither foes nor loving friends can hurt you,
If all men count with you, but none too much:

(And I think this is the climax:)

If you can fill the unforgiving minute
With sixty seconds' worth of distance run.
Yours is the Earth and everything that's in it,
And—which is more—you'll be a Man, my son!"

There is the rub. It is a hard thing to do, but it will pay.

You know as we grow older in life it doesn't make any difference what experiences we may have—listen, I say it doesn't make any difference what darkness, what depths, what floods, what flames we go through—let me emphasize it, it doesn't make any difference what befalls us, it is not the avoiding of these things that counts, but how to meet them—that's the rub!

There isn't a man or woman in the meridian of life who hasn't met things you didn't expect, and some you expected you didn't have, and some you have had you didn't look for. What are you going to do? One reason why there is so much unhappiness in married life is because you haven't been willing to meet the inevitable and adjust yourself to each other.

Sometimes you hear people say, "I like Norris but he is always stirring up trouble." Did you ever hear anybody say that? (Laughter.) "He is always fighting something," they say. My friends, there never was a bigger falsehood told on an innocent man than that statement. Let me explain to you. That same charge was brought against every prophet in the Old Testament, and the Apostles in the New.

The neighbors of Noah accused him of stirring up trouble.

The 450 false prophets of Baal and Ahab accused Elijah of stirring up trouble in Samaria.

In the Roman Empire of Caesars they said the same thing concerning the Twelve: "These men have turned the world upside down."

Rome in the 16th century accused Martin Luther, John Calvin and other reformers, who dared the power of Rome, of stirring up trouble.

Next Sunday night I will show you how this country is facing the greatest crisis since it has been a republic. I will show you how that dark, deep laid conspiracy has now with a most powerful organization throughout this country, laid its hands on Congress, has laid its bloody hands on the press of the country, and undertakes to do what? Break down the greatest piece of moral legislation ever enacted, and when a man gets out to protest against that thing, they say he is stirring up trouble. Depends on your viewpoint.

I came to this city twenty-one years ago last Sunday—I didn't think I would have to take this off—(removing coat and collar) but I have to use this voice until midnight, and if you will permit me I will shell it off—my wife said when I put this suit on: "It's a good thing summer is about over, your coat is worn out." Well, a fellow gave me this one and maybe somebody will give me another one next summer.

Last week four men went to a horrible death down here at a town called West—they came in contact with a live wire and were burned to death—yonder north of Dallas a family of one of them— a mother and her son—a Mrs. Beavers, got in a car and went to arrange for the funeral services of the dead brother and son at Garland, Texas, and on their way a drunken driver ran into the car and killed this 58-year-old mother and 28-year-old son, and they had a triple funeral, the son who was killed by a live wire and the mother and son who were killed by a drunken driver. What did it? It was the accursed liquor traffic that caused two of those funerals, and if a man undertakes to lift his voice in protest somebody begins to say, "He is dabbling in politics, stirring up trouble!"

I say I came to this city twenty-one years ago—I didn't know it, but a friend called my attention to it when he told me I had been here longer than any other pastor in the city. Well, I have had a right interesting time. I will never forget the first afternoon we met in the old church, which would seat about 500—and we are building one now that will hold five times as many—there were 32 men present—I think you will see the reason that I am going into this when I have finished. Some of them are still living —some have long since passed to their reward. I offer no criticism against them, or anybody else tonight; I do not find it in my heart to do so—they began to talk, one at a time, and they told what a wonderful church they had—and it was—and what a wonderful city Fort Worth was, and that was the truth—so when they had all spoken around, they asked me if I had anything to say. I said, "Gentlemen, when we get through with each other we won't look

like we do now." I suppose I said that because I didn't have anything else to say—I had forgotten it, until years afterwards one of
them reminded me of it.

It was a great church, it had a great history.

Murdered Pastors

Can I ever forget, when a young preacher 19 years old, a
drive I had with Dr. A. W. McGaha, who was once the pastor
of this church—a great man. I was just a green country
boy and he was then standing on the crumbling edge of the grave.
He said to me, "Frank, God forbid that you or any other preacher
shall have to go through with the experience that I had to go
through with the First Baptist Church of Fort Worth," and he
told me some of the things, and he called the names of some of the
men I met when I came here, and the very men who fought me
the hardest. They did every pastor that way, and I decided to
stop them. He told me as we jogged along, how they had literally
murdered him, crushed his spirit, and broken his heart—and he
went to an untimely grave. I found that had been the history of
most every pastor for the last 30 years, and when the war started
on me, I told them of their record. I said, "Gentlemen, I understand your record is that you have run off every preacher you
have had, but I tell you now—you may do it to me, but you won't
do it with my consent—you've got a man now you can't run off,
you can't ruin, you can't kill, and if you don't behave yourselves
I'll turn the last one of you out." Well, they went around and
talked about me, said I was "awfully unruly"—a dictator—you
know—we have all kinds of "taters"—imitators, dictators, shoe
string taters (laughter), and some preachers have tater vines for
backbone (laughter).

Oh, if I had been some little Lord Fauntleroy to be bandied
around, booted from pillar to post, like so many preachers—and
good men they are—there would not have been carloads of malicious slanders sent broadcast about me. I fought back with everything at my command and I have no apology to make for it. (Applause.)

We got along two years, just as peaceable and quiet as a
graveyard—I want to say now all my troubles have been inside
troubles, every last one of them; yes, sir. If I had never had any
trouble on the inside I would never have had any from the outside—now you may not believe that, but by nature I am a very
timid man, the most timid man you ever saw (laughter). Now I

knew you wouldn't believe it. I got over a lot of it. I never had any fights in my life, I never did, never had any in school. I was the quietest, most peaceable boy you ever saw. I know you don't believe that, but it's so. One reason why that was so, I was very delicate in health. No one thought I would ever live to be grown —and some people wish I hadn't. (Laughter.)

Crowd Used Pot Plants for Seats

Well, after we had run along two years—we would have nice crowds in morning and an empty house Sunday nights—you know what I mean, just the average Sunday night crowd—I wasn't preaching to any sinners, just preaching to an empty wood yard— I said, "I am going after the crowds of sinners"—and when I did, some of you were there that first night—if Charlie Snelling is here, he remembers what happened that night, some of the rest of you remember it too. The crowd couldn't get in the church that night —the sisters had decorated the platform with nice pot plants, ferns and some other kind of spreading plant—what are they? (Voice: Palms.) That's what they were, great big things that grow up this high—well, they had the whole platform decorated with palms, and I had to stick my head up over the top of them— like at a funeral or a fashionable wedding—when I put on a new program, the Gospel message, the crowds came, a lot couldn't get in—some were converted that night who hadn't been in church for twenty years—here is what they did, some fellow saw all those pots up there and he decided they would make good seats—and he just turned one of those plants bottom-side up—you know one of those fuzzy-wuzzy plants—I can see him now—I didn't know what to do—here is the way he turned that pot—this stool is the pot and here are the plants (showing how it was done with a piano stool) up here—he took that thing and turned it upside down this way and sat down on it. (Laughter.) Well, now that put the plant under the bottom and it made a good seat, and so he set the example. The next morning! Talk about rows! A committee of sisters looked at those pots and anybody could see they were ruined —and they came and jumped on me—I said, "Don't jump on me, jump on the fellow that sat on the pot, he is the one that did it, I didn't have anything to do with it"—and one of them, I shall never forget it, oh how she did talk—she said, "You are going to ruin this church, our church has good standing in the city, and you are getting this crowd in here, you are going to ruin this church." Now, I don't mind arguing with a man, but I am not going to argue with a woman, and I just sat there, a nice little boy, and listened to her—there was no use talking—the pots were ruined, no use arguing about it, but I was never so glad of a thing in my life. (Laughter.)

Here is the thing I am trying to tell you, it didn't matter with that crowd—and they were good women—it didn't matter with them if souls died and went to hell, no, what they thought more of was some old fern in an old jar than the soul of somebody going to hell—that's what I was up against! That's the first row I had —I finally told them to take their old pots—and I told them something else I am not going to repeat. You let a bunch get after you like that gang got after me and you will say things too; yes, sir.

Sometimes people object to my language but they forget what I have been up against. Martin Luther threw ink bottles at the devil and Moses knocked an Egyptian in the head, but how wonderfully God used him—He can't use sissies and cowards.

I had another experience that night—have a seat brother (to a man coming down to the front from the edge of the crowd). Here, I will give you this pot and you can sit on it (handing him the piano stool). Do you like the sample? I'm glad to see a fellow like you—you are like that fellow that night that turned the pot upside down.

MAN SITTING ON THE STOOL SAYS: Well, I like to hear what you say, and I can't hear it on the outside, the crowd is too big.

DR. NORRIS: Well, that same night something else happened—we had a nice little choir—one woman who would start in G and end away up in Gee Whiz, and a beer-guzzling Dutchman for a choir conductor—he had hair as wide as the top of this desk, and he would shake it to the right and to the left. He had been there twelve years, and that night they turned the pots upside down—the crowd had gotten there ahead of time, and I started them to singing some old songs, and this Dutchman came and he couldn't get in, and he wrote me a note and said: "Please open the way so the choir can get in." I wrote on the bottom, "Wait until I send for you." If he had waited he would have been standing there yet. (Laughter.) The next morning that beer-guzzling bunch of hair came around and he shook that head of hair east and west, and north and south, and up and down. Oh, yes, I stood there and watched him shake and tell me what he wasn't going to stand for until the old windmill run down, and I said, "Are you through?" And I said, "Professor, so we can understand each other, you have resigned."

"Me resign!" he said.

"You—have—resigned!"

"Vell," he said, "the deacons! the deacons! the deacons! they employed me!"

I said, "The dickens they did—you are out, you know what that means, you are fired." (Laughter.)

He said, "I will take it up with the deacons."

And bless your life, he did. He went around to see the deacons —there were three or four bank presidents—and they called a special deacons' meeting. I saw one of them and he said to me, "Well, I will see you at the deacons' meeting tonight?" I said, "Are you going to have a deacons' meeting?" "Yes," he said. I began to smell sulphur all around in the air, and that night when I walked in, there stood that beer guzzling bunch of hair and he was just laying it off, and the deacons began to talk, and tell me where to head in—one of them began to tell how the professor had played at all the funerals and the weddings. I waited until they got through and I got up and said, "In order that we may understand each other—I told the professor he had resigned, and Mr. Deacon So and So, you have resigned," and I pointed to another, and said, "You have resigned," and to another, "You have resigned," and so on. "We will understand whether or not I am going to be pastor or janitor or whether I am going to play kite-tail—we might as well understand each other now." I looked at them and they looked at each other—and they all went out—and one of them told me years afterwards, he said, "I knew that we were into it then."

Of course the church voted to accept their resignations upon my recommendation.

I didn't deserve any credit for taking that stand. Here I was with a wife and three children, and so help me God I didn't have any other place to go. I had to stay. (Laughter.) You know I have seen preachers all over this country fired out. Well, it never did appeal to me to be fired, never did. (Laughter.)

So things broke loose—I am just giving you a few things in passing, just a few little inside things. I will get to some other things in a few minutes.

Cutting Down the Tent

In 1911 they had a prohibition election all over Texas—one morning I picked up the Fort Worth Record and saw that the names of three deacons in the First Baptist Church headed the committee that was to receive and welcome the saloon crowd that were coming here for a convention—three deacons in the First Baptist Church! Their names headed the list—one of them was the chairman of the board—he was the chief orang-outang of that committee. I showed it to my wife, and I sat there and looked at her, and she said, "I would go easy." I said, "There is one thing, they are either going out back or front door." I called the deacons up and told them I wanted a meeting before the preaching service on Sunday morning. We met, and I took that paper, held it up, and said, "Here is what we have." And I saw some of them begin to squirm around—one of them is the best friend I have got in the world today. I said, "You can take your choice, you can get out of the church or get out of that crowd, one or the other." I knew I was right about it then and I know I am right about it now. (Applause.) Well, the fur began to fly, you could just smell sulphur in the air. If you would strike a match it would catch fire anywhere.

Things went on. We were holding a meeting in a tent down here—they demanded that we take it down—Bill Davis was mayor at that time—now Bill and I are good friends today. He told me we would have to take it down. I said, "Why, are we breaking any law?" He said, "Well, some of your own bunch, some of your own men and the business men have demanded that it be taken down." I said, "I won't take it down"—and he sent down there some firemen and policemen and they cut it down. Well, all hell broke loose in this old town!

The Mayor's Address to a Mob of Three Thousand

Of course I went after the mayor and his administration. I had no other course.

Then he called his crowd together in the old auditorium with three thousand packed and jammed, and he went after me for two hours. He didn't allow any women or boys under 21, and he invented new words that had never been heard in either the chain gang or gamblers den. I sent a stenographer down and had every word taken down and printed it, and put a copy of it on everybody's doorstep in Fort Worth.

Now what happened in Shushan's palace gives some idea of what happened in Fort Worth that night.

The mayor closed that inflammatory address with these words:

"If there are fifty red-blooded men left in this town there will be a man hanging from the telephone pole tonight."

Somebody ran to the telephone and called me, and told me what was going on, and what the plan was. I came back from the telephone and sat down in front of the fire with my wife and three babies. She asked me about my telephone call, and I told her there was "nothing unusual." And it was about the same thing that had been going on for several weeks. While sitting there I decided that if they were going to pull off an ugly scene like that I didn't want my wife and children to see it. I put on my hat and overcoat, and my wife asked me where I was going, and wanted to go with me. I told her I didn't want her to go.

There wasn't any courage on my part. I just went. I don't know why, but I just went down there, and when I got there in front of the city hall I saw a man standing up on a slab with a rope in his hand, and I walked up to him, since he was calling my name, and said, "Are you looking for me?" He dropped that rope and I had the whole place to myself.

The Story of the Man Who Had the Rope

I'll tell you how we first met. The first time I saw him after this turbulent night, he was on the back seat of the First Baptist Church. I didn't recognize him, and I said to Charlie Butler, who was then directing the music:

"Charlie, do you see that old bear back yonder on the last seat, when the service is over I want you to go back and find out who he is."

He had a mustache long enough to tie behind his ears. He looked like a wild animal just out of Borneo.

Charlie went back at the close of the service, got within a few feet of him and just looked at him.

The next Sunday he was there again in the same place. I said, "Charlie, yonder is that old bear again, don't let him get away tonight without finding out who he is."

After the service was over Charlie went back there and afterwards reported to me that the crowd was too great and he got away.

One day going down Main Street in Fort Worth I saw him. I stopped when I saw him. He had on a white sombrero hat, confederate gray uniform, coat came down below his knees, two rows of brass buttons, and had a heavy walking cane over his arm. He had on boots, with spurs on them and bells on the spurs. I stopped him and asked:

"My dear sir, haven't you been coming out to the First Baptist Church?"

He squared himself up and looked at me with all his two hundred pounds, and said, "What do you want to know that for?"

I said, "I want to meet you—what is your name?"

He said, "Captain George B. Holland, Captain Company B, Confederate Grays, R. E. Lee Camp, Fort Worth, Texas, United States of America."

I said, "Captain George B. Holland, Captain Company B, Confederate Grays, R. E. Lee Camp, Fort Worth, Texas, United States of America, J. Frank Norris, Pastor of the First Baptist Church, Fort Worth, Texas, United States of America, is my name. I am glad to meet you, sir."

He still came to church and a short time afterwards I met him again and said to him: "Captain, why don't you come up near the front where you can hear better?"

He said, "I can hear all right."

I said, "You are not afraid to come to the front seat, are you?"

"Me? I am not afraid of all hell."

Then I said, "I dare you to sit on the front seat of the First Baptist Church four Sunday nights—I double-dog dare you to."

He said, "I never took a dare in my life."

He drew a line, spit on the other side of it, steped over and said, "Here is my hand."

The next Sunday night he came, walked down to the front, that cane on his arm, the sombrero hat in his hand, double breasted Prince Albert gray uniform, boots and spurs, sat down, folded his arms and looked at me right square in the face.

I stepped off the platform, greeted him and he was very cordial, but cold.

Breathing a prayer, "Oh Lord, if you ever helped me to preach help me tonight. I have the meanest sinner in all the country in front of me."

I had gone and checked up on him, and an old timer, a good

friend of mine, when I told him Captain Holland was coming to the First Baptist Church, he could hardly believe it, and told me what a tough character he was. He was captain of the Texas Rangers before the Civil War. He had so many notches on his gun he had lost the count.

At the close of the first night he sat on the front seat, he came up to me, gave me his hand and said, "Are you going to hold me to the other three nights?"

I said, "Captain, are you a man of your word?"

He said, "I am. But you filled my hide full every time you fired tonight."

The next week he came to see me and said, "I have told my gang how you perforated my hide last Sunday night, and I want them to come out and get the same thing. I am going to bring the gang out Sunday night, and I would like for you to reserve a place at the front with me."

I said, "How many will you bring?"

He said, "I will let you know Saturday."

Saturday he came and made reservation for thirty-five. The next Sunday night he brought the whole gang in, after drilling them down in the basement of the First Baptist Church on how to behave themselves in religious services.

Such a gang of gamblers, saloon keepers—well, the dictionary would be exhausted to describe them! They looked bad enough on the outside but worse on the inside.

Time rolled on and I said one day, "Captain, do you have a Bible?"

"No, you certainly don't know who I am. You know, I hadn't been inside a church in forty years when I started to go to your church. Do you know who I am?"

"Yes, Captain, they tell me you are one of the meanest white men in town."

"You have got my number correct."

I gave him a Bible and wrote in it just how we were introduced to each other. He read that Bible through—I know he did for he asked me every question from "Where did Cain get his wife?" to "Who was the seven headed, ten horned Beast of Revelation?"

One morning he woke up in the room over a saloon where he

was living and reached over to get his bottle to take his morning drink, and his hand fell on that Bible, and here are the words he said when he stood before the church:

"I raised up to get my bottle for my morning drink, and my hand touched the Bible first, and as I reclined on my elbow, I said to that bottle, 'I have served you long enough and you have robbed me of my manhood; you have robbed me of my family; you have robbed me of my happiness; and you have robbed me of my soul, and I will not serve you another day. And before I dressed I opened that Bible, spread it out on the bed, got on my knees, buried my face in it and said, 'Oh, God, if there be a God, have mercy on poor old George Holland, the meanest man living'."

And turning to me he gave me the half filled bottle of liquor, held up the Bible and said, "This has won."

Six years afterwards I got off the train returning from an evangelistic campaign. My wife met me and said, "Captain Holland is dying and calling for you."

We rushed out to the edge of the city in Riverside and found him propped up in bed, his eyesight gone. I drew near and said, "Captain."

He said, "Oh, Oh, is it you? I am so glad you have come. I am going to stack arms today. I have fought my last fight. They have come for me, but I am not afraid."

And he reached his thin, emaciated hand under his pillow, pulled out that same Bible, held it up, and in a feeble gasp said, "This has won!"—"This has won!"—"Preach it on and when you are through and tired, and you come to the crossing, old Captain George Holland, the man who had the rope to hang you will be standing at the beautiful gate to be the first to welcome you home."

And together we sang as his last word,

"Amazing grace—how sweet the sound!"

And when we came to the verse,

"Through many dangers, toils, and snares,"

he could go no further, but grasped my hand in his and whispered, "Praise God! Praise God!"

About that time—I want to tell you something—I really hesitate to give this out, all this is being taken down and will be published, and put on the radio.

Pastor Fired in Saloon

They had a meeting—twenty-four of these men, all deacons—they didn't meet in the First Baptist Church, no, I will tell you where they met—they met upstairs over 808½ Houston Street, and they sent for me to come down before them. I didn't know what was up and I didn't know anything about the character of the place—I walked up into that place perfectly innocent—but I had a suspicion that I was going to get notification of my funeral. One of the deacons got up and said: "When we called you here we thought you had some sense, but we have found out now that you haven't and we here and now notify you that your time is up, and we are going to put another man in your place." In other words, I was fired—for there was but one man in that crowd that stood for me. I will tell you what I found on the walls—a retail liquor license in the name of one of the men that demanded I leave here. A man had just joined the church about that time—he wouldn't object to my calling his name, when I told him what had happened and how things existed, he said to me, "I can hardly believe it." I could see he doubted it. His name is Mr. W. C. Pool. I said to him, "You come and go there with me and I will show you the place. I will show you the retail liquor license, and the bar, where they called the pastor of this church to meet in a deacons' meeting. He said, "All right," and we walked down there and went up the stairs and we found the bar and the white apron bartender and the license, and I would like for Mr. Pool to tell you whether or not that is the truth.

MR. POOL: I saw it just like he is telling it.

DR. NORRIS: Stand up, Mr. Pool, and face the crowd and tell them whether I have told the truth.

MR. POOL: You have.

Now, ladies and gentlemen, there is where the fight started.

I told them they could kill me, and they would have liked to do it—"But, so help me God," I said, "I will never leave this fight as long as there is fight in my body." (Prolonged applause.)

Next time you hear one of the gang cussing Norris just tell them what W. C. Pool said here tonight. He is one of the most honored and best known men in Fort Worth.

That's what I had to go up against. That's the crowd that began to send out their propaganda. Yes, sir. And one of them was foreman of the grand jury that turned in a bill of indictment against me. He said "We have got no evidence against Norris," but that man and two others called J. T. Pemberton—Mr. Pemberton was my friend, and said to him, "You go and tell Norris if· he will resign and leave Fort Worth we will not indict him, but if he does not we will—and to indict a preacher will ruin him," and ordinarily speaking that's true.

Mr. Pemberton said to them: "If you have got any evidence, go ahead and indict him, but don't use the grand jury as an instrument to destroy an innocent man." Mr. Pemberton told me what they said. When I went before the grand jury I was very frail in health, and I said to them, "Gentlemen, I know what you have conspired against me and in the name of the best woman that God ever let live, and in the name of three defenseless children, and in the name of Elijah's God, I don't ask any quarter, and furthermore I demand that you do your worst, and if there is a God I will be preaching in Fort Worth after the last one of you have been put under the sod." (Applause.) That's what I said, and the man that led that fight, his name became a synonym—well, let the mantle of charity be pulled down.

Why, they even had detective agencies spying on me. This thing happened years afterward. Preaching one day in the Bible Institute in Los Angeles to five thousand people, I looked over to the right and I saw a familiar face, but I couldn't place him. After the services were over he came up and shook hands with me and told me his name. He was head man from the Pinkerton detective agency in New York and they gave him ten thousand dollars to come here and convict me. He gave up in utter disgust after he had been here awhile, and gave his report to Mr. Pemberton and told him to give it to his preacher. This man and I sat down together and talked and he said to me, "The marvel to me is that you are living today—if I were an infidel I would be compelled to believe there is a God." (Applause.)

I am not saying these things—I don't have to say them as a matter of defense, I am just giving you some of the inside of the cup. I am just telling you of some of the battles. And perhaps there are some here who are discouraged, some man or woman, whose hold on life is slipping. My word tonight is, "Be a good soldier, fight on, fight on, and never give up, and sing as you fight:

"Am I a soldier of the Cross,
    A follower of the Lamb?
And shall I fear to own His cause,
    Or blush to speak His name?
Must I be carried to the skies
    On flowery beds of ease,
While others fought to win the prize,
    And sailed through bloody seas?"

The Demand For Resignation of Pastor

Well, I must go on. There are so many angles to this—I want to say to you, and don't be shocked. I say it kindly—in all the controversies I have had with the outside world, the saloon crowd, they are nothing to compare with what I have had on the inside. Why, ladies and gentlemen, put down this date. I remember it so well because it was Tuesday night in November, the first Tuesday night before the national election, when Woodrow Wilson was elected. I was living right out here at 1201 Sixth Avenue, when six men, and one of them the high priest of the synagogue, wanted to come out to my home and talk to me and they wanted my wife to be present. I didn't want her to be, but they insisted. They knew if they could break down her will and spirit, why of course they could reach her husband—and as we were sitting there after supper I said, "Some gentlemen are coming out after while." She said, "Is that so?" I didn't tell her what they wanted. I felt then, as I have seen her all these years—she has a very quiet way of meeting every situation that rises. After while they came in, six laymen and among them one preacher—so nobody will misunderstand, the preacher was Dr. L. R. Scarborough, President of the Seminary, Fort Worth, Texas. I say these things kindly. They sat down and I began to talk a blue streak about the national election. (Laughter.) I discussed Roosevelt and Taft, and they sat there, and I talked on—I wouldn't give them a chance to say a word, and they squirmed around and cleared up their throats (laughter), and they twisted—and they would start off to say something—the spokesman—they had his funeral within the last 100 years, peace to his ashes—and they twisted, and I kept batting away (laughter), and they would pull out their watches and look at them, 9 o'clock came and I kept talking away (laughter), and I never let up. Finally one of them said, "Well, we have come to"—I said, "What do you think about Roosevelt's last speech?" and I started off again. (Laughter.) After while one of them said, "Well, now it is getting late, and we don't want to keep you up——." "Oh," I said, "that's all right, sometimes we don't go to bed anyway." (Laughter.) My wife was sitting over there taking in the whole show, and laughing to herself. I knew they had come out to put on a show before her, and I thought I would put on one first. (Laughter.) I had the best time in the world—you know I just sat there and watched them—they were nervous—you know in a red-hot fight always keep your eyes on the other fellow—so I sat there and looked at all of those birds, and there couldn't a one of them look at me—they all looked like suck-egg hounds going down a back alley. (Laughter.) I just kept looking at them—and it got late—finally one of them said, "Yyyo yo you kn, kn, know wha, what we come out for?" (Laughter.) I said, "How should I know? I thought you came out to see me—the first time you have been in our home, and I am mighty glad to see you." It was the funniest thing in the world, but not one of them could laugh. One of them began again, "You know, know, know"—"Well," I said, "I have certainly enjoyed your visit and hope you will come again. I don't know when I ever enjoyed two hours more than these two hours this evening." (Laughter.) That's true, I never did. (Laughter.) I enjoyed seeing those fellows sit on hot embers for two hours. (Laughter.) Finally one of them just broke right in and he said, "You know our situation. The church is torn all to pieces." I said, "Is that so? I didn't know there was any trouble." "Well," he said, "we have come out here to make you a proposition." "A proposition about what?" I said. "We want to make you a proposition like this, that if you will, if you will resign and leave Fort Worth, we have decided to give you a year's salary in advance and pay your way for any trip you want to go"—thy didn't say so, but the farther away it was would have suited them better. I said, "Gentlemen, in other words, you have come to offer me a bribe—I want to tell you that your price is too low." (Applause.)

Thirty Days' Notice to Leave Fort Worth

Just giving you a few chapters inside the cup.

Time rolled on, and it rolls fast, but would you believe 156 men met in the dining room of the Metropolitan Hotel, which is now used by the Chamber of Commerce—they met at noon on the first Monday in September, 1916, and drank to my going or death—appointed a committe to notify me of their demands, and believe it or not, this committee actually called on me in the office of the First Baptist Church.

Talk about scared men, they were the worst scared I ever saw, they were shaking from head to foot. It was too funny as far as I was concerned to be very badly scared. Here the whole gang after one poor little preacher. This committee told me they were waiting for my answer down at the hotel and that I had thirty days in which to pack my goods.

I said, "You are very kind to give me thirty days. I will give you back 29 of them and I'll go down to the hotel with you," and so we all four walked out of the church together. When we got to the corner one went east and one went west and the third one and I walked on together but he did not say a word. He is sitting over there tonight and is one of the best friends I have in the world.

I answered their un-American demands that night at Fifteenth and Main Streets. How many of you were there? (Large number of hands go up.) My wife wanted to go with me but I said no. I wore a white flannel suit, didn't have on any coat, went bareheaded and didn't have a thing on earth in my hands or in my pockets.

The crowd was estimated from twenty to twenty-five thousand. I circularized the town with their demands and threats and that I would answer. I had a friend to park a truck at the place of speaking before the crowd gathered. It was a difficult thing for me to get in through the crowd—three saloons on four of the corners where I spoke.

When I stood before that crowd the first thing I did was to lead them in singing "There's a Land That Is Fairer Than Day," and from appearances it looked as if I would be in that land before breakfast. Soon that howling, shrieking mob was quiet and I preached them a sermon on The Prodigal Son. I baptized men for years who were convicted and converted in that service.

Incidentally, the man who presided over that meeting in the hotel met with a most tragic death on the interurban just six days afterwards. I don't want to refer to it, it's overwhelming, it sends the most terrific feeling of awe through my soul, but the record is well known: every hand that has been lifted against the First Baptist Church has failed to prosper, judgment has come on it. Oh, how true the words of Isaiah, "No weapon that is formed against thee shall prosper." (Isa. 54:17.)

For full particulars of these tragic days see Rev. L. L. Cooper who was by my side through all these hours night and day, and he never flickered on a single inch of ground.

Visit From Five Baptist Pastors

About that time I had a visit from five Baptist pastors. They, like the committee that came to my house, had never been to see me. They professed great concern for my welfare, for my life, and for my family.

They said, "Norris, haven't you got any sense?"

I said, "No, I haven't." (Laughter.)

They said, "If you had any sense you would know you have lost out, your influence is gone, you can't rebuild"—we had no building at that time—"you have lost your wealth, the newspapers are against you, city and county officials are against you, all the clubs of the city are against you, all business organizations are against you, your health is gone"—and they just kept piling it up. And three of those pastors are roosting on another limb and I don't know where, but here was my reply, "Go back and tell the gang that sent you, in the name of the Triune God and by the faith that my mother gave me I will be preaching in Fort Worth after all of you have gone to parts unknown." (Applause.)

God forbid that I should boast, just telling you the inside that I may help some struggling soul.

"And we know that all things work together for good to them that love God, to them who are the called according to his purpose. . . . What shall we say then to these things? If God be for us, who can be against us? He that spared not his own Son, but delivered him up for us all, how shall he not with him also freely give us all things? Who shall lay anything to the charge of God's elect? It is God that justifieth." Romans 8:28-33.

Deep Dark Valleys

I don't mind telling you that I have been through some deep dark valleys. I have been criticized because I did not wear crepe on the lapel of my coat—I don't believe in crepe. When King Jehoram walked on the walls of Samaria during the severe famine the wind parted his royal garments and sackcloth was underneath the purple—wear sorrows on the inside, not on the outside. I have told my wife if I go first I don't want her to wear any mourning for me—I don't want anybody to have any suspicion as to where her husband is gone. Death is not a dark valley, not a thing of mystery, it's the opening of the prison door, it's to depart and be with Christ.

The unfortunate dark tragedy that fell across my life—of

course, every man could wish that such a thing would not happen in his life—that record is well known, I need not discuss it. I did not then and do not now have any apology to make for any course when such a necessity is forced upon a man. There was the one supreme moment, rather I should say second, when all that a man holds dear, wife, children, stood by my side, and the God who made me and put the breath of life into me, endowed me first of all with that indescribable something to stand for my wife and children and I did it in that hour, though with deepest sorrow. And whenever the times comes that a man can't defend his own life and his wife and children in his sacred private study then we should pull down the flag—but I need not discuss it further. I had no hate, I had no malice, there was no murder in my heart and never has been against a single human being. I never saw the unfortunate man until he broke into my study. It is a matter of record as to who sent him there and for what purpose.

I repeat it was a great sorrow, a life-long sorrow, but not one tinge of remorse. I have never even dreamed of it. General Lee, the greatest soldier the South ever produced, and Theodore Roosevelt said he was the greatest soldier in history—he was forced to defend his native state but there was no malice, no hatred, no murder, and, therefore, no remorse in his great soul. But there was a Gethsemane of sorrow. A great preacher in Dallas, Dr. Truett, killed a man—it was not murder, it was accidental, inevitable. There was no remorse but great sorrow. So did Moses.

Talk about the inalienable right of self-defense—there is not a missionary in China who would return home alive but for the American and British gunboats. Only fools and pacifists talk otherwise. Missionaries, preachers and women have as much right to their lives as common gamblers, cut-throats, thugs and hi-jackers. When a man breaks into another man's private office to assassinate him, why, he just commits suicide provided he jumps on a man who has love and courage to defend his own life for the sake of his own precious wife and children.

But I repeat, it was a deep sorrow and will always be.

Denominational Controversies

Let me tell you something, how unrelenting hate goes on. They say, some of my enemies. "Norris can't get along with his own denomination." That's a mistake, I get along gloriously with my own denomination, I am for the denomination, but I don't get along with some of the leaders, with some of the ecclesiastical politicians of the denomination. It's all summed up in the one word, "But Mordecai bowed not."

Here's how the denominational fight was started. In 1920 a noted Methodist minister—Dr. John A. Rice—he is dead now—wrote a book on "The Old Testament in the Light of Today." Upon his own request I loaned the book to Dr. L. R. Scarborough, and in his own handwriting on page 24 of this book he wrote the following:

"What an unpardonable comment and interpretation of Genesis and following divinely inspired book! Moses began his Genesis with 'God,' Rice begins his with 'poetry,' 'folk lore,' prehistoric characters, doubt. Wesley would open Old Testament and say, 'Thus saith the Lord,' Rice will open his to teach young Methodist preachers and say, 'thus saith E. J.' or some other figure of the critical fancy of an informed scholar of the Chicago-Berlin school of infidels! Methodism of the old soul-winning Wesley type should rise up and put this invader of Southern Methodist orthodoxy out and rout him out of such a place of influence. 'Poetic fragments,' 'short stories,' versus 'All Scripture is inspired of God.'

"L. R. SCARBOROUGH."

So he helped me put this Methodist modernist out and the Methodists were smart enough to ship him to Oklahoma, C. O. D.

But wait a minute, the Baptists had the same thing and more of it and when I turned the light on Baptist Modernism, Dr. Scarborough and all the rest of the leaders jumped all over me and they are still jumping but not jumping on me for I am not where they are jumping. Trust and mortgage companies are making them jump now. (Laughter.)

High Priest and the Sanhedrin Interferred With Collection of Insurance and Caused Injury to the First Baptist Church

This would not be given out if we did not have the documentary evidence to support it.

Herewith is the report of the Southwestern Adjustment Company of Dallas which was sent to the Insurance Companies in reply to certain statements sent to them by the enemies of the church and among those statements that were sent to the amazement of the Insurance Companies was some from the high priests in the Sanhedrin.

What wrong have these people done? If the gentlemen had hatred against the pastor of the First Baptist Church they had a right to take it out on him, but did they have the right to take it out on several thousand people who put their blood money into this property?

It was hitting below the belt. Every man knows that a Court House trial for collection of Insurance would be seriously affected by the element of prejudice.

The Adjustment Company that handled all the Insurance answered this interference and though it cost us money and much delay, yet if the denominational leaders received any joy out of this injury to the church—may the God of all the earth have mercy.

This report lugged in a lot of things which had no part or lot as to whether or not the insurance should be paid, wholly irrelevant matters. Of course, it was done for the purpose of prejudicing the insurance companies against us and the insurance companies had a special investigation made and I got that report also, and here is what a fair, unbiased investigation reported, the answer they gave the satanic ecclesiastical systems.

Insurance Company Records

"That question has no place in the handling of this fire loss. The most eminent Baptist divines in Texas, including the president of its leading colleges and universities in Texas, recognized Norris last year to the extent of debating with him over their church row. These debates were broadcast over radio every night.

"The Baptists in this State have had one of the biggest church rows that was ever staged, with Norris leading a big faction on one side and a number of eminent Baptist ministers leading the other side.

"In conclusion we want to say we have not tried to find out or decide what manner of man J. Frank Norris is in our investigation of this case. The people of Texas have been trying to decide that question for the past twenty years and they are hopelessly divided. If they were called together now to decide the question it would result in the biggest fight that could possibly be pulled off in Texas. A jury could be picked in thirty minutes that would hang him on general principles, or one could be easily found that would acquit him of any charge that might be brought against him.

If he is guilty of half of the crimes that have been laid at his door, then he is one of the most dangerous criminals that ever ran at large. If he has been wrongfuly accused, then he has been one of the most cruelly persecuted men that was ever the subject of false accusations. In which class he falls only he and the Almighty knows. We are sure the Southwestern Adjustment Company does not. We only know he has been abundantly able to take care of himself and that he has had for 20 years, and still has, the loyal and undivided support of the largest congregation in the world. He is a man of magnetic personality, wonderful ability, a natural born leader of those who believe in him and he divides the world into two parts—those who believe in him and follow him with a loyalty that knows no bounds and those who hate him to the extent that they would like to see him hung."

False Slanders of 4th Degree Knight of Columbus

That "investigation" that Fourth Degree Knight of Columbus, who got fired because he made false statements on the church fire, wrote in his report that "Norris' residence was burned at 1:00 a. m. in a mysterious manner." I had only $7,000 insurance on $16,000 worth of property. You know how my residence was burned. It was not burned at one o'clock at night and nothing "mysterious" about it. Here's what the Record-Telegram said about that fire —I am giving examples of the malicious slanders that have been sent out through the long years. But what has happened to every man who circulated them?

Fort Worth Record-Telegram, Jan. 2, 1928

"The home of Rev. J. Frank Norris, pastor of the First Baptist Church, was destroyed by fire with estimated loss of $16,000 Sunday morning. The fire occurred while the pastor was conducting Sunday services and Mrs. Norris, ill for several months, and her mother, Mrs. J. M. Gaddy, 84, were in bed because of illness. The residence, a one and one-half-story frame building, was outside the city limits at Siding 6, Fort Worth-Dallas Interurban.

"Only a few treasured articles were saved. The pastor's library went up in the flames, origin of which is unknown. Practically all the family's clothing was destroyed.

"An adjoining vacant residence, owned by W. E. Buchanan, also was destroyed. Both dwellings were outside the city limits and were far removed from fire hydrants. Fire company No. 4 responded to the call and fought the blaze with chemicals.

"The fire originated at 11 o'clock Sunday morning while Rev. Mr. Norris, his daughter, Mrs. Charles Weaver, Chicago, and two oldest sons, Jim Gaddy and J. Frank Jr., were at Sunday services at the First Baptist Church. Only Mrs. Norris, Mrs. Gaddy and the pastor's youngest son, George, 10, were at the house.

"All three of the members of the family had been ill, Mrs. Norris having been confined to her home because of illness. Mrs. Norris got her aged mother and young son out of the flaming house. George ran to a neighbor's home, quite a distance away, and telephoned his father after Mrs. Norris attempted to use her telephone to find it was out of order.

"Rev. Mr. Norris, after talking with his 10-year-old son over the telephone, telephoned the fire department and turned in the alarm. The pastor hurried from church services to his home and did not occupy his pulpit Sunday morning.

"Rev. Mr. Norris and members of his family were given shelter in the home of friends Sunday. At the pastor's office Sunday no announcement was made concerning plans for the family's home in the immediate future. Mrs. Norris was reported yesterday afternoon to be prostrate.

"The temperature ranged far below freezing Sunday morning when the flames routed the members of the household from the home. Dangerous exposure to the weather was met especially by Mrs. Gaddy because of her age.

"First indications of the fire were found when the young son investigated barking of his dog.

"The fire was announced over the church radio during the morning. Several persons sent in contributions toward erecting a new home for the pastor.

'While the worst blizzard of the winter raged early Sunday morning, 12 fire alarms were sounded in various parts of the city before 2 p. m. Yet the fire damage was light, excepting at the Norris home."

New Home Built By Friends

But like everything else that has happened to the pastor and church, this was only another example of Romans 8:28—'And we know that all things work together for good to them that love

God, to them who are the called according to his purpose." Friends from everywhere responded most generously and the pastor's family moved into a new modern nine-room home, fully equipped, costing $21,000.00, and not a dollar of indebtedness!

Enemies Being Saved

Through all the tragic and glorious experiences multitudes of sinners have been saved and saved continually. And large numbers of bitter enemies have been saved and baptized. Here are two typical cases, the head of the liquor organization of Texas and dance hall proprietors.

Saloon Gang Plot Assassination

Did not the liquor gang assassinate Rhoderick Gambrell on the streets of Jackson, Mississippi? Did not the same cold-blooded conscienceless liquor gang assassinate Senator Carmack on the streets of Nashville, Tennessee? Did not the same liquor gang brutally attack John Carney and R. H. Coward on Cotton Belt train between Hubbard City and Mount Calm and Coward died from injuries? Did not the same cowardly gang assassinate Fred Roberts on the streets of Corpus Christi? Did not the same liquor gang assassinate the District Attorney in Borger last year, and was he not shot in the back as he went into his own garage? (And to this day the assassin has never been caught.) Did not the same gang make a cowardly attack on Evangelist Mordecai Ham in Fort Worth in 1916? And did not this same gang shoot down in cold blood on Main Street, Fort Worth, District Attorney Jeff McLean? And now we have the testimony of the converted former head of the retail liquor dealers association of Texas of the several secret meetings of the liquor gang where it was discussed and planned "to get rid of Norris because he is ruining our business." This quotation is the exact language of Bill Blevins, now a Christian and honored member of the First Baptist Church. He was converted and baptized into the First Baptist Church some eight years ago. He was in the saloon business for over forty years and had one of the best known saloons in Fort Worth when prohibition came. He organized the retail liquor dealers association of Texas; was its brains and generalissimo. He sits on the front seat of the First Baptist Church every Sunday and now loves the preacher he once hated and conspired with other saloonkeepers to get rid of. Behold, "what hath God wrought" and how true is Romans 8:28— "And we know that all things work together for good to them that love God, to them who are the called according to his purpose." Bill

Blevins is a mounment of Divine grace and tells this whole story—the conspiracy against Norris and his miraculous conversion with tears of gratitude! What explanation can be given of it? It is enough to make infidels fall down and own their Lord, and many of them have confessed Him as their only Saviour, like the Philippian jailer, when they saw the marvelous manifestiation of Divine Power!

Salvation of Dance Hall Proprietors

Time would fail to tell of many strange and glorious experiences. For example, the happy salvation and baptism of dance hall proprietor and wife who, located a short distance from the old church, Third and Taylor, saw two men running from behind the church the night of the shooting through the window of the church where the pastor was sitting. This occurred in January, 1912. But during the courthouse trial these two witnesses were running a public dance hall and were bitter enemies of the pastor who made war on dance halls. Therefore, they kept closed mouths on this most valuable testimony. Years afterwards both were convicted, gloriously converted and baptized by the very pastor they had so bitterly hated, and who refused to testify for his life when he was fought by a conspiracy as black as Haman's. They are two of the most honored, active and consecrated members of the First Church today and never miss a service. Their names are Mr. and Mrs. Ben O. Pulliam, and live at 1209 May Street, Fort Worth!

Incidentally, the "hired prosecution," the state, the conspirators knew of this highly important testimony while they were framing the pastor in the grand juries and the courthouse. Read again what the great Baptist commoner said of "the colossal frame-up" in leading editorial of the Baptist Standard, May 2, 1912.

"A Colossal Frame-Up of Wickedness'

Dr. J. B. Gambrell wrote these words:

"The country has come with great unanimity to the belief that the whole business is a colossal frame-up of wickedness in which the machinery of the law has been seized and used to ruin an innocent man in order to screen guilty men. The complete play-out of the perjury case, the utter inefficiency of evidence, even total lack of any evidence in the case, has settled public opinion as to the grand jury, the legal adviser of the jury, and the whole business. Hon. O. S. Lattimore did not put it too strong when he said it was a disgrace to the state."

"I WAS THERE"

By L. L. Cooper

It was my happy privilege to be associated with Dr. Norris as financial secretary of the First Baptist Church 1913 to 1920. We passed through many very trying times and testing experiences.

We had no protection from the law, so we had to protect ourselves from those who would molest or destroy the property of the church.

Many times the man from the local newspaper in the next block would throw pennies and nickels and have the boys run after them and then jerk our signs down and throw rocks through the windows. One half bushel of rocks accumulated that were thrown through the windows of the church.

In the thick of the fight when the pastor and his associates and members of the church were fighting the devil on every inch of the ground, the pastor came in one morning and said, "I want you to go with me. Are you ready?"

We came to a certain prominent hotel on Main Street where some 81 of the leading business men of Fort Worth had met, and in solemn conclave had agreed that Dr. J. Frank Norris should leave town, dead or alive, within the next ten days. (The mystery is how the pastor knew this meeting was in session.)

As we arrived at the hotel the meeting had adjourned. The men were in the lobby, standing about in groups, discussing the matter that they had so solemnly agreed to.

In one of these groups was the chairman of the State Democratic Committee, who was also owner of one of the largest wholesale grocery businesses in the city. There was also the state secretary of the Retail and Wholesale Liquor Dealers for Texas. Other leading business men and politicians were also there.

Mr. Norris said to these men,

"Gentlemen, you men have met and taken upon yourself the obligation for my removal from the city. I want to tell you now that I will be here to preach any of your funerals if you so desire —Furthermore, it is my solemn conviction that a number of you men will be filling a four by six before the next sixty days go by."

He also took from his pocket a Bible and held it up in their faces and said,

"Gentlemen, when you get me you are coming over that book— good morning!"

Rev. L. L. Cooper,
Great Lakes Bible School evangelist.

The most amazing things happened.

One of the men in this group fell in the same hotel the next morning with apoplexy and struck his head against a radiator. He has been paralyzed ever since.

Another man who owned four saloons was shot at one of his places of business the next day.

These tragedies went on until some seven or eight of these men had fallen. To climax it all, the man that called the meeting of this "Famous 81 Business Men" was leaving his palatial home on the Interurban between Dallas and Fort Worth, with his chauffeur, and just as they came upon the track one of the fast limited interurbans crashed into the back of the car and killed this man on the spot. The chauffeur was not hurt seriously. These things cannot be explained—"But God."

In The Laboratory

The auditorium of the church was running over and standing room was at a premium. For the seven years not more than twelve Sundays went by without souls being saved and people uniting with the church, as high as 60 additions on a single Sunday. The Sunday School grew from some 500 to over 4,000.

The time came for a new Sunday School building. After much prayer a modern miracle took place. A hundred foot square, four story building was erected where the original church building stood. The paving bricks from Main Street were purchased for hauling. This building when ready to be occupied cost approximately one-fourth what the building would have cost.

The method of financing the First Baptist Church was that every member should according as the Lord had prospered him. The standard of giving was, and is, the tithe. One common treasury of the church. The church went from the high pressure method to the New Testament, individual method, using the Sunday School as the educational enlistment agency.

It has been my happy privilege these 17 years since leaving the First Baptist Church to be known as the stewardship evangelist in a number of the states west of the Mississippi River, especially Texas and Oklahoma.

I have been in more than 650 churches with this message of stewardship. We have seen more than 15,000 people unite with the churches in these years by teaching and preaching stewardship enlistment, personal visitation and evangelism.

Our slogan has been, "A place for every member and every member in a place." Get the people and they will give their money.

MY TWENTY-THREE YEARS IN FORT WORTH OR INSIDE THE CUP—No. 2

Sermon By Dr. J. Frank Norris, Sunday Night, September 21, 1930

(Stenographically Reported)

DR. NORRIS: I want to call your attention to the text used last Sunday night when I didn't get through. It is found in the third chapter of Esther and second verse: "But Mordecai bowed not"—"But Mordecai bowed not, nor did him reverence."

This, as you recall, is the very familiar character, a Jew by the name of Mordecai, one of the children of captivity, and Haman had been promoted to be Prime Minister over this great empire that reached from India on the southeast way down to Ethiopia in the depths of Africa, including 127 provinces. So Haman was the mighty man in the empire, and when he rode forth, everybody bowed down and saluted him. That meant that three times their heads went down to the ground. But there was one who refused to bow down when Haman rode forth, and because Mordecai refused to bow down to this unscrupulous politician, Haman sought vengeance, not only against Mordecai, but against all the Jews, and he succeeded in having an Imperial decree written, sealed and signed by Ahasuerus, the king at that time, and sent throughout the 127 provinces of the empire, that every Jew, man, woman and child, be put to death on the 14th day of Adar, or of March. For that imperial decree, Haman paid into the king's treasury ten thousand talents of silver. The decree went forth, it could not be changed, it was unalterable. You are familiar with the wonderful story of how Esther became queen instead of Vashti, and she was doubly related to Mordecai—she was his first cousin—she was the daughter of his uncle and she was also his adopted child. When the decree went forth Mordecai lay in sackcloth and ashes at the king's gate. When Hatach brought word to Esther of Mordecai's weeping in sackcloth, she sent forth royal robes to clothe him and take away his sackcloth and ashes, but he refused to accept them and sent back the word to Esther:

"You go speak to the king that the lives of your people be spared."

And Esther gave command to Hatach to tell Mordecai: "For thirty days have not I entered into the presence of the king and there is a law in Shushan Palace that if anybody goes uninvited into the king's presence that means instant death, unless he wills to extend the golden scepter."

Mordecai again sends back the word: "If you refuse to do this, deliverance will come from another source, but it will not come to you and your household."

Then Esther said: "I will go and if I perish, I perish."

So she went unbidden into the presence of the king and stood in the inner court opposite the king's house. The king saw her and extended the golden scepter and Esther bowed before him.

The result was that Haman was hanged on the gallows that he had prepared for Mordecai, and Mordecai increased in favor, because of the power of God upon him, and the people were delivered.

The theme that comes down to us through the ages of mankind is the one word: "Mordecai bowed not"—he would not bow down to Haman!

It was with no small hesitation that I made up my mind to go into some things, to discuss some things that I discussed last Sunday night and I am going to finish tonight. I'll give you a few more chapters on "Inside the cup."

I want to say to you tonight, to this great audience—that the ministry of this hour is whipped, it is backed off the boards and on the defensive. The last thing on earth God wants and what the world despises is a ministry apologizing for its stand—because we have nothing to apologize for, and if I can help some brother of mine, some fellow soldier in the battle of life, God help me to do it. One of my mottoes I learned when a boy from Henry Drummond, "I shall not pass through this world but once, any good thing therefore that I can do to any human being let me do it now, let me not defer or neglect it, for I shall not pass this way again."

Shall New Testament Churches Be Free?

The issues, my friends, in the history of the First Baptist Church, and I can reduce the plural to the singular, and say the issue in the First Baptist Church through all those years of conflict, is whether or not a New Testament church shall have the unchallenged right to run and order its own affairs according to the Magna Charta of the church. That's the only issue, all others are side issues.

I don't know what I said last Sunday night—it was taken down but I haven't read it over, but I want to make this very clear, that the controversies we have had on the outside are nothing to what we have had on the inside, and when I say on the inside I don't mean altogether members of the First Baptist Church—now for many years we have had no controversies on the inside with members of the First Baptist Church—so when I say on the inside I mean on the inside of the Baptist denomination.

I travel over this country a great deal—I made three addresses out of the city last week, and I am going next week. I like to go. I love to give the message. I spoke in Abilene last week to what the papers there said was more than five thousand. I spoke to them for more than two hours on the fundamentals of the Christian faith, and I am glad to say there were many saved as a result of that meeting. I rejoice to do that kind of service. Of course it is hard. It costs me sweat and blood and nerve and time, but I enjoy it.

I talk a great deal with preachers, and I know what I am talking about, and I say this without fear of contradiction, one of the supreme needs of the hour is that the churches be freed from entangling alliances.

As I speak tonight there are multitudes of people here not members of the church I have the honor to serve, and I am sure you agree with me, whatever be your church faith, that your heart has been made to bleed and your face has been made to blush, as many times you have seen some ungodly clique in your church absolutely rule and dictate to the entire church, preacher included. That thing ought to come to an end. That is not what Jesus Christ established for the church—no, no, no, ten thousand times no! (Voice amen.)

Only last week a pastor told me, "Norris, if I should preach on these things, I have four families in my church. I would have the biggest row that ever was raised."

"Well," I said, "I would have the biggest row before daylight and go on and preach on what I think I ought to preach on; yes, sir." (Voices amen.)

Talk about rows—I have had the supreme delight of firing and cleaning out two choirs since I have been in Fort Worth, and I do not hesitate to tell you that when I made up my mind to do it, I had the most delectable experience I ever had, or ever expect to have this side of Paradise. I have nothing against choirs—how I delight in this large magnificent choir.

Ladies' Parties Rule Pastors

There are some women present tonight who will remember this experience—I am just talking tonight on a few of the inside chapters. We had all these societies—the WMU's, the Ladies' Aid, you know what all the different ones are—everyone of them are just like suckers on corn stalks, and they kept me just juning around all the time, working myself to death, doing what they told me to do, and you needn't fool yourself they will tell the preacher what to do—talk about them being a help to him—why he is just a fifth wheel trying to keep up—just like a boy riding on the coupling pole—everybody else sitting on the front seats, going to a Fourth of July celebration, and there is no room for the boy and he has to sit on the coupling pole sticking out about ten feet behind the wagon—so I got tired riding on the coupling pole and made up my mind I was going to ride up on the front seat and drive the team, therefore, some people said, "Norris is heady, he is unruly, he raises disturbances." They wanted me to be like the little boy—he isn't going to cause any disturbances, certainly not. But I don't believe any preacher should be riding on the coupling pole while some old goozer of a deacon or Jezebel sits on the front seat—that's his place, let him ride on the front seat and drive the team. That's my opinion. (Voices amen.)

A man asked me not long ago if I ever made mistakes. I said, "I make more of them than anything else, if I didn't I wou'd be out of fellowship with the whole church." (Laughter.)

Now talking about those hen parties—now, ladies, don't misunderstand me and get mad at me tonight—if you do it isn't going to do you a bit of good. It is funny to me to hear somebody is mad at me, it doesn't cause me to lose one minute's sleep—it's just like winking in the dark, there's nobody seeing you.

Cause of Envy

A bunch of Baptist preachers went over to see Dr. J. B. Gambrell, and told him that he would have to help them do something with Norris. You can take ninety-nine per cent of the criticism against this church and it is on account of the rest of the fellows are preaching to an empty wood yard and I have a tabernacle full of people. There are plenty of folks for all—like calling hogs—there are some of my hog calling friends sitting over here—they will tell you if you call hogs three times and not shell the corn down to them they won't come any more.

Well back to these societies—I don't want to get off on that—you know what, I used to have some women in the church who would call me before breakfast and another one would call me before dinner and they would call me after dinner and they would call me after I would get in bed and then sometimes call up between times. What did they want? I do not know. I never have found out—only they would want me to make a yard and a half of announcements. How many of you here ever heard a preacher get up and make about a yard and half of announcements and you would wish he would hurry up and get through—and if he didn't make them, here they would come! Well that thing went on, Monday, Tuesday, Wednesday, Thursday, Friday and Saturday, and Sunday—and there I would have to stand up there and read a lot of announcements that nobody cared anything about—until finally one day I decided I wasn't going to read any more, that it wasn't the business of the pastor to read a lot of announcements, so when they were handed to me I laid them aside—whoopee! They came around and tried to lay me aside, and they came very near doing it too. (Laughter.) Now they were all good, fine women—they proceeded to give me my walking papers; yes, sir, and I saw what was going to happen. I am one nervous creature and it doesn't take much to scare me. (Laughter.) You just let a bunch of women get after me—it just makes me nervous, and if you don't turn around and run after them—well, you'll just be out—you preachers, you let a bunch of women run you all night and all day and all the week and you won't feel like preaching the next Sunday.

One of them got after Elijah and he ran 300 miles without looking back or leaving his forwarding address. (Laughter.)

I called all the presidents and the secretaries, and the vice-presidents and all of them together, the whole posse comitatus in one meeting. I didn't even tell my wife. She was there. So when they all met that afternoon, the main ramrod said to them: "We are so delighted to have our pastor with us this afternoon, and he has a word he would like to say."

I got up and said: "Madam President. I just want to say a word—it won't take me but a minute and I don't want to disturb you." Then I said, "As pastor of the First Baptist Church I want to say all your societies have adjourned sine die, to meet no more." Man! I said that going out the door. Yes, sir, I had my hat in my hand, and I didn't lose any time saying it—I think I left my car running. (Laughter.) I heard something going on behind me

New Gospel Sound Truck recently purchased by the First Baptist Church, which will carry the gospel in sermon and song throughout the city and surrounding territory.

—like that black panther of Honeyboy and Sassafras! (Laughter.) And they stayed adjourned! They don't win any souls. The main thing they do is gossip about everybody in the neighborhood— the preachers, the deacons and everybody else. I got tired of it and I said, "I'm through, that's all." Now then talk about getting claw hammers out. (Laughter.)

I'm just giving you a few inside chapters tonight.

Newspaper Refused to Print Norris' Name

I referred to a conspiracy last Sunday night—a man who hasn't been in this city long, and he is talking about joining the First Baptist Church—I hope he is here tonight—I will give him a chance. He said to me: "Say, you said something about newspapers not publishing your name for two years' time, is that actually so?" I said, Yes, it is s-o, so. The morning Record, it was then, came out and published an editorial and said, "We will not publish the name of J. Frank Norris in these columns." How many of you remember that? Hold up your hand. (Large number of hands up.) All right I wanted you to say so, for I want the strangers here to know that took place. All right, listen, instead of discouraging me, I said, "Now you have been delivered into my hands." And I got some big placards and had printed in red ink and black ink in great big letters: "COME TO HEAR THE PREACHER THAT THE LIQUOR PRESS OF FORT WORTH BOYCOTS." How many of you remember that placard? I never told who the preacher was—and I plastered the town with them—well they commenced coming. They called a meeting of the directors and the stockholders of this paper and they said: "This thing has got to be stopped." You know there would be people get married—John Smith and Sallie Brown and no preacher married them, and they would have funerals and no preacher conducted the funeral—if I was the one that did it. I just kept twisting their angoras and I had more fun in a minute over it, than they ever did have—that thing cost that newspaper—a director told me afterwards!—$175,000! And it went broke!

Let me tell you something, now don't misunderstand this— there are three things that a man is a fool to go against, one is the Church of Jesus Christ, the other is a woman, and the third is a preacher of the Gospel—you'd better let all three alone. (Laughter.) There are three things that God is jealous for, first, His word, second, His Church, third, His prophet. He will take care of all three. Here is something I speak of with great hesitation, certainly with great humility. Every hand that has been lifted against the First Baptist Church has failed to prosper. There have been lots of tragedies connected with it.

The Broken Down Denominational Machine

Take the denominational machine—the Baptists are one thing and the machine is another. Most of their machinery is in the junk heap.

If I had been willing to bow down to the unscriptural demands of the denominational Hamans there would never have been any trouble.

If I had never exposed evolution in Baylor University that forced seven evolution professors to resign, there would have been no trouble.

If I had meekly and subserviently put on their post-millennial program of institutionalism there would have been no trouble.

If I had been willing to take the unscriptural assessments of the illfated 75-Million Campaign there would have been no trouble.

Oh, I am a New Testament Baptist, not a machine Baptist. I am for the denomination but I am not for a lot of long-standing high-handed misappropriation of sacred mission funds. The main difference between me and other preachers is I have dared to say so openly and they have not. But I have more people to preach to and most of the preachers are looking for a place to hang their hat.

The proudest thing in the history of the First Baptist Church is that we were put out of the synagogue because of our stand for New Testament principles. In 1921 the papers said in big headlines these words:

"ONE LONE MAN AGAINST FOUR THOUSAND DELEGATES."

But oh things have reversed. We are now in the overwhelming majority and the end is not yet. The machine is broken and rejected. "Mene, Mene, Tekel Upharsin" is the verdict rendered against the Sanhedrin that has fought and maligned a great soul-winning independent New Testament church.

And the church is growing today as never before. In a short time we will enter one of the greatest church auditoriums on the

American Continent. I want the Baptist General Convention to meet in that auditorium. It has been eighteen years since the Convention met in Fort Worth. What are they afraid of? Why don't they come to Fort Worth? (Now 24 years.)

Would it not be a wonderful thing for the machine to meet in a great church that it turned out because that church chose to study the Bible as its only text book instead of the literature of the Convention? This is unbelievable. But the minutes of the 1923 Convention show that one of the charges against the First Baptist Church was that we discontinued the literature of the Sunday School Board!

Isn't that a glorious chapter in the history of any church? We are so grateful for it—strong temptation to boast of this badge of honor, but no, we are humbly grateful that we are counted worthy to suffer for the sake of the pure Word of God, plus nothing and minus nothing. May not this be one reason, the main reason why the abounding blessing of heaven is on the church? Stand by the Word of God and the God of the word will stand by you.

Attempted Blackmail

I have never told this before, only a few friends know about it.

At 10 o'clock one night I received a call to come marry a couple. It was rather a late hour for such a call and it was from a certain section that raised my gravest suspicions. I took the number and found out it was not wise for me to go there, and didn't go. It wasn't but a short time until I got another call to marry a couple, still later in the night, and I didn't go. I was talking to a friend about it and we agreed that if I got another call I would go, and sure enough after while I got another call. I can tell you exactly what the number was, 612 Calhoun Street. When I got this call to come marry a couple, and in view of things going on, and from what I had heard before, I said, "All right I will go." I asked for the names of the parties. They gave me some names—I don't know if there were any such parties. It was a cold night—I never said anything to my wife for I didn't want her to pass on it. I got hold of a man I could depend on to go with me, but I didn't let this gang know anybody was coming with me. We went to that place—we drove by it two or three times then we stopped. The plan was that he was to get out and stay behind a bush or vine that was there until I needed him. I walked to the door, rung the bell and a woman weighing about

225 pounds came to the door. I said, "Is this where a couple wants to get married?"

She said, "Yes, sir, come in."

She opened the door, I stepped in, but I left my right foot against the door facing and the door struck my heel.

She said, "Come on in."

"Where is the couple?" I asked.

"Well," she says, "come on in and I will call them," and she caught hold of the door and gave it a shove.

I said, "That's all right I will keep my hand on the door, get the couple."

She said, "This is my house."

I could see under a portiere a half dozen or so feet of men and women. She insisted on my coming in. I called the man on whom I knew I could depend, and said, "Come on." He walked in and shoved that door wide open, and you never heard such running down the back hall—and there was nobody left but this woman and a girl. I called to the girl, and she broke into tears and told the whole scheme. Two of the city detectives were stationed there and two men in uniform on the outside—the scheme was—there was nobody to be married—she said, "They were to bring you here and then when you got there they were to raid this house and take you to the city hall in order to ruin your name." Well, I wasn't afraid of having my name ruined then and I am not afraid now. I made up my mind not to let any low down gang of the underworld assassinate me or put me in a compromising position. I will tell you the other side of the story. That woman in charge of that house where she lived for three years afterwards, one night, bless God, that woman came and heard me preach and was saved, and I baptized her, and one year afterwards I preached her funeral. I got the whole story from her.

Incidentally, you may be interested to know that place was owned by the chairman of the Board of Deacons of the First Baptist Church. It was one of the most notorious resorts of the city. This chairman of the Board of Deacons was fighting me—trying to fire me—I pulled this ownership of this house of ill-repute on him before the whole church. The number of the place 612 Calhoun Street. It has since been cleaned and is a decent section of the city. Board of Deacons—yes, that is what most of them are fit for, to fire the preacher, but tables were turned in this case and the gang have been mad even since, at least some of them.

It is an old trick of the devil, just as old as the conspiracy of Potiphar's wife against Joseph. The gossipers like to whisper it, the ecclesiastical machines threaten it, but you know such hell-born schemes have never even interested me, much less worried me. Falsehoods, I care not how many and by whom circulated, can hurt no man.

Fight on Radio

Here is something I hesitate to call attention to, but think you ought to know it. This is of more recent date. There was a petition circulated to make a protest against my using radio KFQB, it was then, now KTAT. They tried to put me off the air; I read what they said; I got this from the Radio Commission at Washington. They carried this up there, and I can tell you who took it. His name is "G-l-e-a-s-o-n," Gleason; and the mayor of Fort Worth then—here is what they said—that station KFQB's programs were a disgrace to the citizens of the country, and that these Sunday programs which aroused religious strife were of a type that are broadcast by only the worst and most vicious type of agitator—that was during the Hoover campaign when Al Smith failed to carry Texas. Among the conspirators to put us off the air—they didn't know it would get back down here—was a prominent preacher, the President of the Seminary at Fort Worth. Here was the scheme. The former mayor was to put up the money to pay for it, run it to advertise his department store during the week, and the President of the Seminary was to take my time on Sunday! (Laughter.) Well neither of them have it yet, and that isn't all, they won't get it. (Applause.)

Somebody says, "Why refer to these matters?" Here is why. If you read in the Old Testament you will find where the prophets reviewed the whole history of the Jews, going back to the time God opened the Red Sea and they walked through dry shod, how they came to the wilderness and God sent manna from the skies, and when their feet touched the brim of Jordan, how God marvelously delivered them—that is the one explanation to it.

I am just giving you the records of the Radio Commission at Washington. Sometimes I have folks say, "Norris, looks like it all would run you crazy and ruin your health." There was a time they nearly ran me crazy and did break my health. In fact, I was broken every way. They said I was financially broke.

They told the truth, except I was worse broke than they said. But thank heaven I paid every cent a long time ago. I am not boasting—just trying to help some struggling fellow sailor out in the storm.

You say, how do I have such good health?

Listen, if you want good health, don't go to bed with any hate in your heart.

If you want good health, have lots of good humor.

If you want good health, fight a good fight and if you lose, forget it and get up and go to fighting again tomorrow.

If you want good health don't worry about what folks say about you.

If you want good health, don't worry—go to bed, pull up the windows and let the world go to hell until daylight. (Laughter.)

If you want to have good health, read your Bible.

If you want to have good health, get hold the latch string of heaven when the stars go out, live in eternity and not in time, put your faith in the arm of Jehovah and not in the weak, frail arm of the flesh. Paul says, "I have no confidence in the flesh."

You know there are some people that worry themselves into the grave because they worry about what somebody says about them. Suppose what they say is true, quit it, get on the other side, and if what they say is not true, don't pay any attention to it. A preacher came to see me the other day and he was just wringing his hands worrying about everybody talking about him. I said, "It's not so, is it?" And he said "No!" "Well," I said, "go on and preach the gospel, and eat two square meals a day and sleep all night and you will be all right."

The Insurance

I want to tell you something else. This hasn't been so far back either. One day the church office got notice the insurance on the church's building was being cancelled. I didn't pay any attention to it. I won't go into all that tonight. One of the biggest insurance men in Texas, not a member of anybody's church, called me up and said, "Norris, I think you ought to know what is going on."

"What's going on?" I asked.

He says, 'There is a deliberate plan to have cancelled all your insurance and force the mortgage due and foreclose on the property and take it away from you."

Now that looked like pretty serious business, and we went on for awhile with practically no insurance, and we owed a life insurance company in St. Louis a heavy debt and they held a mortgage on our property. I knew what the scheme was—I never even told my wife this, but I jumped on the old Sunshine Special and went to St. Louis. I arrived in St. Louis and walked over to the office of the President of the company we owed the money to—I didn't know who he was, but do you know I found out that he was a brother to a Baptist preacher who was an old school mate of mine, and that President knew me as well as I know any of you. I just laid the cards on the table, and told him what was up. He says, "The law is that you have got to have insurance."

"I know that," I said, "but, listen, you are not going to bother us until we can get it?"

"Get it just as soon as you can," he said.

We went on talking, and it was about lunch time and we went to lunch together, and his last word to me was, "Go on and preach the gospel and do the best you can."

That's what we have had to go up against. They soon found out they couldn't get anywhere with a great Christian man head of an insurance company—who told them to go where the fires don't go out, and said he had faith in the First Baptist Church: he had faith in the God of the First Baptist Church. (Applause.)

Now who had that done? I will tell you. I want you to know there were certain Baptists in it. Who else was into it? A certain merchant who is not living in Fort Worth or anywhere else was in it, a former mayor.

That's some of the things we have had to go through in this church. My friends, it was enough to run a man crazy, but I felt like it would come out all right, and bless God, it did, and we have one of the finest pieces of property in Fort Worth and we are building our auditorium right on up, and it is going to be so absolutely fire proof that I couldn't even burn it myself. (Much laughter.)

Ecclesiastical Hate Against First Baptist Church

I said a moment ago—I give you this word briefly—now you can go up against the saloon and the underworld, whip them, and they will come and join you. They don't carry malice. Why, I have baptized a large number of ex-saloon keepers. You can whip a man on the political field, and next year he will be voting for you. They don't carry malice. My friends, the meanest and blackest hate on earth is ecclesiastical hate. What was the enemy that pursued the Apostle Paul?

What was it that nailed Christ to the cross? The hate of the ecclesiastics.

What was it cut the heads off the Apostles? It was Ecclesiasticism.

Let me show you something. Just fifteen years ago the First Baptist Church decided to dump all the Sunday School literature, quarterlies, leaflets. You can't learn the Bible with such junk—so we decided to take the Bible only and use it in every class of every age: that we would sit down and study together the same lesson out of the Bible, and we went through the entire sixty-six books, every age, every class and we turned around and started through again. This morning the entire Sunday School studied the book of Esther. My friends, that's one of the charges the ecclesiastical machine made against the First Baptist Church, because we refused to use the literature and took the Bible only. I have no use for something some man says about the Bible, all I want is what God says. This church stands one hundred per cent for the whole Bible from the first preposition "In" to the last "Amen" of Revelation.

The First Baptist Church believes in the direct creative act of God, that He created the earth, the stars and systems; that He created the fishes of the sea, the birds of the air, the animals of the forest and that the climax of His creation was man.

The First Baptist Church believes in every miracle in the Old and New Testament—that when God said, "Let the waters be gathered" it was so, and we believe when it says He split the sky and fire came down from heaven on Mount Carmel, it was so; we believe when it says a fish swallowed Jonah and it made him so sick of his job that it threw him up, that it was so. (Laughter.)

The First Baptist Church believes that the Holy Spirit overshadowed the Virgin Mary and she brought forth the Son of God, the son of man.

The First Baptist Church believes He performed all the miracles the Bible says He did. We believe that He turned the water into wine; that He opened blind eyes, unstopped deaf ears; that He healed the paralytic and the lame man walked; we believe that when He called to the dead, "Come forth," they came forth.

The First Baptist Church believes that He has all power to forgive sins; we believe that He was nailed to the cross that He might bring us to God; we believe that when He died they took His body, wrapped it in linen and laid Him in Joseph's new made tomb, sealed it with hate, and guarded it by Roman Power for three days, and we believe that on the First Day of the week, He burst asunder the bars of death and rose in triumph over the grave; and we believe He was seen on the earth for forty days and that He ascended back to the right hand of the Majesty on high, where He ever liveth to make intercession for us—and thank God we don't need any priest to speak to Him for us through any hole in the wall, to get our sins forgiven; no, sir. We believe that this same Jesus is coming again down the sky in great glory and power to raise the righteous dead, and the righteous living saints will be changed in a moment, in the twinkling of an eye, and together! together! together! we shall be caught up to meet the Lord in the air, where we will ever be with Him, and we believe that He is coming to put down all rule and all principalities and power and chain the Devil and establish His reign on the earth for a thousand years! (Shouting.)

I want to say this last word. Of course nobody is going away and say I am boasting—for there is no ground for boasting—I have my scars; yes, sir. I have them, but I am not going to wear any crepe on the lapel of my coat. I am not going around like a weak kitten—no. My friends, you will never find mine on the outside. It is on the inside. It is the great joy of my life that I can look back over the years and say, "I never asked for any quarter." I haven't done it yet, and bless God, I don't expect to. Let them do their worst. When my funeral comes—I hope that will be a long time off—and the friends pass around my coffin, and when last comes my wife and children, and they look on the cold dead face of their father, I want them to say this and it be the truth—"He never turned his back in the day of battle." (Voices amen.)

"Oh," they say, "Norris is a disturber." That is not the truth by far.

Why do they say that? Because I didn't run at the first crack of the whip.

Why do they say I am a disturber? Because I refused to let a few worldly deacons run me out of town.

Why do they say I am a fighter? Because I wouldn't let a lot of half undressed women raise hell in the church and tell me what to do.

Why do they say I am a disturber? Because I declined to let a bunch of singers tell me where to head in.

Why do they say I am a disturber? Because I refused to let the saloon crowd and their sympathizers rule the church when the prohibition fight was on.

Why do they say I am a disturber? Because I refused to let evolution be taught in our Baptist schools without a protest.

Why do they say I am a disturber? Because I refuse to let any ecclesiastical gang on top side of God's earth tell the First Baptist Church how to run its business. (Applause.)

Why do they call me a disturber? Because I refused to bow down to Haman, that's why.

Yes, there have been some dark, deep waters, I don't deny it, but I have tried with it all, when the darkness deepens, to see the light. When the babel of voices roared there was a song; when the waves were high and the wind tempestuous, I could hear the voice of Him who said: "Be of good cheer, it is I, be not afraid." I have tried as I walked down through the walls of the Red Sea and heard Him saying, 'Come on over on this side"—and when I walked through the wilderness there was the shade of His cloud of grace. I have tried when I came to the waters of the swollen Jordan to pick up the stones, carry them to the other side and build a memorial to our God. I have tried when I walked around the walls of Jericho to sing, "We are marching to Zion," and when the walls fell down flat, give God the glory. When He said go into the fiery furnace, He went in with me, and when I went into the hungry lion's den, I thought, if I am eaten by the lions, I will be through and go on home to heaven, and I will not sell my birthright for a mess of pottage, and like Paul and Silas, I have tried to sing and pray at the midnight hour, for the Lord to come and shake down the doors and have a midnight baptizing. (Shouting.)

I have but one joy, that's all—while ago as I walked down the aisle, I saw a man and his wife standing over there, at first I didn't recognize them, and I apologized to them. Jake Street, are you still here? (Man answers in audience.) Jake, do you mind standing? (Man gets up.) Jake drank for several years. How long was it? About fifteen years, wasn't it? "Yes, sir." Thank you, Jake, be seated. I baptized Jake about two years ago this summer—when I walked down that aisle and saw that man there together with his beautiful wife—he is living a sober Christian life now—why I would rather go out tonight and put my arms around some other Jake down in the depths of wreck and ruin and by the grace of God lift him up, lift him up! lift him up! (voices amen) lift him up! until God reaches down and takes him and gives him back to his wife a sober man, than to have all the wealth of the world—what joy! (Voices amen, shoutings.)

You know that man Shields, that veteran of the 90th Division —whom I baptized a week ago last Sunday night at 1:30 a. m., when I called for him the next Sunday night and he wasn't here, somebody said: "Norris was just telling that, there isn't any such fellow." Mr. Shields, are you here tonight? (Man arises.) Come down here and tell that gang how they lied on you. (Man comes to front.) You are not going to tell this fellow that fought in St. Mihiel and the Argonne battles that I lied about it. Come on up here. (Man walks up on platform.) Friends, this is Mr. William E. Shields, who because when I called for him the other night and he wasn't here some said, there wasn't any such man. Will you tell this crowd if your name is Shields?

MR. SHIELDS: It is.

DR. NORRIS: Where do you live?

MR. SHIELDS: 409 Broadus, Seminary Hill.

DR. NORRIS: Tell this crowd if three Sunday nights ago you called my home about five minutes to 12 o'clock.

MR. SHIELDS: I did, yes, sir.

DR. NORRIS: Tell this crowd whether or not you told me, "I have been a wicked sinner and I have committed every sin in the world, but that I got down on my knees tonight and I am saved," did that happen?

MR. SHIELDS: Yes, sir.

DR. NORRIS: Tell this crowd whether or not you said: "Dr. Norris, I want to be baptized tonight."

MR. SHIELDS: I did.

DR. NORRIS: Tell this crowd whether or not I told you that we didn't have the baptistry filled and I didn't know whether we could or not, and you told me that didn't make any difference I could find some place, and that we could go down to the Trinity River?

MR. SHIELDS: Yes, sir.

DR. NORRIS: Tell this crowd whether or not I told you that I would baptize you if I had to take you to the Trinity River.

MR. SHIELDS: You did.

DR. NORRIS: Tell this crowd whether or not we filled up the baptistry and at 1:30 a. m. on Monday morning I baptized you?

MR. SHIELDS: That's so.

DR. NORRIS: And you have been happy ever since, and got a good case of religion?

MR. SHIELDS: Yes, sir.

DR. NORRIS: My friends, here is this man who had not been in church for many years, this old boy that faced death in the world war for you and me—why long after all the skyscrapers have fallen down and the earth has melted with fervent heat and all the works of the world have been burned up; long after yonder heavens have been rolled up like a scroll and long after the Angel of Time shall stand, one foot on the land and one foot on the sea and lifting his right hand sware by Him that liveth forever and ever, who created the heaven, and the things that are therein, that time shall no longer be—away out, out yonder in the eternity of eternities William Shields and Frank Norris will sit down together and talk about that midnight baptizing! (Shoutings.)

Folks, I am sorry for you who are not preaching the gospel. (Voices amen.) Yes, sir. Sometimes I have had friends say, "Norris, you ought to have made a lawyer." Lord have mercy on the lawyers—(laughter)—there is not much chance for most of them. Why they never have such joy as that.

I must close, your patient hearing tempts me to go on—I want to give you this last word and give an invitation. I am so hot I have preached my collar and tie off. (Laughter.)

I want to give you the greatest story of my life. I wanted my wife to come tonight—but she thought she ought to stay at home and help with the radio—and I wouldn't tell her what I wanted for if I had I knew she wouldn't come, but I want her to stand here on the platform someday and tell her side of this story. I want you to have it from a woman whose faith never fails.

In the darkest darkness of the tragic summer of 1912—the reason why it was so dark—everything was gone, my health was gone—I looked like one of these scare crows they put out to keep the crows out of a watermelon patch walking around—I looked like a poor old horse that was string-haltered with blind staggers reeling around—I felt like that and I looked like it. I couldn't talk more than ten or fifteen minutes until I would begin to cough, and I would tremble like a twig in a March wind, and afterwards I would be so hoarse I couldn't speak above a whisper. Now I believe I could speak for twenty hours and never know what it is to be hoarse.

I want to say this to help somebody. Say, did you ever feel like your feet were going down and down and down? Well, beloved, I know how you felt.

Did you ever feel like everything on earth was gone and something had gone wrong upstairs? Well, I know how you felt.

Have you ever gone to bed and rolled from side to side, and the morning would come and you had not slept a wink? Well I know what you are talking about.

Say, were you ever just worse than broke—I don't mean badly bent—my enemies said I was broke, they didn't know the half of it. I was broke all flat. (Laughter.)

During that day when everything was gone, then something seemed to snap up here in my head and I felt like somebody had a sledge hammer hitting me on the back of the head. About that time a friend wired me to come help him in a meeting—I said I can't hold a meeting I haven't got the strength to hold a meeting, but I wired him I would come without thinking much about it. When I went down to catch the train, I missed it—I was glad of it, and went to send a telegram that I wasn't coming, and George Neace—if he were here tonight would perhaps remember this, said, "Brother Norris, there is another train going at 11 o'clock." It made me mad because he told me. I got on it and went down there and when I got there—a little town of about a thousand people—well it seemed like all the folks and all the dogs were standing there looking at me to see what kind of looking wild animal I was. Brother White came up and took my little old hand satchel—didn't have much in it—and he said, "You are going to be my guest"—well he was a nice looking, civilized man and I went along with him. When we got home he introduced me to his wife and took me to a room—a nice looking room, and said, "This is to be your room." We went out to the tabernacle that night and everybody was there for forty miles around, and when I stood up to speak I was so weak I couldn't stand without holding to the stand for support. I was absolutely exhausted. I read a few Scriptures and said "Good night." I didn't make any appeal. I didn't have any appeal to make. When we got home that night, Sister White wanted to fix me something to eat—I didn't want anything to eat. I didn't have any appetite. I had a dark brown taste in my mouth. I went to bed. I tossed back and forth all night long—the next morning when I was shaving I noticed my hand trembling—my eyes were blood shot—I looked like I had been on a month's drunk. We went down to the tabernacle that day, and talked a little while and quit. That night there was another big crowd—I preached the best I could and we went home—I had not been able to sleep and I was so tired —my breath was short, just cutting off right here—I woke up to the fact that unless that thing changed I would soon be in my grave or in the asylum. Later on that night—Oh, that night, it was the greatest night I ever experienced on earth, the darkest and the deepest and the saddest—the family went to bed—I tried to sleep but I couldn't. I needed sleep I had lost several nights. I hadn't been able to eat and sleep all summer and I didn't weigh but 124 pounds, and I was as tall as I am now—that's a good deal less than what I weigh now—let me see that's about sixty pounds less than what I weigh now. After while as the night rolled on and I tossed and tossed—my limbs from my knees down felt like I was standing in red hot fire, and my temples just felt like somebody had my head in a vise bursting it wide open, and I felt like somebody had tweezers pulling my nerves out one at a time. My body felt like it had been flayed and cut to pieces —it was gone, wasted away. Finally I got up, put on my clothes, the window was open, I didn't want to disturb the family, and I took my shoes in my hand and slipped out, walked out the back way out into the pasture, I walked along slowly until I got way out from the house and I sat down for awhile in the grass— and I sat there—thin, wasted away, broken, discouraged, overcome, overwhelmed—after while I lay down on the grass like

Jacob the first night he was away from home—I put my hands under my tired aching head and lay there looking up at the glowing stars on that hot July night, and I wondered why all these things had befallen me. What wrong had I done? I went to Fort Worth and made the best fight I could and I had lost—I didn't care for myself so much, but my wife and three babies, God pity them! My friends had turned away, everything was gone and I knew I was gone too—I am telling you I knew I would soon be in the asylum or in the grave in a short time. I felt myself slipping, and I was terribly alarmed about it. When I got up the cold sweat was on my brow. I started home and the gray streaks of morning were showing up in the eastern sky— I slipped back into bed, but I couldn't sleep. After while that good old Methodist layman came and knocked gently on my door —I said, "Come in." He came in and said: "Did you have a good night?" "Yes, sir," I said. "Well," he said, "breakfast will soon be ready"—I didn't want anything to eat, but I went in and sat down at the table. I was so sad I couldn't think of a word on earth to say, and Sister White wanted to know if there was anything she could fix for me that I could eat. I felt like a man that was drowning and nothing to hold to—every friend I had on earth was gone. I said to myself, I am going home, get my family and I am going to Southern California where nobody knows me and I am going to get out there on a ranch and I am through with the ministry—not that I had lost faith in God, but I had lost my fight, my courage was gone, health was gone, everything was gone.

When we started to church that night I told the family to go on that I would walk. After they had gone, I got my grip—I didn't have much in it, just a change of underwear and a necktie—and I said I am going home tonight and I am not going to tell a soul that I am going. I walked on to the tabernacle and went through a peach orchard and I hid my grip in some weeds, and I went into the tabernacle. When the services were over I meant to slip out there, get my grip and catch the 11 o'clock train and come home.

When I got into the tabernacle and started to preach, the pastor leaned over and whispered to me, "Do you see that man sitting back yonder?" I had already seen him. He said, "That old fellow with the red bandana handkerchief around his neck—he is the meanest man in all this country, it is the first time I have ever known him to come to church—he has a half dozen notches on his gun. If you could reach that man you could reach this whole country." I can see him now as he sat rared back—he had on boots and spurs, and I learned afterwards bells on his spurs, and he looked at me and I looked at him, we were of mutual curiosity to each other. I stood up, tired and weak, and I looked at him and I thought—"You poor old sinner, it's the last time I ever expect to preach and I am going to give you the best I have got."

So what happened? I looked at him and he looked at me— and I began, "A certain man had two sons: and the younger of them said to his father, Father, give me the portion of goods that falleth to me. And he divided unto them his living. And not many days after the younger son gathered all together, and took his journey into a far country, and there wasted his substance in riotous living. And when he had spent all, there arose a mighty famine in that land; and he began to be in want. And he went and joined himself to a citizen of that country: and he sent him into his fields to feed the swine. And he would fain have filled his belly with the husks that the swine did eat: and no man gave unto him. And when he came to himself, he said, How many hired servants of my father's have bread enough and to spare, and I perish with hunger! I will arise and go to my father, and will say unto him, Father, I have sinned against heaven, and before thee, And am no more worthy to be called thy son: make me as one of thy hired servants. And he arose, and came to his father. But when he was yet a great way off, his father saw him, and had compassion, and ran, and fell on his neck, and kissed him. And the son said unto him, Father, I have sinned against heaven and in thy sight and am no more worthy to be called thy son. But the father said to his servants, Bring forth the best robe, and put it on him; and put a ring on his hand, and he made a great feast"—and about that time I saw that old red-faced sinner bury his face in his hands—it was a hot night and I didn't know what it meant, but in a minute he just reached up behind and tore that old red bandana loose and I saw him bury his face in it and his frame shook like a leaf in a storm—and folks, something happened in this tired weak frame of mine—and I stood up on my hind feet for the first time in a long time and felt strong—and I said if there is a man here who is a sinner lost and will come to the Father's house tonight, come on; come on! come on! and, my friends, I can see that old sinner now as he got up and started down the aisle—he had that old red bandana handkerchief in one hand and his cow-boy hat in the other, and you could hear his bells jingling as he came—listen folks, he didn't stop to shake hands with me, but he fell full length on his face—and when his little old Methodist wife sitting over there, when she saw him, she let out a shout that you could have heard a quarter of a mile and she came running and fell by his side (shoutings) and in five minutes there were more than fifty men and women in that altar seeking Jesus Christ, and salvation came down and that 11 o'clock train whistled and went on and they were still being saved, and twelve o'clock came and folks were still being saved, one o'clock came and they were still shouting, and two o'clock came and were were still there. When I got back home at 3 o'clock and walked in Brother White said, "Fort Worth is trying to get you"—well I knew who in Fort Worth wanted me. I went to the telephone and tried to talk—I have always been able to keep control of my emotions, but sometimes they get the best of me—this was one time they did—I got Fort Worth on the line and they told me Mrs. Norris was trying to get me, and I said, "Bless God, I want her too." When she came to the telephone and said, "Hello, is that you, Frank?" I just played the baby act, and I couldn't do anything but stand there and cry, and central kept saying, "Talk, talk, here they are." Well I was doing my best to talk and I couldn't say a word. I turned to Sister White and I said, "You tell her." She said, "All right, I will tell her," and she came and took that receiver out of my hand, and she drew back and slung it against the wall and shouted "Hallelujah! hallelujah! hallelujah!" and she just shouted all over the room. I said, "Brother White, you tell her"—he said, "All right," and he came to the telephone and he said, "Sister Norris," and that was as far as he got, he just bellowed as loud as he could—and their sixteen-year-old daughter came and she tried it and she just squalled and cried. And I said, "Give me that telephone receiver"—and all the time central was saying, "Talk, talk, talk!" Finally I got my feelings under control enough and I said, "Wife, wife, we have had the biggest meeting you ever saw, more than half hundred sinners have been saved, and they are still shouting all over this country, and the best part of it is, wife, you have a new husband—he has been saved tonight, and he is coming home and we are going to start life over again and lick the tar out of that crowd and build the biggest church in the world." And she said, "I knew it was happening. I have been praying for three days and nights. I haven't slept a wink, and tonight I had the answer to my prayer, I have been praying that this thing might happen, and my joy is complete, my cup runneth over." I said, "Wife, I will be home Sunday."

The next Sunday I preached at 7th and Lamar and the fire from heaven came down and we had sixty-two converts to walk down the aisle. Any of you remember that night? (Hands up.) Many of you.

To God be all the glory. I praise His name for good health and for the opportunity He has given me to testify for Him, and as long as there is breath in my body, as long as my tongue can proclaim, that long will I proclaim the unsearchable riches of Jesus Christ. My only hope of reward, my only ambition, my only joy, is to take some old boy like Shields and Jake Street out there and point them to the way of salvation that shall outlast the shining stars and a life shall be saved for ever and for ever! Who will come tonight? (People came from all the tabernacle.)

DR. NORRIS' OUTSIDE ENGAGEMENTS

In addition to the two large churches, Dr. Norris fills engagements throughout the country between Sundays. A sample of his war on modernism and communism on the one side and an appeal for salvation on the other, is demonstrated in meeting in Rochester, New York, April 14, 1936. The newspapers' accounts of the meeting are as follows:

Kagawa Co-o

Rochester, N. Y., April 7.—(Special News Bulletin)—A score or more of radical Baptists are being brought to Rochester on April 13, 14 and 15 to expound Doctor Kagawa's political philosophy and for the purpose of advocating the extension of the Consumers' Co-operative program. A Committee of Fifty, including some very prominent clergy and laymen has been formed to bring an equal number of ministers to this city at the same time to expound a program that will take the church out of politics and put its ministers back in the pulpit preaching the gospel.

The opposition to the Kagawa program will center its attack under the banner raised by the Reverend J. Frank Norris, D. D., prominent Detroit clergyman, who also has a church in Fort Worth, Texas.

Doctor Norris recently received a letter from the Committee of Fifty which clearly gives the reasons taken by the opponents of the Kagawa brand of religion with its inter-mixture of politics and radical social policies.

The Rochester papers are giving large space to the "War" in that city. The issue is out in the open and clear cut. The Rochester Democrat publishes the following:

"Fundamentalism and liberalism in the church will clash in Rochester next month.

FLAYS KAGAWA AS PROMOTING RADICALISM

With arrival of the Rev Dr J. Frank Norris, Texas and Detroit Baptist preacher and Public Opponent No. 1 of consumers' co-operatives, the battle was on to-day over sponsorship by Colgate-Rochester Divinity School of the visit to this country of Toyohiko Kagawa, Japanese Christian.

Kagawa, principle speaker at the Spring convocation of the divinity school, which opens to-morrow, was to arrive at 3:34 p. m. from New York, and was to be met by the Rev. Albert W. Beaven, president of the divinity school, and Dr. Earl B. Cross, chairman of the Rauschenbusch lecture committee.

Doctor Norris by virtue of his early arrival, in an interview, delivered first blast in which he promises will be a resounding volley, once he gives his three addresses in Convention Hall.

BOTH SPEAK TONIGHT

First of his addresses, sponsored by a local committee of fifty ministers, will be delivered in Convention Hall tonight, while Kagawa is speaking in Masonic Temple Auditorium.

That the Japanese founder of the Kingdom of God movement proposes to do away with general elections, law, Congress and the Supreme Court was only one of the charges brought by Doctor Norris.

The Texas firebrand declared:

"Despite the fact that Dr. Al-

Fiery Texas Cler Blasts at Kaga

Doctor Norris Brands Foes Communists— In Hall Talk

By JEAN WALRATH

Communists — "Christian devils" were names flung at sponsors of Dr. Toyohiko Kagawa's lectures last night by Dr. J. Frank Norris, Texas and Detroit Baptist fundamentalist preacher last night in Convention Hall.

Amid "amens" and handclapping of about 2,500 in the audience and the dissents of a few Kagawa supporters who were present, the fiery preacher centered his attack against the Colgate-Rochester Divinity School and its leader, the Rev Albert W Beaven, D. D., former president of the Federal Council of Churches of Christ in America.

"The Federal Council of Churches that sponsors this gentleman does not represent the 20 million members that it claims, but a small coterie of men hand in glove with the Communists of Russia," declared the Rev. Mr. Norris.

New Attack Tonight

His speech, he said, was only the preparation for the "operation" he would perform in another talk at Convention Hall tonight simultaneously with the appearance of Doctor Kagawa in Baptist Temple.

"And I will prove to you some of those members (of the Federal Council) and one of your citizens, the head of an institution for which I have respect is also part and parcel of this conspiracy," he

BAPTIST SEES 'RED' MENACE

Fundamentalist Preacher Alleges Seminary Connection

Dr. J. Frank Norris, Baptist fundamentalist preacher of Detroit and Texas, will perform an "operation" tonight at Convention Hall.

It will be an "operation" that will throw open to the public, Doctor Norris promised last night in his opening address at the hall, the alleged connection with Red Russia of the Federal Council of Churches of Christ in America of seminaries, including Colgate-Rochester Divinity School, and even of President Roosevelt.

Doctor Norris gave 2,500 persons a taste of what may be expected tonight when he launched out against Dr. Toyohiko Kagawa, Japanese social reformer and economist; against the Rochester divinity school and its president, the Rev. Albert W. Beaven, D. D.

"Amens" Greet Words

"Amens" and applause greeted the avowed foe of Communism. The shouted objection of a dissenter in the audience brought an offer to debate him at any time.

The Rev. Arthur A. Schade of the German Theological Seminary stirred Doctor Norris into the offer to debate, when, from the gallery, he shouted: "Judge not other men that ye may not be judged," and, adding that men "shall be known by their works," pointed out that Doctor Kagawa had never resorted to violence in self-defense.

The Rev. Mr. Schade found himself, together with any other professors he cared to bring along—

It was the likening of a Colgate-Rochester Divinity School professor to a monkey creature in the process of evolution that brought the protest from the Rev. Mr. Schade.

Crediting the sincerity of Doctor Kagawa, whose sponsors Doctor Norris termed "Communists" and "Christian devils," the fundamentalist declared:

"The Federal Council of Churches that sponsors this gentleman does not represent the 20 million members that it claims, but a small coterie of men hand in glove with the Communists of Russia."

Charges Link with Russia

Again, he said: "And I will prove to you some of those members (of the Federal Council of Churches) and one of your citizens, the head of an institution for which I have respect, are also part and parcel of this conspiracy."

In tonight's talk, on "The Stranger Within Our Gates—Is He Friend or Foe?" Doctor Norris promises to discuss the church's going into the business of the consumers' co-operatives. Two other addresses, at 10:30 a. m. and 2:30 p. m. in Convention Hall, were scheduled to precede the evening talks. Tomorrow Doctor Norris will speak at 10:30 a. m. and at 2:30 p. m. in North Baptist Church and in the evening at the Seneca Hotel. His theme tomorrow night will be "The New Deal Exposed."

From the Rochester Journal, April 15, 1936.

Texan Repeats His Attacks On Divinity School, Kagawa

"We'll have a policeman here in just a minute!"

A man in a front seat in Convention Hall last evening, called that out after the Rev. Dr. Frank J. Norris of Texas and of Detroit had declared that Colgate-Rochester Divinity School and its president, the Rev. Dr. Albert W. Beaven, are linked with the "Red Network."

'You needn't call any policeman, and I'll show you why in just a minute," Doctor Norris replied. He then asked for "ten young, single men in this audience who are willing to defend God, country and the home, please stand."

Some 50 men jumped to their feet, and the man in the front seat said no more.

At one or two intervals men in the audience interrupted the speaker to defend Colgate-Rochester, but Mr. Norris told them every word uttered at the meeting was to be printed, and they would have every possible opportunity to reply later. Stenographers took down what was said.

Hall Well Filled

The audience practically filled the large hall's floor and gallery seats, as Doctor Norris, attacking Dr. Toyohiko Kagawa, read extracts from various publicaations.

"Now here's something I hate to do," he said, before reading letter from Doctor Beaven, written in reply to Doctor Norris' invitation to debate on the Japanese Christian leader The letter explained, in substance, that while the Japanese was given the liberty to express his views on co-operations in Colgate-Rochester, this did not mean the school was bound to accept them. Doctor Beaven said that the school did not as an institution sponsor the League of Industrial Democracy. Doctor Norris, commenting it.

"Where is Gannett House?" he asked, then read a report of one or more meetings of a unit of the league being conducted there. He read another account of a branch of the league meeting at an address he gave in McKrs Street, where two Divinity School professors were named as officers

Doctor Norris referred to Doctor Beaven as ."a man of splendid mind," but said that he told an untruth when he said the school didn't sponsor the league, while at that time one already was in that institution

Doctor Norris announced that the issue was no longer between Republican and Democratic forms of government but between Communism and the Christ; and whether the church should "go into this business."

He attacked the Federal Council of Churches of Christ in America and bitterly arraigned radicals saying he foresaw a "great spiritual awakening" in America. During his address in Convention Hall in the afternoon, attended by about 200 persons

Doctor Kagawa was referred to by him as "this apostle of Socialism and of a Duke's mixture of every ism.." He urged the ministers present to "preach and not give Mother Hubbard propositions that cover everything and touch nothing.."

Dr. Norris Closes a Two Hour and Ten Minute Address at Rochester With An Appeal for Salvation

I am interested from the religious standpoint. What America needs is a great revival; come back to the Spiritual; come out of Egypt back to Bethel. The war clouds are hanging low; judgments have come thick and fast.

What have we witnessed within the last five or six years?

The greatest flood, that rose higher, covered more territory, destroyed more homes, land, live stock and people than any flood in the history of America. It destroyed the stupendous sum of $200,000,000 worth of property! But we have forgotten it. Why? Because we are so busy making money.

And Then a Billion Dollar Flood

And soon other judgments came. During these recent years and months we have witnessed the greatest drouth in American history, until the dust clouds were fifteen hundred miles long, and the soil of Kansas and Iowa, and other states swept with the winds across the dome of the capitol at Washington and was buried in the Atlantic Ocean, and there were hundreds of millions of dollars worth of property destroyed; and yet that terrible cloud of judgment failed to warn a wicked nation.

What else? During this time we have had, not a panic, and there is no history, no record to describe it; we called it "The depression," and conservative estimate places the wreck and destructon of values at the staggering sum of two hundred billion dollars! And yet America has failed to recognize God.

What else? During this same period of time we have had more tragic deaths—within the last five years we have had nearly three hundred thousand deaths by tragic accidents, automobile accidents, and more than three millon maimed for life, and yet we roll on at our dizzy rate. Even last year there were nearly a hundred thousand who thus met violent death, and over a million maimed for life—there were thirty-six thousand killed by automobile accidents, and the automobile accidents are increasng so rapidly until the insurance companies and the automobile factories are wondering what shall they do?

What else? During the same five years we have had the worst staggering record of suicides, and we now approach the one hundred and fifty thousand mark!

What else? During this same period we have had more train wrecks, more airplane crashes, and other disasters, such as no nation ever witnessed.

What else? During this time, my friends, this nation has turned itself into shambles of debauchery and drink such as never witnessed since the days of Belshazzar in Babylon. Last year we spent three billion dollars for liquor—multiply that by twelve and you have the national debt.

What else? We have piled up expenses until today the nation, state, municipal, bonded public indebtedness has approached the stupendous sum of sixty billion dollars, until the average man on a salary is fighting for his life as to whether he can even own a home.

What else? Ten years ago it cost two million dollars a day to run this government—today, ten years later, it costs us exactly twenty million dollars a day! The expenses of running this government raised from two million dollars ten years ago to twenty million dollars today, and the end is not yet.

What else? During this period—and here is somethng worse than all the tragedies, all the violent deaths, all the suicides, all the wreck and ruin of property—America has witnessed the greatest decline in church life, in Spiritual life, in history. It doesn't do any good to say the same thing is occurring in other nations—it is world-wide—I can hear somebody say, "Stop, preacher, we know about it, and we don't want to hear it—I repeat they didn't hear it in Noah's time—they refused to hear it in Enoch's time—they refused to hear it in Jeremiah's time—they didn't want to hear it in John the Baptist's time—they didn't want to hear it when Paul preached it—they didn't want to hear it when Jesus, our Lord, preached it—but as long as the grace of God remains on this preacher, I am going to preach it—and I want you to pray God to give me grace to do it, and when the battle is over, no man can put his finger in my face and say, "Preacher, you didn't warn us."

Yonder, when that ship was burning last September a year ago, when there was a wild party, when three hundred or more people burned up in horrible death, as they drank and danced—the first officer of the ship, when he testified, said, "I sounded the note of warning"—when the ship was wrapped in flames they went down to the state rooms, and they would arouse the men and women, and the women were so drunk that when they would arouse them out of bed, there they would stagger and fall on the floor to meet with a horrible death in the flames!

"Oh," I said, "what a picture of this present hour when the prophets of God are sounding the warning, as it was before the flood, when He said, "My spirit shall not always strive with man"—And today this world shuts its eyes, stops its ears, and is surfeited with the wickedness of this present hour—I tell you, friends, judgment is coming on the earth—Judgment! Judgment!

The issues are clear-cut: Shall we tear down the Stars and Stripes and unfurl the Red Flag instead? Shall we make the capitol at Washington an annex to Moscow? Shall we make our universities and colleges of America the breeding ground of Russian Communism? And, most tragic of all, will the pulpits of our land become the representatives of this atheistic communistic conspiracy?

In this year we are celebrating the Centennial of Texas' independence; through a successful war that gave the Union, not only the Lone Star State, but gave to the Union the states of New Mexico, Arizona, California, Oklahoma, Colorado—the great empire that put the cap stone on the greatest nation on earth, from ocean to ocean. Three historic battles were fought—the Alamo, when 183 men sacrificed their lives; Goliad, when 553 were massacred, and after they had made an honorable surrender, having been surrounded by overwhelming odds; and the battle of San Jacinto, where 783 men annihilated 6,000 well-armed Mexican soldiers of Santa Anna, the Napoleon of the West.

Every time I go to San Antonio, I go to the Alamo; when I walk to the back wall a distance of more than 150 feet, I hear again the words of Col. Wm. B. Travis, who called his little band of 183 men around him and said:

"We can yet escape; soon we will be completely surrounded, and all hope of escape will be gone. All who choose to die with me that Texas may be free cross over the line!"

Then with his unsheathed sword he drew a line the length of that old mission, and every man leaped across. David Crockett, lying on his cot bleeding from a dozen wounds, lifted his head and said:

"Take my sword; take my hat across."

Then he said:

"Take my cot that I may die with you."

A woman escaped to tell the story.

Well did Senator Benton of Missouri declare in the United States Senate:

"Thermopylae had her messenger of defeat; the Alamo had none."

I come tonight and say to you as true patriots, as Americans, who love God, home and native land, who still believe in the Bible, who still believe and love our homes, who still believe in the immortality of the soul, who still believe in Jesus Chrst the Son of God—that we will stand, and having done all, stand, and never turn our backs in the day of battle, but cross the line and die for all that we hold dear, and when dying join in that imortal song:

> "Must I be carried to the skies
> On flow'ry beds of ease,
> While others fought to win the prize,
> And sailed thro' bloody seas?
>
> Are there no foes for me to face?
> Must I not stem the flood?
> Is this vile world a friend to grace,
> To help me on to God?
>
> Sure I must fight, if I would reign;
> Increase my courage, Lord;
> I'll bear the toil, endure the pain,
> Supported by Thy word."

THE WORLD WIDE MINISTRY OF THE TWO CHURCHES

Dr. George Palmer of Philadelphia and Haddon Heights Baptist Church writes:

"It is a great joy to have had you with us recently in Philadelphia in connection with our special meetings.

"The evening services in the Lulu Temple were greatly blessed of God. Your messages given in the power of the Holy Spirit went home to the hearts of the people and we thank God for the definite work done by the power of the Holy Spirit in the lives of thousands who attended these meetings.

"We were amazed at the large attendance Sunday afternoon in the Scottish Rite Temple. Philadelphia is one of the hardest places to get a good Sunday afternoon audience and we are especially grateful to God for the wonderful service Sunday evening at which time there were a number saved. We thank God that you were able to come to Philadelphia and the thousands who heard you will join me in thanking God upon every remembrance of you.

"The blessing you brought to our church, the Haddon Heights Baptist, Sunday morning when you preached there has meant much to us all. The whole church was profoundly stirred that morning and we will never forget you."

Dr. H. G. Hamilton, First Baptist Church, Buffalo, New York, writes:

"One of the new features of our trail blazing efforts was the promotion of what we were pleased to call 'A Bible Evangelistic Conference.' We have long wearied of the terms 'Bible Conference' and 'Evangelistic Meeting' and have desired that someone give us a new name for these great rallying efforts sponsored by evangelical Christianity but it was left to Dr. J. Frank Norris not only to give us the name 'A BIBLE EVANGELISTIC CONFERENCE,' but also to give us the program of the entire conference.

"Since the baptism of the church at Pentecost, God has raised up his men for the carrying on of the work such as Paul, Augustine,

Savanarola, Calvin, Zwingli, Luther and Spurgeon and here on the horizon comes a man by name of Norris, pastor of two great churches at the remote ends of the nation—Fort Worth in the South, with a membership of 12,000 souls, and Detroit in the North with a fast growing membership of three thousand erecting an auditorium to seat the growing congregations of 5,000 that gather Sunday after Sunday to wait on his ministry. Jealous minded souls will have a tendency to envy him because of his successes but spiritually minded people will pray for him that God will use him as a channel of blessing in these dark and apostate days to inspire the hearts of the saints and to call the church back to the Faith once delivered."

Dr. Howard C. Fulton, Belden Avenue Baptist Church, Chicago, writes:

"Just these few lines to express my appreciation to you and gratitude to God for your ministry during the three days of Bible and Evangelistic Conference held in our Church December 12 to 14.

"The meetings were a great success in every way. Our people say they were the best special meetings we have had during our ministry here.

"The crowds were splendid, all expenses were very happily taken care of without any undue pressure or burden upon any one, and there was deep, rich, abiding and far reaching spiritual blessing.

"We had a very unusual prayer meeting Wednesday evening after the meetings. A great spirit of praise and prayer, some confessions and many reports of rich blessings. And our people are going out into the homes two by two in New Testament fashion witnessing for the Saviour.

"And how happy we are also to know that a great group of ministers from Chicago, Cook County, and out through the states of Illinois, Indiana, Wisconsin, Minesota, Michigan and Missouri were able to attend these meetings and receive much needed encouragement, inspiration, instruction and rich blessing which God was pleased to shower upon us by His blessed Holy Spirit.

"May God richly bless you and your two great churches as they make it possible for you to spread revival fires throughout the length and breadth of our land."

Rev. J. J. Van Gorder, Butler, Pennsylvania, writes:

"It was a great meeting and the above expressions give the

concensus of all who attended. Such crowds! We have never seen such attendance in our fourteen years of pastorate here.

"We feared that the weather had wrecked the whole conference. Imagine our joy and amazement when we found the main auditorium filled at the ten o'clock session with preachers making up a large portion of the audience, some having driven more than one hundred miles over the hazardous mountain roads. The afternoon audience overflowed into the Sunday School rooms. The evening audience filled every nook and cranny of the building, both upstairs and down, with many standing. We learned later that many were turned away, that is, they would come and see the crowded condition of the building and go away. On Friday the crowds were even greater. On Friday evening, the church was filled an hour before the time for the services. The Grace Lutheran Church, just across the street, was secured and it was soon filled. After Dr. Norris finished his message, he went across and gave a message to the people there, also.

"The congestion was so great at the evening services that registration was impossible but we feel safe in saying that at least one hundred preachers were in attendance. A check was made on the audience and it was found that five states and more than fifty towns were represented.

"One of the most helpful features of the two days was the 'pastors' clinic' conducted by Dr. Norris at the close of the afternoon sessions. For one hour and a half he would answer questions concerning the various problems of the pastor. We shall never forget the expression of one pastor with snow-white hair who said, 'I am going home to begin all over.' Another pastor was heard to pray, 'O, Lord, forgive me for the time I have wasted.' Yes, the Christian worker was right in saying, 'It was a mountain top experience'."

Rev. Clarence Keen of Kitchener, Ontario, writes:

"We are all still rejoicing in the blessing of God that was upon us through your ministry of last week. Our prayers were answered and our expectations realized. Truly we had a great time and I want to thank you again for your coming. It was a joy to us to have you in the home and we sincerely hope that the privilege may again be ours.

"Yesterday was a great day for us. There was liberty in the services and a fine spirit maintained. I baptized four last night and three others came at the close of the service for baptism and church membership.

"Saturday afternoon a phone call came for me and I went to the home and led a father and his twelve-year-old boy to the Lord.

"Many of our folks listen to you on Sunday morning over the air and be assured of our prayers and abiding Christian love.

"Many of our folks testified to the fact that they had never been in such a meeting as we had on Friday night. It will long be remembered by many. One of the men said to me Saturday, 'I went home and told my wife that it was the first time in my life that I had seen a man intoxicated with the Spirit of God'."

Rev. A. B. Crossman, Worcester, Massachusetts, writes:

"I have just been checking over the registration cards of our conference in Worcester and find that members from twenty-four churches in Worcester alone registered. Besides this, there were members from forty churches throughout the state but outside of Worcester that registered. Also there were about twenty churches that registered from outside the state. Six states being represented in all. When we realize that practically all registration was done at the day services and none at the evening service and that registration was by no means complete I feel that the great inspiration we received at these services has been scattered all over New England.

"I have had many letters from those who attended telling of the great help they received and what a blessing they were able to take back to their churches. All these reports of course make one feel that the Lord has used us to His Glory. Some have already reported that the revival spirit has broken out in their church because of these meetings. The Sunday night following the meetings, there were two men about forty years of age who came forward and were saved as in tears they knelt at the front of the church and prayed for salvation in the Lincoln Square Church. I feel that we are on the verge of a great awakening in this church and pray daily that I may be the greatest soul winner of all.

"In regards to the anticipated tour of the New England States, it would seem advisable to me that this should be done in the Spring. The winter snows will soon be here and in New Hampshire, Maine, and Vermont the traveling from one city to the other would be almost impossible until the winter's snow has gone. I did not get to talk to you very much concerning this tour and would like to know just what you expect and I will do everything in my power to carry out your wishes. I feel that such a tour would be the means of awakening and encouraging a great many fundamental pastors who are at present very much discouraged."

Rev. L. G. Whitelaw, Kitchener, Ontario, writes:

"It was an epoch gathering, long to be remembered by all who were there. It was unique in its diversified personnel. There were Baptists of several different groups coming together as ONE to study the Word of God under that great man Dr. Norris. It was the coming together of many who for some time had been separated.

"TO SEE two old College Class mates, once workers in the same Fellowship but separated by schism in the body of believers, ONCE AGAIN brought together, to see them standing as brothers, locked in an embrace, did one's heart good!

"TO SEE the Convention Baptists, the Regulars and also the Independents, AGAIN, freely intermingling with smiles and hearty handshakes and praising God was a sight rejoicing to the heart and long to be remembered. God was TRULY in their midst.

"TO SEE a self-abandonment and a self-effacement and a humility strangely absent at some former gatherings, and an absence of that spirit of 'measuring themselves by themselves and comparing themselves among themselves' (2 Cor. 10:12) so much in evidence at other times was truly most refreshing. The Holy Spirit was doing the measuring and hearts were being searched by the LIVING WORD spoken from the lips of God's appointed messenger. ALL seemed to be working TOGETHER and once more being welded TOGETHER, through the love of Christ, through that same blessed Holy Spirit.

"Hearts discouraged and some defeated and others depressed got a new grip of their Lord and took courage and returned to their work with new determination to preach the Word with all boldness and with great fervor to pursue the work of winning precious souls. Oh it was simply wonderful.

"Each day of the Conference was a mountain-top experience. The audiences were filled with the joy of the Lord. The old time Gospel was preached. Christ and His Word were exalted and magnified. The evangelistic zeal of Dr. Norris is truly remarkable. Hearts were deeply stirred by his spiritual messages each morning and on Friday afternoon, and evening, like a prophet of old, he rehearsed and enumerated God's footsteps down the sands of time, finally bringing us to the present crisis in Europe and the world at large, showing us that God's hand is still in control, guiding, ordering all according to His sovereign Will for our good and for His glory."

Dr. D. B. Clapp, Paducah, Kentucky, writes:

"Your visit of three days will never be forgotten by our people or by the great crowds who waited on your ministry. I confess I was not prepared for the mighty Spiritual power that seemed to accompany every message. I had read of the great conferences you had conducted in many churches in the northern territory. We did not expect it to happen to us. One noble preacher said he received more benefit in the three days than he had ever received in a three weeks meeting.

"This conference will result in a perennial revival in our church. A very spiritual and well rounded Methodist pastor said he would like for you to hold a conference for their body and have all the college of Bishops present in the meeting.

"Your visit to us will go far to remove the prejudice uninformed people had against you as well as giving the people an understanding of the things we are seeking to accomplish. Many people had an idea you were a fire eating monster and were surprised to find you as tender as a mother nursing a sick child.

"The brethren of the ministry went home with new courage and with a determination to study the Bible and preach the Word. Our own people are humbled and will meet the great responsibility thrust upon them."

Rev. Harold L. Harsh, Madison, Illinois, writes:

"I want you to know how much I enjoyed the two days meeting at Alton, Illinois.

"I am sure that meeting will go down in history as the greatest meeting ever held in that town; the Spirit of God certainly led all the way through.

"I have talked to a number of preachers since then, and their testimony is that they have a new conception of the ministry; many of those men were discouraged. They have been fighting for the Faith once for all delivered to the saints, for a long time. They were not confessing defeat, but they were discouraged.

"You will never now just how much that meeting meant to them, and all of us for that matter."

Rev. C. Edgar Dowing of Reynoldsville, Pennsylvania, writes:

"I was one of the preachers who came to Butler, Pa., to hear you preach. Three of us drove the two hundred miles to hear you, returning to our homes on Thursday night. I didn't sleep much that night and something just drew me back to Butler to hear you again on Friday. So I drove the two hundred miles all over again, but may I confess it was the most glorious two hundred miles I ever drove or ever will drive.

"I am writing this because I think you would like to hear my testimony. I have been preaching for the past seven years and am in the second pastorate since I left school. My father also being a fundamentalist, I attended a fundamental school, Gordon College of Theology and Missions in Boston, Massachusetts. For the past four years I have been pastor of a Baptist Church and have been considered a good preacher and pastor. I thought so too until I heard you at Butler. And the Holy Ghost revealed to me what a fool I have been.

"I found so many things wrong with my ministry, and myself that there was nothing else to do but start at the beginning which I did Sunday morning in my pulpit. I confessed to my people with tears my condition before God and as their pastor and I asked their forgiveness. Well my brother, no one told me what a fine message I brought yesterday morning how fine I had presented it. But there was a firmer handclasp and many moistened eyes, but if everyone would turn against me tomorrow I wouldn't care, for you see, Dr. Norris, for the first time in my ministry, I came clean before my God. I held nothing back. My heart has been very joyous today and for the first time I believe my ministry will begin to have a backbone instead of a wishbone."

Rev. Wilbur Small of Napoleon, Michigan, writes:

"Now as for myself I am still in a daze and can hardly make myself believe that it was true. My heart was truly blessed. While I have always believed in the preaching of the old time gospel I am more than ever determined to go forward for my Lord and I personally want to thank you for your coming and for the wonderful way in which you poured out your heart and upheld the Christ of Calvary.

"I am more than grateful inasmuch as my churches (The Brooklyn and Napoleon Baptist Churches) both are affiliated with the Northern Baptist Convention, and although I had asked for the co-operation of the Convention and had tried on previous occasions to get some of the leaders to come down and speak to us, not once have I had a speaker from the Convention. However, when the Michigan Baptist Convention heard a rumor that we were intending to withdraw, it was only a matter of a few days until an official from Lansing arrived. On the other hand, I called at your office in the Temple Baptist Church on Wednesday, November 17, and you graciously consented to come the following Monday and give us a whole day of meetings. This, to my way of looking at it, was really helping a brother in Christ and was the height of co-operation.

Rev. E. C. Shute, Decatur, Illinois:

"In recounting the events of those days to my congregation I told them that when we speak of a 'Bible Conference' we usually think in terms of study periods, set programs, discussion hours, addresses on Christian life and service, etc., with varying degrees of interest and helpfulness, but that the gathering in Alton, Ill., was an experience that will not be forgotten by any who were privileged to attend, this side of the thin vail of time.

"Not since the days of the great Welsh revival that swept like a mighty tidal-wave from one end of the land to the other have I ever witnessed anything to compare with it, and it is my deep out-breathings to God that this blessed work that He has seen fit to entrust to you shall indeed sweep like a prairie fire from one end of this country of ours to the other, and over into the heart of the distracted nations of the earth."

THERE ARE TWO UPHEAVALS WHERE THERE IS ONE

It was an exodus of the Children of Israel out of Egypt and across the sea.

Then there was the rebellion of Korah who said to Moses:

"Ye take too much upon you."—jealousy.

In both the First Baptist Church at Fort Worth and the Temple Baptist Church at Detroit, there were these same two upheavals. To use a more modern and another illustration, there was the World War, and the backwash of the war. The two leading men, chairmen of both boards of deacons in Fort Worth and Temple Baptist Church, who were most active in my call to the two churches, had to be eliminated, and they were both good men.

Both had many similar traits and in addition to the many good qualities both possessed, they had the common weakness of a lot of good men in official position; namely, they took themselves too seriously and lacked the necessary broad vision in the building of a great church, and there were some other good people that fell into the same error, under their leadership in both churches.

These two men and a group who followed them wanted to put Saul's armor on David. They wanted to cut the cloth according to their measure. Both chairmen would come to the church almost every day and would even give particular attention to the weekly announcements for the paper, and even went so far as to suggest to the pastor what to preach on, and when one of them called up one morning early and suggested the text for the next Sunday, I waited patiently until he was through. He even went on and gave an outline of the text, and suggested some illustrations. I very quietly asked him if he could come by the office that afternoon, which thing he was very happy to do according to his daily habit, and when he came I said in just a few words:

"Brother Deacon, your ticket has expired, and when the train slows down at the next water tank you will have your baggage ready to get off."

The deacon looked surprised and wanted to know what I meant, and the few words I said to him removed all doubt from his mind that his ticket was actually out!

Of course he went off and told everybody, "Norris is a dictator."

But one thing was dead certain I made up my mind that that deacon was not going to dictate to me or dictate to the church any longer as he had through the years.

The Elder Son Spirit

And another thing is true, in the growing of a great church— I am now talking of that second exodus after the coming out of Egypt. There is always in a red hot fight a small group of people, and good people, who feel they have a priority, an inside track on everything, and especially the pastor, and in both the First Church and Temple Church, the elder son spirit had to be met.

Take for example, in the women's work, and in both churches.

We got rid of the whole cut and dried Ladies' Aid program only to find that as one faction moved out another faction moved in and the same dead, fruitless program.

And when I exercised Acts 20:28, was willing to shoulder the dangerous responsibility of being pastor of the women of the church and unscramble this second faction, and broke up the other nest that was also full of mites—there was weeping and wailing in the wilderness, and some of the dear women, good women too, just thought it was the unpardonable sin that they should not have been considered and allowed to name the leader, program and outline the work.

So now there is a great day in each week in both churches where the good women come and do personal work and visitation, then come together in happy fellowship—not a gossiping society—and with tears and joy report the souls · that have been won.

Another example of the elder son spirit was in the deaconship of both churches, both had what in practice amounted to a self-perpetuating board—one-third go out and two-thirds remain. Of course the two-thirds named the successor to the one-third which meant one-third remained in office. The deacons had complete control over everything and dare the pastor to go against this closed corporation, and with them the Scriptures were perverted to read, "Let the deacons take heed therefore unto themselves, and to all the church over which the Holy Ghost hath made them overseers."

The pastor had about as much to say as to how the church should be run as a weaned yearling calf tied to a stob on the outside of a cow lot looking through the cracks of a new gate wanting to be where he is not.

And in the case of both churches the stob was pulled up and the gate knocked off its hinges and the deacons ran under the barn.

All over America, North, South, East and West, pastors stand in holy horror and constant fear of their "official boards." Oh, how the word "board" has been overworked, when in truth it occurs only one time in the whole 27 books of the New Testament, and that's when Paul had a shipwreck, it said, "And the rest, some on boards and some on broken pieces of the ship."

The New Testament church should not be run by the boards or any official clique. The New Testament plan is that the church is composed of baptized believers, recognizing Christ as the only head, the Holy Spirit as the only Administrator, the Word of God its only message, and salvation of souls its only mission.

The older I grow the happier I am in this conviction; namely, that you can trust a great body of believers and trust them absolutely, and it is the first duty of the pastor to keep any factions or cliques from forming, don't let them even get started, don't let them lift their heads up.

The tragedy of tragedies is that most churches are held down by a lot of long personal grudges, personal envies, and the poor little preacher stands up, and between the factions is scared to death.

Envious Preachers the Worst Slanderers of the Two Churches

Through the years it has been very funny that when Bro. Diotrephes would be eliminated, when I told him his ticket was expired, and when Mrs. Zebedee found out she couldn't have her way, and they had their exit, then the little jealous time-serving pastors, who study the railroad guide more than they do their Bibles, they run to these pieces of excess baggage, give them comfort, and the amusing thing would be they would peddle it all over the country, "Norris lost a prominent member"—"Norris lost an important deacon."

Just like it was in the spring of this year, '37, a man and his wife who held official positions, and there were 998 more just as good, some better, they both got the Diotrephes spirit, got jealous of some others, and when they found out they couldn't have their way they too went the way of all the earth. They are good people, but when good people go wrong they have further to go wrong than bad people. The very next Sunday after their elimination two men joined the church, one put in a thousand dollars into the work, and the other put twenty-five hundred dollars in the work, and this thirty-five hundred dollars over against fifty dollars of the man who had been eliminated. The fifty dollars was the amount given by the man who was eliminated since the first of the year. So it was a good financial deal.

But the little gossiping preachers never tell of the blessings that come and of the growth of the work.

Jealousy reaches its highest, rather I should say, its lowest, foulest expression among two classes; namely, among society women and some preachers.

In both cities where the two churches are located, large numbers of members come from all the other churches, and they go back to their dead churches and if they tell of the glorious services and a large number saved there, then the little envious preachers get on the war path, and the one song of the ages that has caused the undoing of more preachers, "Saul has slain his thousands, but David has slain his tens of thousands."

Pilate said concerning the crucifixion of Jesus, "For he knew that for envy they had delivered him."

A very strange thing has been true of both churches, every preacher in both cities that has fought these two churches has had to move sooner or later. There is not a single one of the pastors in Fort Worth now that passed resolutions of condemnation years ago against the pastor of the First Baptist Church.

And they are shuffling around in Detroit.

But For Every Judas There Are Eleven True Apostles

It has been indeed very tender and beautiful, the vast multitude of true ministers around the world who have understood, prayed for and entered boldly into the fellowship of His service.

"Dr. J. Frank Norris
First Baptist Church
Fort Worth, Texas

"Dear Dr. Norris:

"The spirit of your telegram yesterday was indeed full of cheering encouragement to all of us. Our purpose is to go as never before for 'that which is lost.'

"You will not know, in this life, how you have set the holy fires to burning in the hearts of hundreds and caused them to seek the salvation of others. Personally, and with abiding gratitude, you have been a living joy, inspiration and help to me. I shall always be sorry that my own prejudiced heart kept me from the joy of knowing you during my three years in the Seminary there in Fort Worth. Of course I was, with others, taught to ignore you and the great church. But now I see and I am so thankful to you for so many ways in which you have helped me that I have long ago forgiven all, and am happy to let it die in the past. The blessings of your ministry, your friendship and blessed fellowship far out-strips any evil against you falsely accused.

"Calls are now coming to me from many places—San Francisco, Jacksonville, Florida, and I have just returned from a glorious revival in Des Moines. I am increasingly happy in my work. I'm beginning my ministry! My greatest ministry is truly in front of me. I have a deep settled peace in it all but I want you to know that I owe you a tremendous debt of love. You have been a Paul to me and all these calls come to me because of your helping me through your pulpit and radio. God forbid that any word or deed should show ingratitude on my part.

"Through future months may I prove in some way my abiding love and thanks to you and your great church. I will be loyal to our dear cause and thankful for every help both divine and human.

"A greater ministry for '38.

"Your friend,"

(Signed) T. D. Sumrall.

$3500.00 Sound Truck of The Temple Baptist Church. Recorded messages on Salvation by Dr. Norris are given throughout the city of Detroit.

THE TRIPLE MAJOR OPERATION IN DETROIT

(Two hour ten minute address of Dr. J. Frank Norris at the Temple Baptist Church, 14th and Marquette, Detroit, Michigan, Sunday, January 13, 1935, at 3 P. M.)

DR. NORRIS: There are many Scriptures which I could read to you clearly setting forth the absolute necessity of a separated church life. Second Corinthians 6:14-18 is an unequivocal command for a separated church life. "What concord hath Christ with Belial—or "What communion hath light with darkness?" And Revelation 18:4 says for us to come out from among them and "be not partakers of her sins."

It is all right for the boat to be in the water, but when the water gets in the boat, you had better get out. We are in Babylon but we should not be of Babylon.

Next Sunday this church is going to adopt a one hundred per cent fundamentalist Confession of Faith. It is not enough to affirm certain things, but we must deny some things. For instance, every great truth in the Scriptures first denies error and then affirms truth.

To illustrate the New Birth, negatively, "Which were born, not of blood, nor of the will of the flesh, nor of the will of man,"—"But"—affirmatively—"But of God." "Being born again,"—negatively—"not of corruptible seed, but"—affirmatively—"but of incorruptible by the word of God, which liveth and abideth forever." Take the method of inspiration of the Scriptures, first, negatively, a denial of error, "For the prophecy came not in old time by the will of man:"—now affirmatively—"but holy men of God spake as they were moved by the Holy Ghost."

Take baptism, "The like figure whereunto even baptism doth also now save us"—How? First, negatively—"(not the putting away of the filth of the flesh,"—not the forgiveness of sins, and now affirmatively—"but the answer of a good conscience toward God) by the resurrection of Jesus Christ."

In this proposed Confession of Faith which the Temple Church will adopt next Sunday morning, notice how carefully the great doctrines are stated; first, negatively; second, affirmatively—following the twofold Scriptural method.

Take for example the article on the inspiration of the Scriptures, here it is both negatively and affirmatively stated.

And we have both negative and positive statement of the doctrine of creation.

"We believe in the Genesis account of creation, and that it is to be accepted literally, and not allegorically or figuratively; that man was created directly in God's own image and after His own likeness; that man's creation was not a matter of evolution or evolutionary change of species, or development through interminable periods of time from lower to higher forms; that all animal and vegetable life was made directly, and God's established law was they should bring forth only 'after their kind.' "

No Modernist will sign that. If he does he will join the Ananias group the day he signs it.

Of the Virgin Birth, we say:

"We believe that Jesus Christ was begotten of the Holy Ghost in a miraculous manner; born of Mary, a virgin, as no other man was ever born or can ever be born of woman, and that he is both the Son of God and God the Son."

No Modernist will sign that.

The point I am making is that error must be defined and repudiated. A simple affirmation is not sufficient. Modernists, dishonest as they are, will sign any affirmative statement, with mental reservations, then give their own interpretation.

This is the Scriptural method of all the inspired writers.

Why do we have the letter to the Galatians? First, to deny Judaistic legalism on the one hand, and affirm justification by faith on the other. Why do we have the letter to the Colossians? First, to deny the false philosophy of the Gnostics on the one hand, and affirm the fullness and preeminence of Christ on the other.

Thus I might illustrate with all the books of the Bible.

I want to talk this afternoon particularly about this 13th Article.

"We believe that a church of Christ is a congregation of baptized believers associated by a covenant of faith and fellowship of the gospel; observing the ordinances of Christ; governed by His laws, and exercising the gifts, rights and privileges invested in them by His Word; that its officers of ordination are pastors or elders and deacons, whose qualifications, claims and duties are clearly defined in the Scriptures; we believe the true mission of the church is found in the Great Commission; First, to make individual disciples; Second, to build up the church; Third, to teach and instruct, as He has commanded. We do not believe in the reversal of this order; we hold that the local church has the absolute right of self government, free from the interference of any heirarchy of individuals or organizations; and that the one and only superintendent is Christ through the Holy Spirit; that it is Scriptural for true churches to cooperate with each other in contending for the faith and for the furtherance of the gospel; that every church is the sole and only judge of the measure and method of its cooperation; on all matters of membership, of policy, of government, of discipline, of benevolence, the will of the local church is final."

By this time next Sunday afternoon the will of this church is going to be one of love and unanimous membership; we are going to adopt that article!

(Applause.)

If anybody doubts this, let them come and see. Our authority is supreme and it can be in all things affirmed by the people of this church, and cannot be controlled by the Michigan Baptist Convention. But they claim to judge everything. We come today to discuss that question. They are not final on all matters. A Baptist church has the right to run its own affairs. I am going to tell you, my friends, that is the biggest issue today among Baptists. It is the issue in the South, in the West, the issue in the North; the issue in Michigan. It is the issue in Detroit. It is the issue in the Temple Baptist Church right here this afternoon!

CONGREGATION: Amen!

To show you that is the issue in Michigan, you, Brother Pease, from Jackson, stand up, please.

My friends, this is Dr. J. J. Pease, pastor of the Loomis Park Baptist Church of Jackson.

DR. PEASE: I was born in Michigan, and most of my 27 years in the ministry has been in this state, and during the last six years I have been pastor of the Loomis Park Baptist Church in Jackson.

The Baptist Association where my church is located is composed of 26 churches. Without any boasting, but that you may know the character of my work during this six years, our church had a larger increase than any other church in the Association. In one year we took in more than all the other churches in the Association.

I have spent most of my ministry in trying to cooperate with the Michigan Baptist Convention. But a long time ago I saw the drift of things, and more and more as a matter of conscience I could not cooperate with what I considered unscriptural practices.

The issue came up in our church, and the church stood by three-fourths' majority with me in my contention for the Truth against error, in my stand for old time Baptist beliefs and practices.

But this minority went to the Convention headquarters to get aid and support in seeking to overrule and set aside the will of three to one majority. They received that aid, and caused much trouble in the church.

The Convention officials in control started the whole trouble, and requested a meeting with the Jackson Association. The officials did this with the announced purpose of getting the Jackson Association to recognize the minority group of our church; and if the minority should be recognized, the majority would be repudiated, and that would mean that the minority would control the Loomis Park Baptist Church. Their plans were to lay a predicate for court action, showing that the majority was not regular, but that the minority was regular because recognized by the Convention headquarters.

We had a Board of twelve members, and it was unanimous. The Chairman is here with me on the platform. There was a Committee of five appointed, and two members of that Committee reported to me what took place. They told me that the State Secretary, Dr. Andem, labored for more than two hours with that Committee. The whole purpose was to turn the property over to the minority by going through the courts. Here is where the Convention officials did everything in their power to defeat the will of the local church.

And this forced the church to take drastic action on certain leaders of this minority troublesome group who were in official position.

The property and land contracts were in the hands of this minority, and we were forced to hire a lawyer to protect the rights of the church and force the property to be turned over to the church, the rightful owners. We had to come to Detroit and hire a good lawyer, for we were afraid to trust a Jackson attorney. (Laughter.) (The name of the Detroit lawyer is Hon. John C.

Winter.) This lawyer sent several notices to these people, yet they refused to turn the property back to the Trustees, and when the Convention officials saw what was about to take place, the officials backed down, and in two or three days the property was in the hands of the Trustees of the church. But they kept up the fight.

DR. NORRIS: Where is the Chairman of the Board? This is Brother Kent. I am not going to call on you to speak. This is the Chairman of the Board of Trustees. What is your occupation?

MR. KENT: I am a dentist.

DR. NORRIS: Then I don't want to have anything to do with you.

(Laughter.)

MR. KENT: S. E. Kent.

DR. NORRIS: This is S. E. Kent, Chairman of the Board. Has Dr. Pease stated this correctly?

MR. KENT: Yes, only he hasn't told half.

(Laughter and applause.)

DR. NORRIS: Here is Brother E. Roloff Jackson. He has had a similar experience. I just want him to say whether or not they have been interfering with his church and trying to regulate them.

REV. E. ROLOFF: Well, our experience was something similar to Brother Pease's, except that the Convention was successful in removing us from the Wall Street Baptist Church. They had a secret session. An active member was Judge Hate—

DR. NORRIS: What is his name? (Laughter.)

REV. ROLOFF: Judge Hate, of the Michigan Baptist Convention, was in the city. They were successful in getting us out. With the pastor of the church, 75% of the active members went out, the whole Board of Deacons, half of the Trustees, the whole Sunday School staff of the church, and one Sunday School teacher, and the Church Treasurer and Financial Secretary. 75% of the active church membership remained loyal to the pastor and to the Lord Jesus Christ, and we have stepped out now, and, as in Romans 8:28, we are all doing work. We are happy in our work, and have no bones to pick with the Michigan Baptist Convention. We are just glad we are rid of them.

(Applause.)

DR. NORRIS: My purpose in calling attention to these two churches is that they are right here under our door, right in front of us. What you have heard this afternoon has been going on from one end of this land to the other, and in Heaven's name, it is time for it to stop!

CONGREGATION: Amen!

(Applause.)

DR. NORRIS: That is what is going on right here in Temple Baptist Church, and we are going to stop it!

(Applause.)

DR. NORRIS: We have already stopped a part of it, and we are going to take care of the rest of their hides, beginning with a Mr. Tanner, and not Simon the Tanner.

(Applause.)

DR. NORRIS: Let me tell you something. This thing called Modernism—I have ten thousand times more respect for any Catholic that is faithful to Roman Catholicism than I have for Modernism, because they do believe in God and in Christ and in immortality, and these modern infidels don't believe in anything! It is high time that the Christian world was waking up to the fact that Modernism comes like Absalom stealing the hearts of Israel and at the same time stealing the crown of our Lord. It comes like Judas Iscariot with "Hail, Master!", and with a sardonic smile with the price of blood in its hand. "Come out from among them," is the Word of God, "and be ye separate."

That is what Modernism does. They are doing that everywhere. They "cuckooed" the Congregationalists when the Unitarians took charge of the Congregationalists of America, and they have been "cuckooing" the Methodists, and they are trying to "cuckoo" the Baptists, but bless God! we have got that old cuckoo bird by the neck, and they are not going to cuckoo the Baptists and break them down!

(Applause.)

Somebody says, "Well, we have just a few in our church." You get a barrel of apples. You put three rotten apples in the barrel and which will change? You put a pole cat in this room and which will change? (Laughter.)

Let me tell you what has been going on, no matter what anybody says. In 1925, the Northern Baptists held a convention in

$30,000.00 Tabernacle Temple Baptist Church, Woodward Avenue, Detroit.

Seattle. Dr. W. B. Hinson submitted a resolution requesting our foreign missionaries to say they believed, first, in the inspiration of the Bible; second, in the virgin birth of Christ; third, in the atonement of Christ on the cross; fourth, in the resurrection of the Christ; and fifth, in the New Birth of the soul. You would have thought any Baptist on earth would have signed that, but the Northern Baptist Convention turned it down two to one, and said, "We will send out both modernist and fundamentalist missionaries." That is what they said.

Send out missionaries that don't believe in the inspiration of the Bible! Send out missionaries that deny the atonement of Christ! Send out missionaries that deny the Virgin Birth of Christ! Send out missionaries that deny the resurrection of Christ! In Heaven's name, what are they going to preach? They cannot walk together except they be agreed. "What accord hath Christ with Belial," or "What communion hath light with darkness?" That is what is going on.

The Modernism of the World Baptist Alliance

The World Baptist Alliance is run by a bunch of modernists— and as proof of the rank modernism go back to the Stockholm meeting when the late Dr. A. C. Dixon offered a simple resolution that the World Baptist Alliance give to the world a platform of principles. The resolution stated:

We believe,

1. In the Divine inspiration of the Scriptures.
2. In the Virgin Birth of Christ.
3. In the Diety of Christ.
4. In the Atonement of Christ.
5. In the resurrection of Christ.

And the World Baptist Alliance turned it down overwhelmingly, and instead thereof adopted a platform of "internationalism," "fraternalism," et cetera.

And let me say here the World Baptist Alliance is the biggest cuckoo frame-up ever known among Baptists. Dr. J. H. Rushbrook is a rank modernist, and when he comes South he preaches orthodox sermons—he is the Secretary of the World Baptist Alliance.

Dr. A. W. Beaven of Rochester University is one of the smoothest modernists, and he too when he goes South speaks oily words of orthodoxy. His is the hidden hand of the North American Continent that is directing this modernistic World Baptist Alliance, and he reached down South and got Dr. George W. Truett, and uses him as a wall-flower, and their next meeting is scheduled to be held among Southern Baptists, but the great majority of Southern Baptists are not in sympathy with it, for they have long since learned to "beware of the Greeks when they bring their gifts." And this modernistic machine has got Dr. George W. Truett going up and down the land speaking in behalf of their scheme; although he extends the hand of orthodoxy, yet the hidden voice is that of modernism.

By the way, do you know who Dr. George Truett has as a pulpit supply? Dean Shailer Mathews of Chicago University! (Groans from the audience.)

No wonder you are surprised. But he is the best defender or representative the modernists of the North have in the South. Oh, he is orthodox, he plays the part of Jehoshaphat.

Mr. Chairman, would you allow Shailer Mathews, the arch modernist of Chicago University, to preach in this pulpit?

CHAIRMAN: No, sir.

DR. NORRIS: That's what happened in the First Baptist Church at Dallas. That is the hidden hand behind all this upheaval.

We have had a great many upheavals in Texas and in the South, over Modernism.

The Texas Fight

There have been all kinds of falsehoods sent broadcast throughout the Northland.

But what are the facts? Some fifteen years ago I exposed the first evolutionist in my Alma Mater, Baylor University. This evolutionist was one of the head professors, and wrote with his own hand that man came from the anthropoid ape, and this book was published by the Baylor University Press. I didn't believe it then, and I don't believe it now, and I protested against it, and I made no apology for it then, and I do not now, that man came from the ape.

(Applause.)

Before we were through there were eight anthropoid apes twisted out of the faculty of Baylor University.

But the interesting thing about it all was that the powers that be, and the Board of Trustees, and the President of the University stood for the last one of these apes, and they only resigned when the aroused sentiment of the denomination forced them to resign.

And Dr. George W. Truett, instead of standing against these materialistic evolutionists, defended every last one of them, on the one hand and lost his temper, and denounced in a public address the man who had the courage to expose the evolution. He called him "damnable and despicable."

All these things are matters of record.

Talk About Ecclesiastical Dictation

In the beginning of the Seventy-five Million Campaign, put on at the same time you had your One-hundred Million Dollar Promotion Drive in the North, a group of denominational despots called on me in my office, and demanded I take their apportionment of $100,000.00. I quietly informed them I did not believe in that method, and my conviction was then, and is now, every church has the right and the sole right of naming how, what, when, and the method of its liberality, and that no set of men on the face of the earth has a right to even suggest what the local church will do, much less dictate to it. But this group of political, ecclesiastical dictators, headed by Dr. L. R. Scarborough, the head of the Southwestern Baptist Theological Seminary, said to me:

"Now, Norris, if you don't cooperate and put on this drive, we will brand you to the ends of the earth as a non-cooperating Baptist, and you will lose out; you will not have any crowds to hear you, your church will disintegrate."

That was fifteen years ago!

You can look around this afternoon and judge whether or not they were false prophets. (Laughter and applause.)

Just think of it, a Baptist Church excluded from the Convention for the two following reasons:

First, because the church decided to exercise its sovereign right and throw the literature overboard and use the Bible only, plus nothing and minus nothing.

Second, because the church decided it had the inalienable right to order and run its own affairs, rather than take the dictation of the unscriptural Seventy-Five Million Dollar Campaign Committee

But the interesting and amusing thing, this ill fated action on the part of the machine cost the Convention—well, they were ou of debt, and now they owe over six million dollars. Then they had three thousand churches cooperating with the headquarters, now they have only about six hundred that send in contributions each month. The records speak for themselves. Then they had a great army of laymen, now they have practically all quit.

The machine must be congratulated, however, in finally waking up to the terrible consequence of their course toward the First Baptist Church. Instead of it putting the church out of business it put it in business. They gave it hearing around the world, and thousands upon thousands have been saved at home and abroad through the ministry of the First Baptist Church. How true is Philippians 1:12: "But I would ye should understand, brethren, that the things which happened unto me have fallen out rather unto the furtherance of the gospel."

Then the church had no radio, and it now has a radio that covers the great Southwest and part of the East.

The church had no paper then, now it has a paper four times the size of the average denominational paper.

But that is not all. Last fall at the State Convention at San Antonio the Convention repealed the article in its constitution that put the First Baptist Church out of the Convention, and now they want the church to come back, but sooner would we break into a graveyard or crawl in through a jail door—we are free!

We are happy; we are united—"For that a notable miracle hath been done by them is manifest to all them that dwell in Jerusalem; and we cannot deny it."

They sent out this unscriptural demand, dictating to the churches how much money they should raise, in a large envelope that had on the outside in crescent shape red letters these words:

"Seventy-five Million Campaign."

I had received that letter some few days before the excathedra demand of this coterie of these ecclesiastical dictators. I reached over on my desk and took the envelope with this demand and tore it to pieces without saying a word, and then crumpled the pieces in my right hand and cast the pieces at the feet of these dictators, and said: "That's my answer to your papal demands."

(Proloned applause.)

And, ladies and gentlemen, I would not have had any self respect if I had done otherwise. (Applause.)

They proceeded at once to carry out their threats, and they went after me hot and strong, and believe me, we had a merry-go-round for many years in the Lone Star State.

I didn't have any paper or radio at that time. I told them they had the advantage of me. They circularized the whole country. They published article after article in all their machine papers. They misrepresented my church. They sent out hundreds of thousands of tracts—one series of six—and the President of the Seminary, Dr. L. R. Scarborough, sent out one hundred thousand tracts, paid for by corrupt mayor of Fort Worth, because I exposed his crookedness. The tracts were entitled, "The Fruits of Norrisism." They even hired time for seven nights on the radio and called me everything on earth—the most blistering and vitriolic terms that ever fell from the lips of man. It is doubtful if even John Dillinger would have used the language that they used. Concerning that ill fated course of their hate fest, Dr. W. B. Riley wrote in his magazine the following:

"The Texas Baptist Controversy"

"The air in Texas has been blue during the month. Six or eight outstanding Baptist men connected directly with the Texas Baptist machine, undertook to give Norris a black eye over the radio. It would seem that they went in for a straight killing. Norris, in order to put past dispute what they said, arranged for a wax cylinder reception, and he gives the following as samples of speech employed: 'Malicious,' 'diabolical,' 'falsifier,' 'perjurer,' 'liar,' 'thief,' 'scoundrel,' 'reprobate,' 'despicable,' 'damnable,' 'devilish,' 'infamous,' 'murderer,' 'criminal,' 'dastardly,' 'heinous,' 'infamous liar,' 'malicious falsifier,' 'wicked,' 'corrupt,' 'hellish,' 'malicious liar.' At the close of these addresses delivered by Drs. Brooks, Scarborough and others, Frank was immediately upon the air for an answer. We heard him but once, but were told by those who listened in nightly that this time was a sample of his regular procedure. He begged the air audience not to think hardly of his opponents, to remember that they were excited and heated up, and that their strong language did not represent their better spirit. He ignored very largely their hard names and malicious charges, and moved straight to the preaching of a first class evangelistic sermon, concluding with a soul-winning appeal.

"We say without hesitation that, while we have heard of men building platforms, adjusting nooses about their own necks, tying the upper end of the rope over a limb, and then kicking the plat-

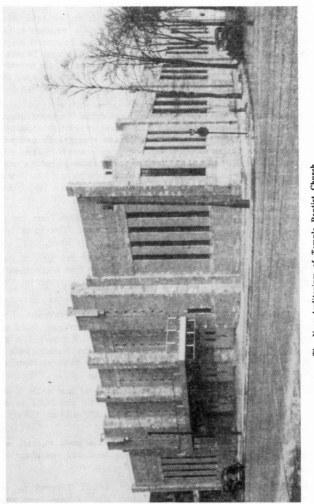

The New Auditorium of Temple Baptist Church

form from beneath themselves to dangle till death, we have seldom seen so many high class and apparently sensible men commit the same folly at one time as occurred in this procedure. Since it began, I have been in Kansas, Oklahoma, Arkansas and Tennessee, and everywhere there was one judgment of 'a foolish procedure injurious to those who inaugurated it,' and advantageous to their enemy.

"The procedure can be explained, however, on the same ground that is going to render desperate leaders in the Northern Baptist Convention in the near future. The Texas machine is going to pieces; the whole Southern machine is badly crippled; and when men's vested interests are touched, they lose equanimity and often behave foolishly. We predict that the comparative good nature of the Northern modernists among Baptists will not last much longer."

Great Revival Followed Hate-Fest

What an indictment of the Texas Baptist Machine from the pen of Dr. W. B. Riley as published in his magazine, "The Pilot"!

And this was the prevailing opinion among all fair people East and West, North and South. While they were on the air I thought of the old adage, "Whom the gods destroy they first make mad."

I went on the radio immediately when they signed off, preached the Gospel of salvation.

There was something coming back through the darkness of the night—it was between 10:30 and 11:30 P. M. Everybody could feel the hush! Presently a telephone rang and a call for me. The girl at the telephone said: "He is on the radio and cannot talk to you," but a woman in tears said: "I must talk to him. My husband is saved!"

And a note was put on the desk in front of me while I was talking and I called the quartette to the radio and said to the listeners, "Excuse me, I have an important call at the telephone."

The first I heard was the shoutings of this good woman, and she said: "My husband is saved, and he wants to tell you about it."

He came to the phone and said:

"This is J. R. Thompson, Greenville, and I listened to the bitterness and vilification with joy and delight. I have been your bitter enemy—I have hated you. I have cursed you, but I realized a few minutes ago that I was going to the judgment, and I fell on my knees and called on God for mercy and my wife prayed for me and I am saved, and I wish you would tell the brethren and all the world that I know I am saved."

I went back and reported it over the radio. A mother phoned from Tyler, Texas, saying: "My boy was at his filling station tonight and heard what they said against you and then listened to your Gospel message and came running home and is here and I will let him tell you how he was saved."

And all the way through the eight nights and on the Sunday following 142 people united with the church, most of them for baptism. Perhaps the most remarkable case of conversion through the radio hate-fest was Mrs. A. Ellig. She had a large party in her home with liquor on the table and while they were drinking and gambling they wrung their hands with glee at the cussing and abuse that was heaped upon the head of J. Frank Norris by the denominational leaders.

But when the next hour, the message of salvation, of sin and judgment, went into that same drinking, wicked company, this woman fell on her face and cried out before them all, "I am lost, I am lost!" And she was most gloriously saved.

And it ended that drinking party!

The next Sunday she stood before the great audience and told the whole story and she and her dear husband are two of the most active soul winners in the First Baptist Church today.

If there was ever an occasion where the Scriptures were vindicated it was during these eight nights of the hate-fest, "But I would ye should understand, brethren, that the things which happened unto me have fallen out rather unto the furtherance of the gospel";—Philippians 1:12.

And the following Sunday 142 people united with the First Baptist Church.

The Master Mind Behind the Radio Hate Fest

As is now well known, and has been known for many years— it is no longer a secret as to the master mind back of the radio hate fest. In truth there was no secret at the time. His highness, the chief priest of that year called several secret councils and all for one purpose—"This man"—"This man"—"This man"— "This man must be eliminated."

Some who passed to their reward protested in the council, and among those who protested was Dr. S. P. Brooks, President of Baylor University, even though he was pulled into the debate and against his will.

Immediately after the debate started the first morning, this high priest that had pushed everybody into it sent out an S. O. S. call and said,

"Scarborough fumbled the ball last night. Norris went rings around him. It is a regular tom cat fight. He is conducting a revival meeting. My telephone has been ringing all night long. Telegrams are pouring in. Just one week of this will ruin everything."

Dr. Scarborough was not present and they called him by long distance and told him that the radio hate fest must be called off. And Scarborough was consistent and said,

"What we have begun we must finish"—and it was finished.

Dr. F. S. Groner at that time was superintendent of missions. He was also pushed off into it by the same high priest, and after this high priest cut Groner's throat, and he did it after he had entered into solemn agreement that "We will stand together to the last ditch"—Groner and the high priest had one final meeting at a restaurant in Dallas when he told the high priest,

"Your course and conduct in my affairs is the most diabolical and cowardly that was ever known."

For full particulars of this whole mad radio hate fest, communicate with Dr. F. S. Groner, President Marshall College, Marshall, Texas. And for further information communicate with Dr. E. C. Routh, Editor of the Baptist Messenger, Oklahoma City.

Ecclesiastical Hate When Born of Deep and Long Standing Conspiracy Goes to Any Length to Accomplish Its Purpose

That the Sanhedrin would bribe one of the twelve, is characteristic of the Ecclesiastical Sanhedrins of all the ages. As was to be expected there were many who were unstable, others who were untrue and some who played the part of Judas Iscariot.

More than once it was found that the First Baptist Church was actually paying the salaries of tools of the enemies of the church but this is a characteristic of the nations when they go to war, and the First Baptist Church was in a greater war than with flesh and blood, than when the nations of the earth go to battle with each other. "For we wrestle not against flesh and blood, but against principalities, against powers, against the rulers of the darkness of this world, against spiritual wickedness in high places."—Eph. 6:12.

Statement of H. M. Harris, One of Fort Worth's Best Known Citizens

There was a young man converted and baptized into the First Baptist Church and was in its office force as bookkeeper and then as superintendent and later entered the ministry. He did not have the courage to resist the inducements of the Sanhedrin and he went on the radio. Here is the statement of one of the best known business men in the city of Fort Worth which tells the true story of the pitiful treachery of the former employee of the First Baptist Church:

"In the fall of 1927 I was listening to a red hot debate between a group of Baptist preachers on one side and Dr. J. Frank Norris on the other, and I heard one of these Baptist preachers state substantially as follows:

" 'That you may know what kind of man Dr. J. Frank Norris is, the First Baptist Church sold certain properties and he, Dr. Norris, charged the church with $7,500 commission and charged it to the name of a firm called Harris and Hyde. I was bookkeeper of the church at that time, and there was no such firm of Harris and Hyde, and Dr. Norris used this name as a fake to collect from this sale $7,500 for himself.'

"When I heard this my amazement knew no bounds because I and my partner, Mr. Hyde, did make the sale, and we did receive the $7,500 commission. And Dr. J. Frank Norris did not receive one cent of it.

"And while the radio discussion was going on I called up and made this statement and it was given to the public. And the preacher who made the false charge never had the decency to make the retraction and apology." (Signed) H. M. Harris.

Mr. H. M. Harris' address is 1415 Petroleum building, Sixth and Throckmorton, Fort Worth, Texas, and his telephone is 3-1997.

The above answer to the $7,500 false charge could have been published to the world, but the policy was never to answer and let the God that answers by fire—let Him be God. Thousands heard this slander by this preacher over the radio. He was forced to tell it.

A pitiful thing is that this preacher afterwards sold his influence to the gamblers of Fort Worth and in return his son received a small mess of pottage. All the lawyers and citizens of Fort Worth know of this deal. And Fort Worth is wide open and gambling dens abound on every hand.

This information is public property, therefore privileged to repeat. Only the most pitiful attitude should be held for this twice sold preacher.

The mantle of charity should be pulled down over the conduct of the preacher who made this false statement over the radio. He came into the office of the pastor of the First Baptist Church and wept and said he was forced to do things against his will. He told how one of the high priests called him into his office, and this was in the beginning of the denominational controversy. The high priest scared the young preacher out of his wits and convinced him that they were going to "ruin Norris."

This is in keeping with the methods that the Sanhedrin followed. For instance, they sent another young fellow out to see an old man by the name of P. P. Pierce. The old man had been in the asylum and went again afterwards, and this representative of the Sanhedrin got him to sign a statement that he could not read, and said afterwards he never did read it, and the statement read as follows:

"This is to certify J. Frank Norris stole $50,000 from me and still has it." (Signed) P. P. Pierce.

Honorable R. V. Patterson, a great lawyer at Decatur, Texas, and who was with the machine, made a thorough investigation of the Pierce Affidavit.

Dr. J. L. Ward, President of Decatur College, had the dear old man at Decatur and was going to give out the affidavit to a huge crowd, but Mr. Pierce told Judge Patterson,

"I did not know I signed it and J. Frank Norris never stole any money from me."

But Dr. Ward went on the radio and read the above affidavit and the Sanhedrin photographed and sent it throughout the Southern Baptist Convention.

That it was proved to be a fake did not lessen the circulation of it, and even after they found it out they never had the courage to confess their sins.

But the $7,500 false statement and the $50,000 fake affidavit were just samples of the floods of propaganda over the radio and in the denominational press.

The pitiful situation is that the same former employee of the First Baptist Church was the same tool that was used by the Sanhedrin before the young preachers at the Seminary, giving the false testimony that Norris owned the property of the First Baptist Church. Also he gave circulation to the fake $50,000 affidavit as well as numerous other slanderous reports.

But he probably should not be blamed, for it may be an inherited weakness. And when the young priests are tempted by the high priests with promotion—things have not changed since Samuel's day—I Sam. 2:36, "And it shall come to pass, that every one that is left in thine house shall come and crouch to him for a piece of silver and a morsel of bread, and shall say, Put me, I pray thee, into one of the priests' offices, that I may eat a piece of bread."

Norris Owns the First Baptist Church

It was amusing as well as pitiful the volumes and volumes of propaganda that the denominational leaders broadcast throughout the land. It was indeed the serpent casting out of his mouth tracts, leaflets, publications "as a flood."

A typical example of their proganda was "NORRIS OWNS THE PROPERTY OF THE FIRST BAPTIST CHURCH." Young preachers were called together in the Seminaries and denominational colleges and instructed to tell this to their people.

And they did!

The young preachers believed it and so did other people!

And it did not matter with the leaders that the deed of records were open to the public and showed that the property, every bit of it, was owned by the First Baptist Church, and Norris did not own one square inch of it.

But the mischief was done!

Anything to destroy Norris!

"And there were above forty in this conspiracy."

Tracts Circulated Ahead of Norris

There was a series of six tracts, telling the world who Norris was, and in addition, "The fruits of Norrism" by the President of the Seminary. Everywhere I went for a meeting these tracks were sent on ahead.

Take for example, the Euclid Avenue Baptist Church in Cleveland, Dr. W. W. Bustard was then living and the pastor. This great church wired me to come and hold a meeting for them and the week before I arrived every member of the church received these tracts.

Of course, tracts from the leaders of the denomination greatly disturbed many good people. The pastor and deacons met and discussed it but decided for me to come on, and again: "But I would ye should understand, brethren, that the things which happened unto me have fallen out rather unto the furtherance of the gospel."

Everybody came—some out of curiosity, some out of sympathy, some out of contempt, but the Lord came also and more than two hundred new members came into the church, and at the close of the meeting over $500,000.00 was raised to build a new building and one woman who was converted and baptized into the church, led the offering with $55,000.00.

Tracts on Door-Steps of People of Fort Worth

On Saturday nights these tracts would be distributed on the door-steps of the homes of the people of Fort Worth. While they prejudiced a great many, yet they interested a large number and they came to hear the Gospel and were saved.

"Norris Refused to Pay for Literature and Was Cut Off"

This is the statement that the Secretary of the Sunday School Board, Dr. I. J. Van Ness, told his field men to circulate throughout the South and they did. Something had to be done to counteract the rapid decrease of the literature of the Board by churches that were throwing it out of the window and putting the Bible only, plus nothing and minus nothing, as their only text book.

This was far from the truth because the First Baptist Church paid cash on delivery for all literature that it received from the Board, but the mischief was done.

Incidentally there was an audit of Dr. Van Ness' books and for ten years or more it was found that he had been giving huge contracts of printing to a printing company without competitive bids, and he had connection with this company.

There was an estimated over-pay of more than $300,000.00.

Dr. Van Ness "resigned."

This is just a simple statement of the inside facts with malice toward none and love for all.

"So they hanged Haman on the gallows that he had prepared for Mordecai."

Old Auditorium, Temple Baptist Church, which has now been converted into a modern Sunday School building.

WHAT HAS BEEN THE RECORD OF THE MACHINE IN TEXAS

Before the fight started, Texas Baptists were out of debt, and today they are six million dollars in debt. Already several of their institutions have been foreclosed, or are in bankruptcy, and professors are unpaid, confidence is broken down, and of the over 3000 former cooperating churches, not one-fifth of that number, are cooperating today.

What has been the record? It has been a long record of misappropriations and embezzlements.

The seminaries conspired together, after they had received their apportionment out of the Seventy-Five Million funds, and by political scheming voted two million dollars out of the Foreign Mission funds and left the Foreign Mission cause stripped, stranded and bankrupt, and over 300 missionaries had to be called home.

What else?

There was the infamous million dollar steal from the Home Mission Board, and in order to cover up the higher-ups, a light sentence was given to one man, and he has long since been out.

What else?

Surely the curse of Almighty God has been on the Southern ecclesiastical machine. There was a $100,000.00 steal from the Foreign Mission Board by the treasurer, for which he was sent to the penitentiary.

What else?

There was a $150,000.00 steal from the Baptist Hospital in Dallas, and the court record shows it had been going on for ten years, and if it hadn't been for outside interest it would have never come to light. But one of the guilty parties was sentenced to the penitentiary for a term of years.

What else?

There was another big steal in Howard Payne College, and the professor—and the woman in the case—she was sent to the penitentiary and the professor went free.

What else?

There is the big scandal in connection with the Sunday School Board, that all efforts have failed to cover up, and now the main high-cockalorum is going out in a short time, and time would fail to call the roll further.

They said I would not have any crowds to preach to!

I have no hurts; they can't bother me any more, but by the grace of God I am determined that they are going to let the ministers alone—like these pastors sitting here on this platform, and I am going to do to them what Samson did to the Philistines when he took the jawbone of a certain well known animal and went after them. (Applause and laughter.)

They say that I enjoy a fight. I didn't enjoy it to begin with, but now I have a deep down feeling that I was predestinated to attend to this crowd of ecclesiastical dictators.

Murdering Pastors

I am tired of these ecclesiastical machines murdering pastors in cold blood. The average pastor, say to his credit, is a modest man, he is timid. He is not a fighter. I wasn't to begin with. I was very timid. But the machine crowd forced me to fight.

You know how the average preacher spends a sleepless night?

Do you know I think Daniel had certain deacons in mind when he wrote about that one horned Billy Goat. (Laughter.)

The average pastor overworked, will go to bed seeking a needed night's rest, and that one horned Billy Goat will be ramming the head of his bed, and the pastor will turn from side to side—who can sleep with such buttin' at the head of his bed. And then some Jezebel, president of the hen parties in the church, will get her claw hammer and sit on the foot of his bed, then he is getting hell at both ends. (Laughter.)

But that isn't all: then some marcelled-hair, striped breeches, worldly choir director, and his gee-whiz soloist will kick the slats out from under his bed. (Laughter.)

The modernists say there is no hell hereafter, but one thing dead certain that poor pastor is having hell on earth. (Laughter.)

And I am opposed to it.

The average pastor is like the mule's tail, goes wherever the mule goes, pops when the mule brays, and that is what the average pastor does, just goes switching and popping around whenever the mule brays.

I know what I am talking about. I have taken a post-graduate course. I had ten of these hen parties in my church at one time. Like the ten lepers that came to the Lord. And just let me fail to make an announcement for one of them or read it just like they sent it up!

Therefore, ladies and gentlemen, I am opposed to all the one horned Billy Goats, or Jezebel hen parties, or these marcelled, striped breeches choir directors with their hell raising, card playing, high kicking soloists, dictating to God's called and anointed pastor how he should conduct his ministry, preach or do anything else. (Applause.)

But that isn't all. In addition to this inside clique that dictates and dominates a pastor, there is the bunch of political herarchies, formerly known as the "headquarters," now known as the hindquarters, that dictates to the average preacher. Now I am through with it. I finished my course twenty years ago. My business now is to give diplomas to my brethren. (Laughter.)

Speaking of these cogs and wheels on the inside, hen parties, et cetera—don't misunderstand me, I am for the work of our good women. I am for the work of the young people, but I am not in favor of them running the pastor or running the church, for it means the ruination of everything, pastor and church included. We don't need any Diotrepheses, or any Jezebels.

I had ten hen parties once, as I told you, and I called all of them together one afternoon, never even told my wife what I was going to do. I was afraid to. So they all met, presidents, vicepresidents, secretaries, and what a nice delightful occasion, and the general president arose and very graciously said:

"We are very happy to have our beloved pastor with us this afternoon. It is not often he appears in our meeting. We don't know what he has to say, but we know it is something good for his words are like apples of gold and of silver, and we only regret that he is so busy that he cannot come oftener."

(I said to myself, this is my last time.) I left my car running. I held my hat in my hand—I was standing as close to the door as was polite, and I said:

"Ladies, I am very happy to be with you. I think very highly of all of you. I have no speech to make, only an announcement— you have all adjourned sine die."

And as I said the last word I was going out of the door. You talk about pandemonium, consternation, brick bats, sulphuric acid —I was like the old negro preacher who got up before his congregation and said:

"I'se gwine to preach today on The Two Roads—one road leads to hellfire and damnation, the other leads to heaven—as for this nigger I'se gwine take to the woods."

Do not misunderstand me, I am for the work of the good women. Paul said, "Help those women who labored with me in the gospel," and a good woman is God's greatest gift to a church and pastor, but what I am striking at is this worldly hell raising element that breaks the heart of the pastor and destroys the spirit of the church.

Modernism Right Here In Michigan

Let me give you an example of Modernism right here in Michigan. I have here an address of a very distinguished gentleman from Kalamazoo, pastor of the church there, Dr. George H. Young, First Baptist Church, Kalamazoo, Michigan. Here is an example of it.

I will not take the time to read this exposure, but it is by a well known minister, pastor, First Baptist Church—he has published it and sent it broadcast—he charges in this address that the faculty is composed of modernists and rank unbelievers—he charges that the faculty is not in sympathy with even religious worship.

And yet this college is in the "whole cooperative program," and unless you support this modernistic college you are branded as "traitor"—"non-cooperative," and I will say here and now that it is not only your duty not to support it, but you are guilty of high crime before Almighty God to put your money in an institution that denies the authority of the Scripture, that denies the Virgin Birth of Christ, that denies the Deity of Christ, that denies the resurrection of Christ—in short, it is high treason against our Lord and Saviour Jesus Christ to support or patronize such an institution. (Applause.)

The Scheme of Modernists To Capture Temple Baptist Church

Now we are coming right down to where we are living. For 25 years I have dealt with the schemes and underhanded methods of Modernism. There is no crime it will not commit. There is no law it will not break. There is no slander it will not circulate. It is like its father, the Devil, without conscience or character. Their method is to sow tares while the men sleep. They come like Joab, with pleasing words, but with the hidden dagger of death. They come with the soft velvet footfall of the tiger to spring on their unsuspecting prey. They come and deceive the very elect. They come crying, "peace," "peace," when there is no peace. They have captured church after church while the truly orthodox have been asleep at the switch.

Now this same relentless, serpentine, modernistic machine has interfered with the sovereign right of the Temple Baptist Church, and, thank God, has failed to capture it. (Applause.) Fortunately this church has a fine body of men, some of the noblest deacons I have ever met, they know the tracks of modernism. They know its shibboleth. They know its smell. They recognize its voice, although it comes with soft words.

Two Opposing Forces In Temple Church

There have been for years two conflicting forces in this church. The former pastor, a good man, is a Fundamentalist, and the associate pastor who has been hand in glove with the Detroit Baptist Union—he has been in charge of the Sunday School, and the Sunday School is separate and apart and independent of the church. That is, it has been until now. I will give you an example of the separate and divisive condition existing between the church and Sunday School: The first Sunday I was here for the meeting I asked all the crowd to assemble in the auditorium for services. The chairman of the Board, made the request of the various superintendents, but it was checked and cancelled by the associate pastor, and I was politely informed that the Sunday School was under separate management.

I never sought this call—the pulpit committee and deacons of the church knew my situation. I have been in the same place for more than a quarter of a century. I was raised near where I now live. I have had my conflicts, my lights and shadows, joys and sorrows, have gone through the fires of the furnace made seven times hot. I have no hurts. I have faced every foe, and have never dipped my colors in the presence of any foe. I am happily situated, have the greatest church on the whole face of the earth.

After this church made the call I went home to be with my little family on Christmas Day, as the various ones were returning from school and elsewhere. While I was at Chicago visiting my daughter on my way home, I received a message that the modernistic machine crowd had started trouble. When I reached home I heard the news of their sniping and spreading their false propaganda. I immediately left my family and returned. If they had gone on and behaved themselves I would have sent a nice telegram thanking them for the call and that would have ended the matter. But if anybody thinks a bunch of these machine, ecclesiastical politicians can make a fight on my wife's husband, and I will do like a flop eared, "pot-licker," suck-egg hound, when he tucks his tail between his legs and runs down tin can alley—well, they have another think coming. (Applause.)

Therefore, I have come back here to find out how many people in this church have enough nerve, backbone, and red blood in their veins, to clean up things—and, bless God, we are going to clean it from cellar to garret. (Prolonged applause.)

We are going to find out whether or not H. C. Gleiss and his little machine of Detroit can dictate to the Temple Baptist Church. We are going to find out whether A. W. Beaven, the political whip of the Northern Baptist Convention, can capture this church for modernism. We are going to find out whether a bunch of traitors will be allowed to do the Trojan horse act.

That's what is involved. You know what I am talking about.

Cancelling of Auditorium

Let me give you an example of how this Detroit Baptist machine interfered with the independence and rights of the Temple Baptist Church.

When this church invited me to come and hold a meeting, the deacons went and rented the Cass Tech Auditorium, which has 3500 capacity, for which they paid $300.00 Now what happened?

The day we were to enter that auditorium, the Superintendent of Public Schools cancelled the contract instanter. And why?

He said there were so many protests that had come—he gave that as his reason.

Where did the protests come from?

Not from bootleggers, not gamblers, not from the underworld.

Not from the Roman Catholics.

So they laid it on the Jews. That was a good camouflage—anything or anybody to blame, just do the Hitler act—blame the Jews.

Now I want to prove something to you—the chairman is sitting here on the platform—he is chairman of the Board of Deacons—I will ask him if, when he called Mr. Cody and asked why he cancelled the auditorium, if the superintendent did not tell him he made the mistake, in that he ought to have brought the matter through the Baptist Union—through the office of Dr. H. C. Gleiss?

CHAIRMAN: That is correct.

DR. NORRIS: Why did the superintendent of the public schools raise the question of Dr. H. C. Gleiss and the Baptist Union?

Furthermore, Dr. Gleiss was with a group of teachers the day the auditorium was cancelled, and he told this group that he knew that the auditorium was going to be cancelled.

How did he know it?

That is enough evidence to hang a man.

But wait a minute—the president of the Detroit Baptist Union, one Mr. Judson R. Forrester—he told the superintendent of the public schools, Mr. Cody, if they allowed Frank Norris to preach in that auditorium that the public school authorities would have a dozen libel suits on their hands.

There are many witnesses present this afternoon who know Mr. Forrester said that. He told a great many people that

How many here that know this? (Hands went up.)

VOICE: Yes, sir.

DR. NORRIS: Now, ladies and gentlemen, you have the whole inside story. It was not the Jews, it was the president and secretary of the Baptist Union of Detroit that engineered and brought about the cancellation of that great auditorium.

And I want to say here and now, in the presence of Almighty God, when the flaming day of judgment comes, I would not want to stand in the place of these two ecclesiastical politicians with the blood of souls dripping from their hands!

And you will be interested to know that Mr. Judson Forrester was a member of this church, and caused the former pastor much trouble. He is a modernist. But henceforth he is not a member of this church, and read the records as to why he was excluded from its membership. (Applause.)

Another Part of the Conspiracy to Cancellation of Auditorium

The women's organization has what is known as the political department. I call it that—you have a department where public questions are discussed, that is, by the invitation of this political committee, they invite speakers to discuss social and political questions, and a woman member of the school board came out a short time ago at the invitation of this department.

Now here is another inside chapter. Certain women in this

church who are in sympathy with this modernistic machine went to this school board and brought pressure to bear to have the contract of the high school auditorium cancelled, and for that reason I want to announce here and now that the political department of the Temple Baptist Church is henceforth and forever more adjourned! (Prolonged applause.)

Another Example of Machine Interference

I am not through, nor will I get through. I have been going to school for twenty-five years and studying the underground methods of these ecclesiastical politicians. I not only have no fear of them, I have a profound contempt for them. All right, what happened? I took my Seminary course at the Seminary at Louisville. I passed every course, and there is not a blot on my record. But that doesn't matter—it doesn't matter with these ecclesiastical slanderers that I have been in one church for a quarter of a century, and built up the largest membership on the American Continent. These ecclesiastical slanderers are of Satan, whose first business it is to accuse and slander the saints of God. Just let a minister have enough courage to challenge the principalities of darkness, then begins the slander of innuendo and insinuations that will be carried on against him. They have no authority, they always quote, "And Gashmu saith it," which is the Bible name for, "And they say."

Now, one Mr. L. H. Tanner, who ran this church for many years, was chairman of the Board, who held all the finances of the church, never made a report or had an outside audit—he, Mr. Forrester, president of the Baptist Union, Mr. Gleiss, secretary, and the associate pastor—they undertook to defeat the will of this church by following the snake-in-the-grass methods—never to come out in the open. Mr. Tanner went to a minister, a dear friend of mine, and told him that he had some letters and things on Norris that he was going to spring. When I heard it I wired Mr. Tanner to appear before the deacons of this church and spring every record he had, and read the records to the Board of Deacons. To this day he has never come, but on the contrary refused to.

Why didn't he come?

And when charges of misconduct were preferred against Forrester, President of the Baptist Union, he refused also to come before the Board of Deacons, and what do you reckon his reasons for not coming were? He said he would not come if Norris was going to be present.

Why didn't these fellows meet me face to face before the Board of Deacons?

VOICE: They were yellow. (Applause.)

A fine young preacher was used, and later he apologized—he was one of the finest young men who ever went out from this church or any other church. He went to the Louisville Baptist Seminary, and Mr. Tanner wrote him insinuating that he could find out some things about Norris at the Seminary, and the young man innocently and sincerely, went to one Prof. Frank Powell, and this professor told the young man student he had plenty on Norris, also told him that he, the professor, would sign his name, or would write a letter if it was necessary. The young preacher innocently, and thinking he was doing a good service, wrote the Chairman of the Board of Deacons of this church a letter giving the results of his interview, quoting the slanderous attacks of this professor. The Chairman of the Board called up the young preacher at Louisville and asked him to get the letter from this professor. I will ask now the Chairman of the Board, if that is correct?

CHAIRMAN: Yes, sir.

DR. NORRIS: When this young preacher went and called on the professor did he sign his name as he agreed to?

CHAIRMAN: No, sir.

DR. NORRIS: I will ask the Chairman also if I haven't stated the truth about the young preacher writing this letter under the advice, repeating the charges of this professor, and didn't the professor say that he would write a letter to the Board, signing his name to it?

CHAIRMAN: Yes, sir.

DR. NORRIS: Now, I will ask the Chairman when the professor refused to make good what he had charged to the young preacher, then what did the young preacher do?

CHAIRMAN: He apologized.

DR. NORRIS: And herewith is his telegram of apology:

"Dr. Frank Norris:

"I will never forgive myself if I have interfered with the Lord's work even if in ignorance. I have just been a go between. Forgive me in the name of Christ. I plead with you to be content with an apology from my professor. You have already removed all doubts I had but if you show the Christian love and grace to do this, you will do much more than just that. For my sake, please reply at once. 1 Cor. 6:1.

"DAVID EWART."

(Applause.)

Going To Operate On This Professor

Now, ladies and gentlemen, I have written this professor a registered letter, delivered to the addressee only, notifying him that I am going to operate on him. I have offered him his expenses to Memphis and back that I may operate on him during the Southern Baptist Convention, and if you don't think I will operate on him, you wait and see, and if the Lord let's me live there will be one professor's hide hanging from the top of a telephone pole on the banks of the Mississippi, in old Memphis, Tennessee! (Applause.)

I have his record. This is not the first time he has been guilty of blackguardism and slander.

Oh, there will be some who say, "Why go into these matters?" Here is the answer: I say to you, ladies and gentlemen, the time is long past, when Seminary professors and ecclesiastical machine politicians should be allowed to interfere with or dictate to a local church how it shall run its affairs. (Prolonged applause.)

Oh, I hear some little two by four simlin headed sentimentalist say, "I don't think that is the thing to do." You don't know what Christian thinking looks like. (Laughter.)

Let me tell you something, brother preachers, and I am glad to see a lot of you here this afternoon—many on the platform and throughout the audience, what we need in this modern twentieth century dealing with these modernists, is the spirit of old Elijah when he dealt with the 450 preachers on the Board and on the pay roll of old Jezebel—we need the spirit of John the Baptist.

I have not yet started. Now if this is getting too hot for some of you, it will be all right for you to go. (Two people got up and walked out)—You "ain't" seen nothing yet.

What we need is a little of the courage of Martin Luther when he stood before the Diet of Worms, presided over by Charles V. surrounded by 72 red capped cardinals, and that old Monk said: "I cannot, I will not recant, so help me God!"

And if you think that I am going to allow H. C. Gleiss, who is one of these ordinary two by four denominational time servers, dictate to me, or if you think this church is going to allow it, you will wake up disappointed. (Laughter and applause.)

Do you know what he reminds me of? One day a boy went out hunting in the tall piney woods, and looking up he saw up there, way up on the top limb, a hundred feet from the ground, a red headed woodpecker, just boring away with his bill like a steel riveter on a skyscraper—after a while there came up a heavy storm cloud, and a bolt of lightning struck that tree right in the top and split it all the way a hundred feet to the ground, and that woodpecker thinks to this day that he split that tree! (Laughter and applause.)—Go and give H. C. Gleiss that with my compliments. (Laughter.)

Talk about a closed monopoly—let me tell you something else, there is no secret about it—this Detroit Baptist machine has for years been buying lots and building church houses and financing them with money they get from the headquarters. Here is a very strange thing. Listen at it:

One real estate company does all the buying of the real estate.

One architect does all the drawing of plans.

One contractor does all the building.

One material supply company supplies all the materials.

One plumbing company does all the plumbing.

One insurance company does all the insuring.

Why, friends, if the Republicans had that on the Democrats they would be put out of office before breakfast. (Applause.)

But even the Democrats, as low down as they are, would never have been guilty of grafting on the cause of Jesus Christ. (Applause.)

But I am not through. Here is what has been going on among the large number who have been converted in this meeting. There came to this front seat one night a Roman Catholic with his wife. They got down on their knees, and they were gloriously saved, and the associate pastor, who is no longer here, what did he do? He not only did everything he could against the meeting, as I told you awhile ago, and he is hand in glove with the modernistic Baptist machine—he took these two converted Roman Catholics to one side, and they thought, of course, he was their friend. They wanted to know how to get into the church. They had never been about a Protestant church. You would have thought he would have advised them how to join the church—no, he told them "to wait." He discouraged them, and they did not come in. They went away disappointed and heart broken. They wondered what was the matter, whether it was their fault. A few days afterwards their little two-year-old baby took sick, and they wanted a minister—they didn't want to go back to the Roman Catholics, but they had been turned down, as they thought by the church— the result was they sent for the Roman Catholic priest—but some of the good women heard about it and went there and ministered to them, and that is their testimony after they went into that home.

Is Mrs. Fitzgerald present? If so stand up. Yes—Mrs. Fitzgerald, I want to ask you if the facts are as I have stated?

MRS. FITZGERALD: Yes, sir.

DR. NORRIS: How many others know these facts to be true, hold up your hands. (Numbers of hands went up.)

I told you I was going to take the lid off some crowds who went around and said I would not do these things here in Detroit—that I could pull them off in the Southwest—well, they have already been pulled off in Detroit! It is easier to pull them off here than in the wild and wooly west. I am showing you, my friends, this same identical crowd, is the same ecclesiastical politicians, West, East, North and South.

Here is what it all means. This associate pastor, the piston rod of the machine and their crowds, did everything they could to defeat the meeting. They didn't want anybody to join this church. They saw the handwriting on the wall, and for them it is, Mene, Mene, Tekel, Upharsin.

The Choir Director and Choir

I am not through yet. (Laughter.)

Now I am for great choirs, great choir directors. The First Baptist Church has a choir with a membership of 300, and a waiting list, and I want to say to you, not one member engages in dancing, card playing or other unscriptural and forbidden worldly practices. Last Wednesday this church passed a strong resolution that every deacon, teacher, choir director and choir member must either quit these things or get out. (Applause.)

We have had resignations retail and wholesale. The choir director resigned and stated frankly that he was "Not in harmony."

(Applause.) Well I appreciated him saying he is not in harmony, for we are going to have the most harmonious church you ever saw. We are going to get rid of some more tonight. This is just a sample. Some may say I have spoken very plainly. Well I have —my only apology is that my language is so poverty stricken I couldn't do the subject justice. (Laughter.) This is one time the modernistic machine crowd met its Waterloo in the Northland. The time has come for judgment to begin at the House of God.

The time has come for preachers to be set free from ecclesiastical tyranny. The time has come for the Church of Jesus Christ to be set at liberty to win souls at home and abroad. The time has come for true believers to cease to support modern infidels, and I am going to take this throughout the state of Michigan. (Laughter.) (Applause.) I have already spoken in quite a number of places throughout the state and have many more invitations.

The machine crowd are scared to death, and they are a fulfillment of the Scripture where it says, "The wicked fleeth when no man pursueth." But these modernist machine cowards run swifter when courageous Fundamentalists get after them.

A Revival the Only Hope

And you can't have a revival with machine methods. God never did use machines, He uses men. You can't have a revival by preaching institutionalims. There is only one message, and that is the Word of the Living God. We have lost our faith in the power of Almighty God to save souls instantly, and we have put our faith in machines.

One of your daily papers came out editorially yesterday afternoon and said: "Unless there is an immediate change, we are headed for a terrible upheaval and revolution in America." May God forbid! We don't know what a day may bring forth, but there is one thing I do know: If there was ever a time in the world when the people should turn to the Word of God that time is now. If there was ever a time when preachers should cry from the pulpit and from the housetops, that time is now. Let them call on God for every need, and put their faith in God as their only hope. We are in a terrible storm, but, my friends, I have a stronger faith in the second coming of Christ today than I ever had in my life. What shall we do? What shall we do, preachers? Shall we close the church? Shall we turn our back on God? No! "Having done all, to stand."

Let me give you an example of what we need—the revival that

must come. Mr. and Mrs. Quint, will you please stand—these good people have one near and dear to them by the ties of flesh and blood. He is the father of four children, and for sixteen years has been a heavy drinker. That little wife stood at the marriage altar and put her little white hand in his, and that man promised before Almighty God to be true to her, to provide for, to protect her, to love, cherish and honor her until death do them separate, but instead of joy there was sorrow and when Christmas would come there was no laughter, no joy bells ringing in their home, no Santa Clause, no Christmas tree.

But what happened, at this last Christmas, there was a big Christmas turkey on the table, there was a Christmas tree in the home, there was a sober husband and father, there was joy unconfined, heaven came down and Christ was head of the household for the first time in sixteen years.

Is that true, Mr. and Mrs. Quint?

MR. AND MRS. QUINT: Yes, sir.

DR. NORRIS: That's the issue involved.

Modernism hasn't anything in its shop that can take a drunkard of sixteen years, father of four little children, and a helpless wife, and reach down and lift him up and up until God's grace takes hold of him, changes him, saves him, makes him over, and gives him to his heart broken wife and little children a changed, sober, saved husband and father. (Applause.)

That is the issue of this present hour in the Temple Baptist Church. And that is the issue as we go forth to battle.

"Oh Thou That Killest the Prophets and Stonest Them That Are Sent Unto Thee"

The biggest issue in this present war is not even the Word of God, important as that is, not the salvation of souls, as everlasting as that is, but the issue is the ministry, "and that I am thy servant." There can be no preaching of the Word if there be no ministry. There can be no salvation of souls if God has no man to proclaim His message.

Everywhere there has been a revival, the salvation of souls, it has been through God's called and anointed men.

The greatest crime of the ages has been committed by this modernistic ecclesiastical machine in murdering pastors in cold blood. The Episcopal form of church government takes care of its preachers, and never murders them. I say it to you deliberately after a quarter of a century of careful observation that these present-day Baptist ecclesiastical machines have been guilty of the martyrdom of more Baptist preachers—oh, their crimes, how great, how many! And the blood of innocent preachers cries out from the ground to high heaven for vengeance!

There sits here this afternoon a minister of high reputation who has held some of the best churches on the American continent in both Canada and the United States. He is out today. Why? He had enough independence to get him into trouble, but the storm was too great. His wife's health is broken, and that in turn has broken his spirit. He is one of the most cultured, Christian gentlemen that I ever met, refined and tender as a mother.

What happened? There was a little inside clique in his church which joined hands with this very Detroit Baptist Union that drove him from the ministry. I repeat the time has come for judgment to begin in the House of God.

I could call the roll. Ten years ago I held a meeting in the First Baptist Church, Houston, Texas. Dr. J. B. Leavell was pastor, and no nobler, finer, greater soul ever walked on shoe leather. It was the greatest revival in the history of Houston, 1010 joined the church as a direct result of the meeting, the present auditorium was built, and the church saved from financial bankruptcy. That should have been enough to have caused rejoicing everywhere. But no. No. We would expect the devils in the lower regions to gnash their teeth at such a glorious victory.

But the denominational headquarters at Dallas, the Sanhedrin, including the president of the Seminary, and the now president of the World Baptist Alliance, all went to Houston ostensibly to hold a denominational rally for a fall round-up. But what was their real purpose?

Dr. Leavell tendered the First Baptist Church for the rally, but the invitation was curtly refused, and this Baptist crowd, the leaders of the Sanhedrin, went several blocks below the First Baptist Church, on the same street, and held their rally in the First Methodist Church. They wanted to show that the headquarters disapproved of Jim Leavell. And why?

All day long they hurled their barrages at him. They broke his heart. And why?

Jim Leavell was a Premillennialist, and he had committed the unpardonable crime of having Frank Norris to hold a meeting for him.

I begged and plead with him to clean house of a little worldly element that was working hand in glove with the denominational politicians. He was a good man, and too credulous. He didn't believe what I already knew, namely, that there was no conspiracy, no scheme, no crime that they would not stoop to commit or perpetrate. They persecuted him. He resigned heartbroken. And at the St. Petersburg Convention I met him in the lobby of the hotel. We went to his room and he fell on his face across the bed and wept his soul out like a whipped child, and said, "Frank, they got me."

In a short time afterwards I saw in the paper, "Dr. J. B. Leavell Dead."

Like the voice of Abel's blood, the voice of Jim Leavell's blood, courageous, noble, consecrated, cries to high heaven today against the tyranny and the persecution of that bunch of ecclesiastical politicians.

Therefore I have dedicated my life to turning on the light, and I will never stop over the radio, on the platform, and in the printed page until I expose the ecclesiastical tyranny which for cruelty would make the Spanish Inquisition blush. (Applause.)

That is the issue that is invloved. And to sum it all up the Word of God is involved, the church of Jesus Christ in involved, the word of Jesus Christ is involved, and the ministry of Jesus Christ is involved.

I call upon you to pray. A revival is on the way, and the work, the stand, the revival of Temple Church, the influence will girdle the globe.

Many Notable Conversions

You recall the answer that Jesus sent to John: "Go and shew John again those things which ye do hear and see: The blind receive their sight, and the lame walk, the lepers are cleansed, and the deaf hear, the dead are raised up, and the poor have the gospel preached to them."

The Sanhedrin, the machine crowd, should sit like Saul of Tarsus at the feet of one Gamaliel, who said: "For if this counsel or this work be of men, it will come to nought. But if it be of God, ye cannot overthrow it."

I have never seen more remarkable conversions than during

these recent weeks. Here is a sample. A man whom I met the first day of the meeting, sad, lost and wicked—he attended the meeting, and the last night when I preached on "Crossing the Dead Line"—and what a day that last day was, when more than half a hundred people came to the Lord Jesus Christ! He was among the last who came. He came to the front, knelt in prayer —then I took him into the pastor's office, locked the door, and I said, "Mr. Ford, what is there in your way?"

He said to me: "I have been a great sinner; have committed every sin; I have plunged into drink. There was born to my wife and me a beautiful baby girl. She lived for more than two years, and was taken away. I feel that I have crossed the dead line."

We knelt together and prayed, and I said, "Pray this prayer: 'God be merciful to me a sinner.' "

He did, and then again.

It was soon over. He was saved then and there, instanter, miraculously, by the power of the grace of God.

I baptized him. His sadness was turned to joy. The old life was gone, and they spent their first happy Christmas together. He is present this afternoon. You know his testimony.

In this hour of world confusion, revolutions, wars, bloodshed, the one and only need and hope is an old fashioned, heaven sent, fire baptized Holy Ghost, sin convicting repentance, born again revival.

Great Revival On the Way

It is already here. There is a "sound of a going in the tops of the mulberry trees."

I was coming up to Chicago the other night on the train, and a distinguished lawyer from Dallas and I were talking over the present world conditions. He said, "I don't look for another revival. I am discouraged. Our civilization is doomed. Look what happened to prohibition, we voted the saloon out, and now the liquor traffic is back worse than ever. Look what happened to the League of Nations. I thought we would have world peace, but now we are rushing to another war. Look at the increase of crime, lawlessness, the breakdown of marriage—I am discouraged over world conditions. Chaos is just ahead."

In part that lawyer is corret. This present civilization is doomed. We are certainly in a time of great chaos, but did you ever stop to think that the very conditions that now confront us through the world conditions of chaos, crime, loss of confidence, the abounding and increased iniquity—these are the very conditions that preceded and characterized every great revival in the history of the world?

Enoch had a great revival before the flood, and iniquity filled the earth, and violence covered the face of the world like the waters of the flood that came immediately afterwards.

Take every great revival in the days of the judges, prophets, priests, and kings—they were confronted with the same conditions.

Take the revival in the days of good king Asa for example. In all the revivals of the ages what do you find? Let the scriptures speak. II Chron. 15·1-10, "And the Spirit of God came upon Azariah, the son of Oded: And he went out to meet Asa, and said unto him, Hear ye me, Asa, and all Judah and Benjamin; The Lord is with you, while ye be with him; and if ye seek him, he will be found of you: but if ye forsake him, he will forsake you. Now for a long season Israel hath been without the true God, and without a teaching priest, and without law. But when they in their trouble did turn unto the Lord God of Israel, and sought him, he was found of them. And in those times there was no peace to him that went out, nor to him that came in, but great vexations were upon the inhabitants of the countries. And nation was destroyed of nation, and city of city; for God did vex them with all adversity. Be strong therefore, and let not your hands be weak: for your work shall be rewarded. And when Asa heard these words, and the prophecy of Oded the prophet, he took courage, and put away the abominable idols out of all the land of Judah and Benjamin, and out of the cities which he had taken from mount Ephraim, and renewed the altar of the Lord, that was before the porch of the Lord. And he gathered all Judah and Benjamin, and the strangers with them out of Ephraim and Manasseh, and out of Simeon: for they fell to him out of Israel in abundance, when they saw that the Lord his God was with him. So they gathered themselves together at Jerusalem in the third month, in the fifteenth year of the regin of Asa."

What do you find?

First: Atheism—"Without the true God."

Second: No religious worship—"without a teaching priest."

Third: The reign of lawlessness—"and without law."

Fourth: No peace and prosperity—"there was no peace to him that went out."

Fifth: The reign of bandits and gangsters—"but great vexations upon the earth."

Sixth: War—"and nation was destroyed of nation."

Seventh: Repentance:—"If ye seek him he will be found of you." "But when they did turn in their trouble unto the Lord God of Israel and sought him he was found of them."

What else?

1. Destructive work.

A lot of denominational leaders go around and say we must not have a destructive work. Well, that is exactly the first thing that took place in this revival and in every revival. Listen at these words: "And when Asa heard these words, and the prophecy of Oded the prophet, he took courage, and put away the abominable idols out of all the land of judah and Benjamin, and out of the cities which he had taken from mount Ephraim." That is exactly what Elijah did. He first destroyed the altars of Baal.

That is exactly the first characteristic of the revival lead by John the Baptist. He used his broad axe and cut down their tall trees of Phariseeism, ecclesiasticism, and hypocracy.

Destructive work?

Every housewife must do a destructive work, or else the cobwebs would cover the walls, and the bed bugs would eat up the family.

Every farmer must do destructive work. He destroys the weeds that the corn may grow.

What is needed today in the churches is wholesale destructive work. Use the broad axe of John the Baptist, not a little pearl handle pen knife on the worldly card-playing, dancing, hell-raising choir, the board of deacons, and the teaching force—clean out all worldliness.

There can be no revival in a church that is run and dominated by the worldly element—"For the time is come when judgment must begin in the house of God."

2. A constructive work. Notice these words—"and renewed the altar of the Lord."

Anybody can destroy, but it takes the spirit of God to build.

Therefore there must be two things in every revival. First, destructive work; and second, constructive work.

"The Days of Mass Evangelism Over"

That is what these machines or ecclesiastical politicians are saying. I don't believe it. They are now going up and down the land, and filling the machine papers full of it saying that "the days of evangelism are over." What they mean to say is that we can't reach sinners by the multitudes any more. If this be true, then the Bible is not true. If this be true, then the Spirit of God no longer works.

I believe that there can be multitudes saved today as never before. I know it is true. I have seen it. We are witnessing it.

Talk about world conditions! Where are we?

Isa. 21:11-12, "The burden of Dumah. He calleth to me out of Seir, Watchman, what of the night? Watchman, what of the night? The watchman said, The morning cometh, and also the night: if ye will enquire, enquire ye: return, come."

What does this mean? Here we have darkness and light coming at the same time. How could this be?

The answer is that we have natural darkness and supernatural light, and the darkness is not able to overcome the light.

Revival Certain

Every century is characterized by a great revival. At the close of a thousand years of darkness there was a great awakening led by Martin Luther, Zwimgli, Melancthon, John Calvin and others.

Papal Rome held the world politically and religiously in its death grip, but God touched the hearts and lives of a few men, and they took as their solgan, "The just shall live by faith," and broke the shackles of Rome.

Another century rolled by, and in the beginning of the seventeenth century darkness again was over the earth, the voice of the priest, not of the prophet was heard. And what happened? God touched the hearts and lives of the Puritan fathers and they shook the world.

Another century rolled by. What happened? Deism reigned supreme. God was out of His universe. But God touched the hearts of John and Charles Wesley, George Whitfield, and others. John Wesley was not permitted to preach in his own church, but he stood on the slab of his father's grave and preached a sermon that was heard around the world.

A part of the crowd attending revival led by Dr. J. Frank Norris in five-pole tent at Oakman Boulevard and Grand River Avenue, Detroit, Michigan. The tent covered 45,000 square feet and seats over 8,000.

Another century rolled by, and darkness again was over the land. What happened? God touched the hearts and lives of a few brilliant minds in Oxford University, and on this side of the waters was a hay-stack prayer meeting, and God called that brilliant scholar Adoniram Judson, and took that shoe cobbler from his bench in England, and another world movement was born. And now in the twentieth century we ask, "Watchman what of the night?"

I am a premillennialist, but I don't support the unscriptural views of some of my premillennial brethren, namely, that while the darkness increases there is not also a light. I believe there will be a great awakening as we come to the closing days. In fact, we are already in the awakening.

I believe with all my soul that future generations will write about this Fundamentalist Movement as historians now write up the Reformation and Wesley Revival and other great awakenings. And as the revolutions have rent and torn to pieces all political alignments and governments of the world, so we are now in the greatest religious revival that time has ever witnessed since, perhaps, Pentecost.

What if the present day denominations are smashed to smithereens? It ought to be. They are unscriptural. I believe as never before in Matthew 16:18, "And I say also unto thee, That thou art Peter, and upon this rock I will build my church; and the gates of Hell shall not prevail against it."

I believe in the scripture which plainly says, "The church of the living God, the pillar and ground of the truth."

And this revival that is now beginning will be characterized by the preaching of "all the counsel of God" from the creation of the universe to the Premillennial Coming of Christ. And the church and no outside organizations, but the one and only institution is the one that Jesus Christ established. There was the "Church of Ephesus," the "Church at Antioch," the "Church in Pergamos," the "Church at Philadelphia"—you will find the local church mentioned in the New Testament 112 times.

Also I believe that this great revival that we are now entering will be characterized by an absolute free ministry, called of and anointed by the Spiirt of God. Our God is not limited. When He wants to have a great revival He can go to the depths of a coal mine in Wales or to a haystack prayer meeting in New England, or he can go to the gang land of Chicago and touch and save a Zeoli.

I am looking for the coming of the Lord, and I believe there is coming a revival, and as the last days approach there will be a mighty spiritual awakening in the body and bride of Christ. Ours is not to redeem the world, ours is to get ready the bride of Christ, and when the midnight hour comes, and we hear the call, "The bridegroom cometh, go ye out to meet him"—Oh, what joy!

> "O'er the gloomy hills of darkness,
>   Look, my soul, be still and gaze;
> See the promises advancing
>   To a glorious day of grace:
>   Blessed Jubilee,
> Let thy glorious morning dawn.
>
> Let the dark, benighted pagan,
>   Let the rude barbarian, see
> That divine and glorious conquest
>   Once obtained on Calvary:
>   Let the gospel
> Loud resound, from pole to pole.
>
> Kingdoms wide, that sit in darkness,
>   Grant them, Lord, the glorious light;
> Now, from eastern coast to western,
>   May the morning chase the night:
>   Let redemption,
> Freely purchased, win the day.
>
> Fly broad, thou mighty gospel
>   Win and conquer—never cease:
> May thy lasting, wide dominions
>   Multiply, and still increase:
>   Sway thy sceptre,
> Savior, all the world around."

"For Many Years I Felt That Frank Norris' Preaching Was a Bit Too Radical"

Since the above address was delivered we have received a multitude of letters from all over the country expressing keen interest in the spiritual awakening at Detroit. The house cleaning resulted in the exit of a small group, but ten times over the numbers have

have come in to take their places, and the revival is increasing.

The far reaching effect of what is happening at Detroit is evidenced by the following letter:

5 Park Street, Boston, Mass., Jan. 21st, 1935.

Dear Dr. Norris:

I have been following with intense interest the swift moving events which have been taking place in your life and in the life of Fundamentalism in these last few months. Your recent triumph in Detroit is a great victory for the forces of conservatism in the United States. The leaders of spiritual life throughout the breadth and length of the land rejoice at this wonderful demonstration of the Lord's power which has been so manifest in the Detroit meetings. The thrilling scenes of reclaimed men and a church revived bring back the halcyon days of revivalism under the Wesleys—and under others who were mighty warriors of God. This is what we need. We are praying here in New England for just such a manifestation of the Lord's power in the hearts of men and women and in the very life of our church. We are Unitarianized here to the point of stagnation. Yet, there is a movement of God's people toward just the very thing which was enacted in Detroit. God is going to meet His believing people. We are praying for a definite outpouring of His Spirit upon our fair land which for so many years has been ground under the heel of modern cults and modern theology.

The Baptists of the North need just such preaching as the Holy Spirit effected in your ministry in Detroit. I have been praying daily that there may be some way in which you can see your way clear to take the Detroit pastorate, if only for a few years. It would be the answer of many praying people for definite leadership in the denomination or at least for leadership among the fundamentalists of the group. A sweeping evangelism of just the same nature would even do more, I believe, to awaken and arouse the church to renewed activity and bring the need of the hour to many who, though earnest and sincere, know little about the inroads that modern skepticism and apathetic leadership are making in our beloved Baptist faith.

Let me say that it was at one of your meetings in the Old Tent Evangel in New York City that I was stirred up with the realization that we were at the cross roads in the faith and a very definite stand must be taken. Your preaching during those meetings inspired me beyond anything that I can express. I had only been converted about a year and was studying in preparation for the ministry when your series of messages put the fiber and faith of our fathers into my soul and subsequently into my preaching. I have been preaching about four years and up until last summer was pastor of a Baptist Church in Lynn, Massachusetts.

For many years I belonged to that group of men in the North who, though conservative to the limit, felt that Frank Norris' preaching was just a bit too radical. But today I realize that the "faith once delivered" is radical, and what we need is a mighty dynamo of such radicalism unleashed here in the North. God grant that you may be instrumental in starting a work in the North that shall ride from east to west on the wings of ministering angels.

Enclosed you will find a money order for a year's subscription to the "Fundamentalist." All that I have learned recently has come through the generosity of a friend who has let me have his papers of the Detroit series. I should like this subscription to begin with the first week of September, 1934. As I begin a campaign in New Britain, Conn., next week will you send all the back issues to me c/o General Delivery, Britain, Conn. From then on send the paper weekly to 5 Park Street, c/o New England Fellowship, Boston, Mass.

Once more may I say, press on, continue to push the battle into the enemies' territory. The battle is the Lord's, not ours. Though we be in the minority, yet Gideon's band has always God on its side. One man plus God or a minority plus God can put to flight the majorities of unrighteousness. As heretofore you have triumphed over those whose cry is always, "Contention brings barrenness" by the multitudes who have been won to the banner of the cross in your meetings, so again may such triumph come with even a greater measure of success as the Holy Spirit speaks and woos through you to the salvation of souls. With prayer and interest in all your undertakings for God, and hoping to have the privilege of meeting you in the near future, I am

Yours in Christ Jesus,

WILLIAM P. WHITTEMORE.

February 9, 1935.

THE RADIO HATE FEST

By Beauchamp Vick

"I Expect to Look Over the Parapets of Heaven and See Frank Norris Frying in the Bottomless Pits of Hell."

I heard the entire radio debate, and here is a sample from the records as taken down:

That is a quotation from the address of President J. L. Ward of Decatur College, in the ill fated radio hate fest where the denominational leaders went on the radio for eight nights to damn Dr. J. Frank Norris. Their addresses were all taken down on wax cylinders and the air was blistering with the bitterest epithets ever heard or spoken.

There is no hate or malice equal to religious persecution. Seventy millions of human lives have gone down to death on the field of battle because of religious wars. There is no hate equal to the hatred of a church row.

Dr. Norris fooled his traducers and did not answer them in kind. They rented the time from the KTAT Broadcasting Company. They contracted for it, but never did pay for it, and after they had made the announcement they were going to expose Dr. J. Frank Norris, he secured the hours immediately following and as they signed off, he signed on. He advertised their time for several weeks before over the radio, in the Fundamentalist, and even took paid advertisements in the daily papers. That a great crowd heard goes without saying—both friend and foe.

As soon as the first speaker, Dr. L. R. Scarborough, was through, telling the world all the mean things he ever heard, thought or felt about Dr. Norris, and that everybody else ever felt, thought, published, circulated, whispered publicly or privately, and there was no prayer, no Scripture, no song.

Immediately when the distinguished President of the Seminary signed off, four young ladies stepped to the microphone in Dr. Norris' study, without any announcement and sang in perfect harmony:

> "For you I am praying, For you I am praying,
> For you I am praying, I'm praying for you."

Without a word of announcement there stepped to the microphone a number of sinners who had been redeemed under Dr. Norris' ministry—men who had been saved from drunkards' graves, saloon-keepers, gamblers, and they all with one accord told the listening audience in a score of statements:

"Go home to thy friends, and tell them how great things the Lord hath done for thee, and hath had compassion on thee."

Then Dr. Norris went on and said: "These men are good men but are mad. I feel sorry for them and I want you to forgive them. I have been mad myself and I know how bad it makes one feel.

"You are not interested in what they think of me, or what I think of them, but I want to take this occasion to call this great listening audience to repentance, and after the world is on fire and the heavens have passed away with a great noise, out in the eternity of eternities, you will have no concern about a denominational row between one insignificant preacher and a group of denominational leaders. Therefore, I want to talk to you on:

"The Great White Throne Judgment

"I quote to you these solemn words from Revelation 20:11-15:

" 'And I saw a great white throne, and him that sat on it, from whose face the earth and the heaven fled away; and there was found no place for them. And I saw the dead, small and great, stand before God; and the books were opened: and another book was opened, which is the book of life: and the dead were judged out of those things which were written in the books, according to their works. And the sea gave up the dead which were in it; and death and hell delivered up the dead which were in them: and they were judged every man according to their works. And death and hell were cast into the lake of fire. This is the second death. And whosoever was not found written in the book of life was cast into the lake of fire.'

"This is the final verdict and doom of the universe. Time is no more. And I pray tonight for some prodigal boy that is away from home, some gray haired father who has gone down in sin, some unfortunate girl without hope, and the moral man without Christ, I pray you one and all to listen to these solemn words, when every one of us, these preachers who are saying all these mean things about me, and I with them, together we will stand before the flaming bar of God's eternal judgment.

> "ETERNITY! stupendous theme!
> Compar'd here with our life's a dream:
> Eternity! O awful sound:
> A deep, where all our thoughts are drown'd!"

Facing the Mob At Decatur

Dr. J. L. Ward, president of Decatur Baptist College called a mob together to "hang Norris" on the court house square in the city of Decatur. He sent wide announcements, circulars, newspaper notices and told in blunt speech that the purpose of the gathering was to "hang Norris."

Hearing about it I drove to Decatur, 40 miles from Fort Worth and pushed my way through the mob and stood in front within ten feet of Dr. Ward while he was making his inflamatory speech.

They refused to give me the chance to reply, but I had already arranged for a truck to be parked on the other side of the square and after three hours of denunciation, I walked out and went around and got up on the truck and the crowd broke from Ward like a stampede of cattle and I had a lot of good humor and told many amusing stories and after a time of laughter and genuine Texas good humor I preached a sermon on "The Prodigal Son," and there were many saved.

Another Mob At Waco

"Whom the Gods would destroy they first made mad." This was the slogan, though unannounced, of the Texas Baptist leaders. In the midst of the red hot evolution fight which ran for a period of seven years during which time the Baptist convention did two things every year, "Hang Norris," and whitewash evolution. However, the convention would pass strong resolutions denouncing evolution, while saving the evolutionists. Debts piled up by the millions, confidence was broken down, but the First Baptist Church grew by leaps and bounds and great crowds turned out to hear me where ever I went.

"Take the War Into Africa"

I called up the auditorium in the city of Waco and rented and paid for it at a cost of seventy-five dollars and announced that I was going to "hang the apes and monkeys on the faculty of Baylor University." The President of Baylor called a mass meeting at the Chapel, and not only did all the students attend, but they came from down in the various sections of the city, Jews, Gentiles, Protestants, and Catholics, and the chapel was packed while they "hung Norris in effigy."

When I arrived in Waco the sheriff and chief of police came to the hotel and said, "You had better not stay here five minutes,

Norris, we cannot guarantee you protection and you must not dare to speak tonight." These two officers, sheriff and chief of police, were quietly informed that this was still a free country and that there was a contract with the auditorium and the address would be delivered.

I arrived at the auditorium an hour ahead of time and every available space was taken and it was impossible to get in through the main door and I had to go into a side entrance and never was there such cat calls, hooting, booing, and yelling. They were plainly, sympathetically, and bluntly told: "You are running true to form and are giving the finest evidence that your ancestors were braying asses, screeching monkeys and yelling hyenas."

Soon the howling mob spent its force and the address was delivered calling the names and giving the records of the evolutionists and at the close of two hours and ten minutes address the audience was in profound silence and their hearts were moved and when the question was put to them whether they believed the Bible versus evolution the entire audience leaped to its feet as one man.

This two hours and ten minutes address was published and it was the end of evolution in Baylor University.

At the next session of the convention Dr. J. B. Tidwell read the clearest address that perhaps was ever delivered against evolution and that address is the official statement of the Baptist Convention of Texas and Baylor University; and the evolution discussion swept through the entire Southern Baptist Convention and at the Houston session I had a huge tent and the leaders were seized with panic and stayed up all night long and the late George W. McDaniel, president of the convention told the leaders the convention would stampede to the tent unless they passed a resolution against evolution. Dr. McDaniel himself opened the convention by offering the following resolution:

"This convention accepts Genesis as teaching that man was the special creation of God, and rejects every theory, evolution or other, which teaches that man originated in, or came by way of, a lower animal ancestry."

New Sunday School Building, Temple Baptist Church, Detroit.

THE FOLLOWING WAS PUBLISHED IN THE BAPTIST STANDARD:
"THE HOUSTON TEXAS REVIVAL
By J. B. Leavell

In the midst of the red hot controversy, my two good friends, who are both now in glory, Rev. I. E. Gates of First Baptist Church, San Antonio, and Dr. J. E. Leavell, First Baptist Church, Houston, asked me to hold meetings for them, which I did.

Then the Sanhedrins did gnash their teeth—"When they heard these things, they were cut to the heart, and they gnashed on him with their teeth."

Dr. E. C. Routh was Editor of the Baptist Standard and got fired because he published the following account of those two great revivals, which are as follows:

(It is no secret that one man in Dallas did the firing. Ask Dr. E. C. Routh of Oklahoma City, and ask Dr. F. S. Groner of Marshall, Texas, who also was fired by the same man.)

"Houston has just seen pass into history what is probably the greatest evangelistic meeting in the history of the Southern Baptists. The meeting was under the auspices of the First Baptist Church of Houston. Dr. J. Frank Norris was the preacher.

"Mr. J. Dalbert Coutts led the choir, furnished wonderful music at the piano, and throughout the campaign directed the orchestra and large choir of two hundred or more voices. Other members of the working force from Fort Worth assisted in the campaign. All the forces from the First Church, Houston, stayed faithfully in the campaign from start to finish. The meeting was planned for six weeks, but was continued through its seventh week. Dr. Norris preached twice each week day and three times each Sunday for the eight Sundays.

"1010 Added to the Churches.

"I wonder if any meeting ever saw as large and definite results. 720 people united with the First Baptist Church alone. Most of these came by baptism. This brings the total membership of this church to nearly 5000. 1010 came to all the churches in the city. All the Baptist churches in the city received additions, and probably every Protestant church. Pedo-baptists were borrowing baptismal pools to take care of those who came to them and would not be satisfied with anything but immersion for baptism. The work was definite and thorough with all who came forward. The pastor had a conference with each one individually at the front seat before they were received into the church. People joined from every faith and sect. Every Pedo-baptist denomination made its contribution, and many Roman Catholics. Christian Scientists, Russellites, Spiritualists, etc., made profession and received baptism.

"The Tabernacle was the largest ever built in Texas; seating capacity estimated at from six to eight thousand. It overflowed several times, was always taxed to its capacity on Sundays, the crowds were vastly increasing on week days during the entire period. The Tabernacle was situated at Main and McKinney—in the very heart of the business section. A building had just been torn down for larger construction, and we fortunately used this strategic point during this interval.

"The meeting presented many unique features. Notable among these are the following:

"That a campaign of such proportions should be launched and carried by one church. The magnitude of it will compare favorably with any big campaign in which all denominations and churches participate.

"The expenses of the meeting ran to over $12,000. This was cared for by plate collections.

"Again it is noteworthy that the evangelist received not one cent personally for his services. It was Dr. Norris' proposal that the meeting only take care of such expenses as were incurred in his own church because of his absence, stating that he felt the prolonged absence had encumbered upon him to supply the program at his own church. Every personal contribution went in this fashion, the checks were made payable to the First Baptist Church of Fort Worth amounting to approximately $2,000.

"Another notable feature was that Dr. Norris felt that his greatest compensation was in the fact that his labours went to the establishment of the life of a down-town church. He shares the conviction, with many, that the down-town church is the greatest factor in modern church life. Never did a man find a more critical need in a great church, and never was a church more firmly established by an evangelistic effort. During the meeting it was announced that the pastor had fully refinanced the entire project and included in the deal was sufficient funds to guarantee the completion of the large auditorium. This auditorium will seat 3,400 people. This unit of construction will complete the actual needs of the First Baptist Church, at least, for the present. It leaves also a valuable lot on Main Street, which carries a potential value of nearly a fourth of a million dollars.

"Probably the most prominent and glorious feature of the meeting was the exaltation of the Word of God. Few, if any, living preachers have so mastered the Book. Surely no living preacher is so zealous in its defense. The preacher not only unfolded the Word in a most masterful fashion in every service, but flayed error and the enemies of the truth in the most fierce and fearless fashion, that the mind could imagine. Even the old soldiers of the cross would cringe in the midst of these attacks.

"Again, there was a total absence of emotionalism. The appeal was rather made to the intellect; often more than half of the time used by the speaker would be in reading the Word of God.

"During the campaign the people were led through the Books of Genesis, Revelation, Daniel, Malachi, Acts, and in almost every sermon there was reference made to every portion of the Book from beginning to end. The issue was clearly drawn in the Word of God, and the fruitage from such sowing will be flowing in for years and years to come.

"Dr. J. Frank Norris is a unique man. He is a far broader and deeper man and more resourceful than anyone could ever imagine except through a period of association, fellowship and service. It seems to me that any unbiased student of his life testimony and tactics would be forced to the conclusion that he is actuated by the holiest and purest passion for the Cross, the triumph of the Word and the hastening of the return of the coming King. Amen."

THE BAPTIST STANDARD PUBLISHED THE FOLLOWING:

"DR. J. FRANK NORRIS LEADS FIRST BAPTIST CHURCH OF SAN ANTONIO IN THE GREATEST REVIVAL MEETING EVER HELD IN TEXAS, AND, AS FAR AS I KNOW, IN THE SOUTH.

By I. E. Gates

"I have been pastor of the First Baptist Church of San Antonio for nearly six years, and, only attempted one revival meeting in all that time. However, we have had great ingatherings all through the months and years, from the regular services. But I felt, and my church felt that the time had come to have the greatest meeting in the history of this city. We have tried evangelist after evangelist, but we always failed to do what we had hoped to do. In making preparation for this meeting, my heart turned to my old boyhood friend, Dr. J. Frank Norris, as the only man who could lead us in this great revival, and do for us what we wanted done. I have known Dr. Norris for twenty-seven years. I knew he had built a great church in Fort Worth—the greatest in America. But I did not understand fully how he could hold, for fifteen years, such multitudes every Sunday.

"I found out the past six weeks more than I ever knew about him.

"The First Baptist Church made the greatest preparation for this revival that any single church in America has ever undertaken to do. We erected a tabernacle, costing $5,000.00, with a seating capacity of around 5,000. We conducted pre-revival services for weeks ahead, making the best preparation possible for this great meeting.

"After we had engaged Dr. Norris to hold the meeting in the Spring, he felt that he ought to go to other engagements and postpone our meeting until fall. I was determined that this should not be done, for so much depended upon a great revival just now. My church building program was hanging in the balance, and so many other things were depending upon this meeting that I got on the train and went to Fort Worth and spent some time with him. I told him we could have five hundred additions, and stir all Texas. And when I laid out my plans before him, thoroughly, he agreed to come.

"I never saw a campaign in my life, and never hope to see one that has produced so many results. We had more than six hundred additions to the First Baptist Church alone, most of whom came by baptism, while hundreds of others joined other churches —Methodist, Baptist, Presbyterian, Campbellite, etc. We did not count the 'reclamations,' 'reconsecrations' and 'conversions' as is commonly reported by the thousands in many of the modern evangelistic campaigns. We could have made a greater show, but the church, myself and Dr. Norris were unanimously against it.

"I was not prepared to appreciate what was coming, for I never heard such gospel preaching in my day. Dr. Norris is the greatest Bible preacher that I ever heard. He is familiar with every book of the Bible, and can quote more Scripture in every sermon than any man I ever heard. He made all of his evangelistic appeals on the Word of God. He preached one whole week on 'Hell,' until I could hear the wails of the damned, and smell the smoke of their torment. And upon his first invitation, on Sunday night, one hundred and seven people joined the church. I never heard such sermons on 'Hell.'

"I am convinced that we are preaching too little on the doctrine of 'Hell.'

"He gave one whole week on 'The Work of The Holy Spirit,' and I never heard a man magnify the Holy Spirit as he did in Creation, in Regeneration, and in the Resurrection.

"He preached on every doctrine held by Baptists, including three sermons on 'Baptism'; two on 'The Lord's Supper' and one on 'The Final Preservation of the Saints'; several on 'The Church' and a dozen or more on 'The Second Coming.' He named and denounced every modern sin in no uncertain terms. I never saw people cringe and tremble under the power of the Gospel like they did under this modern John the Baptist preacher. I saw men rush up to the mourners' bench and cry out, 'Men and brethren, what must I do to be saved?' I saw men and women who couldn't speak the English language, come to the front under the power of one of his sermons, and ask 'What must I do to be saved?'

"He spared nobody. He denounced sin in high society, in low society and in no society; in deacons, preachers and elect sisters, until all of us came to the mourners' bench and got right with God.

"He preached a whole week on 'Roman Catholicism.' I never heard such an exposition as he poured out his soul. He preached on:

" 'The Romanists versus the Bible on the Lord's Supper.'

" 'The Romanists versus the Bible on Papal Infallibility.'

" 'The Romanists versus the Bible on the Confessional of the Priesthood.'

" 'The Romanists versus the Bible on Saint Worship.'

" 'The Romanists versus the Bible on The Purple, Scarlet-Robed Woman of Prophecy and History.'

"I never dreamed that any man had the courage to stand up before thousands of people in San Antonio, dominated by Romanism and speak out as clearly as he did for one whole week.

"His sermon on 'The Infallibility of the Pope' was a masterpiece. I have heard B. H. Carroll in his palmiest days, but I never heard a sermon with more fire and logic than when he exalted Christ and proved that the Papacy is unscriptural. I did not know what might happen, but I sat behind him and gripped my chair with my hands and prayed God to give him the message, and he put it across and settled for all times the Fundamentals of Protestantism in San Antonio, till Christ comes. Large numbers of Roman Catholics have joined our church and I have baptized them. This series of sermons was the talk of the town. In fact, the whole meeting was the talk of the town. Never did a man dominate a city like Frank Norris dominated San Antonio. Of course, the devil got busy, as he always does, when God's people move.

"His first great fight was a newspaper fight, and what he did to the Express Publishing Company cannot be written down. The night he took them to a skinning, it seemed to me he had five acres of people present, besides those who were on the roof, trying to look over the banisters to see what was going on. Razor blades were in the air, one hundred feet high, as this John the Baptist wth his broad axe, stood up there before ten thousand people and denounced the Express Publishing Company for boycotting the meeting.

" 'About a week later, we had another great fight, brought on by a combination of a Jewish Rabbi and the Knights of Columbus, and when he got through with them, the dust was settled in San Antonio for the rest of the meeting. He gave them 24 hours to apologize, and the last paragraph in their apology is as follows:

" 'For all of this, as well as any and all words of criticism direct or implied, I have ever expressed concerning you, I again sincerely and unqualifiedly apologize, and I fully retract any and all derogatory statements made by me concerning you as unfounded and unjustified.

" 'Again expressing my deep regret and apologies for this entire unfortunate affair, for which and its consequences, I accept full personal responsibility, I am,

" 'Very sincerely yours,

" '(Signed) ....,'

"I never saw a man who could keep his head and speak with such deliberation and calmness and courage as Frank Norris can, in a great battle. I think he is the most courageous Baptist preacher living on the face of the earth. He looks like a timid, modest man until he becomes aroused, and then his eyes flash fire and his words bite and sting those who are guilty of sin.

"Sometimes I felt like pulling his coat tail and asking him, 'Is there no mercy?'

"No other man living could have done for San Antonio what ought to have been done right now, but Frank Norris. We have been dominated in this city so long by Romanism, that large numbers of our people felt that there was no use to protest. But this great meeting has put new courage and fighting spirit in every Protestant and Baptist within one hundred miles or more of this place.

"I will never be the same man any more. I have always been a peaceable man, and tried to get along with people, but my firm conviction is that Gospel preaching ought never to be defensive, but offensive, and aggressive, with the fighting spirit of a Savonarola, Martin Luther and John the Baptist. This is Frank Norris' style and manner of preaching. He never pussy-foots. He never compromises, he never palliates the Gospel, he never spares anyone's feelings, because he knows he is right, he knows his Bible, and he knows the Lord, and loves His Church.

"He preached three times a day while he was here and gave conference lectures on the side, to our Sunday School teachers, officers and deacons. He taught us more how to organize and make effective the working forces of a great church, than any man who ever came to see us. His plans are the most simplified I ever heard expounded, and when you have heard him, you know it is the only way to make it go. He never theorizes, he never tells you what the book says—he talks from experience, but he knows what he is talking about, and he makes you feel it. I never heard a man, in my twenty-five years of ministerial life, who knew as much about church life, and organization, as Frank Norris. I do not wonder now why he holds the multitudes in Fort Worth, and has the greatest church in America.

"Of course, nobody can do exactly as Dr. Norris does. He would be a fool to try it. But a man can be himself and take his methods and double any church in the world. I have found out several things from him that are the secret of any pastor's success.

"There must be a Spiritual leader somewhere, and the pastor is that man. Several of my deacons learned that while he was here. Some of the elect sisters and the choir director, and the pastor.

"He is the most loyal man to a pastor in a meeting, that I ever had to help me. He allows nobody to talk about anybody else in his presence, nor to criticize and find fault and grouch around.

"He is the most untiring worker that I ever knew, and he has no patience whatever with men and women who will not work, but who seek to give advice. He just cuts them off at the knees and lets them alone.

"When I asked him to come and hold this meeting, I made up my mind fully to let him be the boss and give his directions, and there I showed sense. I never crossed him in any suggestions; I tried to do what he wanted done, for I knew that he knew what ought to be done. I backed him up to the limit, in all of his fights, and urged him on—and our people did likewise. I found no white-livered cowards among our crowd when he got in a scrap with the devil, or the forces of evil.

"Of course, there was some prejudice on the part of some people in San Antonio, to Dr. Norris' coming here. But when they heard him, they became his most enthusiastic admirers, and so far as I know, everybody here is for him now—Baptists, Protestants, and the man of no church. I never saw such a campaign, going six weeks, with such sustained interest. The fact is, the last week was the greatest of all, and he did his best preaching that week.

"Some of the Results

"I repeat, over six hundred people joined our church, most of them by baptism. I am not counting 'reclamations' and 'conversions.' If we had counted these the results would number into the thousands. Our church was completely reorganized, with doubled efficiency. The great doctrines of the Baptist Church were emphasized as I never heard before, in a revival. The cause of Christ was put forward in this wicked city, as no man had ever done or could do. Our new church enterprise was brought to completion, with the breaking of dirt, and the raising of the money to build the first unit of a million dollar enterprise.

"After we heard Dr. Norris for six weeks, we were ashamed that we had done so little, and we have undertaken a ten year program, with a million dollar objective, and with ten thousand membership in the First Baptist Church.

"All these things were made possible by this great revival. There will not be bad after-effects, for his sermons were not sensational, yarn-telling and clown performing; nor were they a bundle of grave-yard stories.

"He built his sermons on the Word of God, and our people will never be the same any more, and will never put up with sop and cider preaching.

"One of his greatest sermons was one on 'The Bible Versus Evolution.' That sermon attracted as much attention as any sermon ever preached here, and it was unanswerable. I know the fight, I know the big fight we are in now is between Fundamentalism and Modernism, and I am lining up, and my church, with the Fundamentalists.

"The revival will continue, for we are going to move our platform and seats out into an open lot near the church and continue this meeting until Christmas, and the First Baptist Church expects to have 1,200 additions, or more, this year. We have had over 800 up to now, with half the year to go. We are going to set the world's record for 1924, in church additions.

"When the new church is done, I have invited Dr. Norris back to hold another meeting, and he has agreed to come, and I look for the next meeting to go beyond the present one. I want everybody to know that San Antonio appreciated Dr. Norris beyond words to express.

"He not only captured the Baptists, bag and baggage, but all other denominations, and thousands of Catholics as well."

"Signed I. E. Gates."

A section of the large crowd that heard Dr. Norris in Berlin.

"J. FRANK NORRIS IS AN OUTCAST"—"HE HAS NO STANDING"—"I RETRACT AND APOLOGIZE"

These two quotations are from the pen of Dr. H. C. Gleiss, Executive Secretary of the Detroit Baptist Union. Dr. Gleiss holds a most responsible position among Baptists of the great city of Detroit. One of his principal missions is to have men called to churches who are in sympathy with the State Baptist and Northern Baptist Conventions. He was very active in the call of a pastor to Temple Baptist Church, following the resignation of Dr. Albert Johnson.

When it was evident that the mind of the church turned toward Dr. J. Frank Norris all the "organized forces" led by Dr. Gleiss did everything in their power to prevent the church from calling him. Therefore a strong minority opposed the call. Not on personal grounds but on denominational grounds. The same issues have been involved in every call of a pastor throughout the Northern Convention.

After the call it is well known that the outside convention forces interfered continually with the work of the church.

Dr. Gleiss came out in the daily papers and said, "J. Frank Norris is an outcast and has no standing."

Another concrete example of the conspiracy against the work of Dr. Norris was a telegram which Dr. H. C. Gleiss sent to Pittsburgh.

This telegram fell into Dr. Norris' hands and he demanded proof or retraction by Dr. Gleiss who was gentlemanly enough to write a "retraction" and "apology."

Telegram To Shut Dr. Norris Out

WESTERN UNION

"936 FEB. 1 A.M. 8:15

"GM. 86 NL. PITTSBURGH, PENN., JAN. 31

   "W. A. MORGAN
   "410 PENNY AVE. KD

   "YOUR LETTER RECEIVED. DR. GLEISS OF DETROIT WHERE MAN HAS BEEN RECENTLY WIRED IN AN-

SWER TO MY INQUIRY AS FOLLOWS: HE HAS NO STANDING. HE IS FIGHTING BAPTISTS EVERYWHERE, ATTACKS CHOICEST LEADERS AS TRUETT AND BEAVEN. HE HAS NO STANDING IN ANY BAPTIST CHURCH IN THIS SECTION. HE IS GREAT AT DESTROYING, BUT NEVER OF USE IN BUILDING UP ANYTHING. IT WILL BE RUINOUS TO HAVE HIM COME. CONSIDER WELFARE OF YOURS AND OTHER CHURCHES. MY ATTITUDE EXPRESSED BY EZEKIEL 33:6.

"LESTER BUMPUS,

Sec. Pittsburgh Bapt. Assn."

THE "RETRACTION" AND "APOLOGY" BY DR. GLEISS

"Detroit, Michigan
"February 13, 1936

"Rev. J. Frank Norris,
Temple Baptist Church,
14th and Marquette,
Detroit, Michigan.

"Dear Dr. Norris:

"Replying to your letter of February 6th, I beg to say that it was a mistake to send the telegram. I very much regret that it was sent and I apologize.

"When the telegram says, 'He has no standing in any Baptist church in this section' it is an error. Since you are in excellent standing in your Temple Baptist Church, it is evident that the statement is incorrect, hence I retract it and apologize, as you request.

"I am sending a copy of this letter to each, Mr. W. A. Morgan, of McKeesport, Pa., and to Rev. Lester W. Bumpus, of Pittsburgh, Pa., explaining its purpose.

"As to your statements three and four, concerning me, you have been misadvised, and as to the statement as to why I left Pittsburgh, that is also untrue.

"Respectfully,

"H. C. GLEISS."

DR. GLEISS SENDS APOLOGY TO SECRETARY
PITTSBURGH BAPTIST ASSOCIATION

"Rev. Lester W. Bumpus,
Pittsburgh Baptist Association,
239—4th Avenue,
Pittsburgh, Pa.

"Dear Dr. Bumpus:

"Dr. Norris sent me copy of telegram you sent to Mr. W. A. Morgan, McKeesport, Pa. You quote me as having said things objectionable to Dr. Norris, and in part incorrect.

"I regret very much sending the telegram.

"I have written Dr. Norris my apology, copy of which is hereto attached.

"Respectfully,

"H. C. GLEISS."

DR. GLEISS SENDS APOLOGY TO McKEESPORT, PA.

"Mr. W. A. Morgan,
410 Penny Avenue,
McKeesport, Pa.

"Dear Mr. Morgan:

"Dr. Norris sent me copy of telegram you received from Rev. Lester W. Bumpus, February 1, 1936. It quotes me as having said things objectionable to Dr. Norris, and which are in part incorrect. I regret very much the telegram was dispatched.

"I have written Dr. Norris my apology, copy of which is hereto attached.

"Respectfully,

"H. C. GLEISS."

The above is just one of the chapters of the inside story and there are many others similar.

During his 26 years in Fort Worth Dr. Norris conducted 81 tent or open air meetings. The above picture was taken of his meeting on East Weatherford Street, Fort Worth, 1934.

WHY TEMPLE BAPTIST CHURCH WITHDRAWS FROM NORTHERN BAPTIST CONVENTION

Northern Baptist Machine Officially Endorses Two Principal Russian, Communistic Organizations in America

"WE WILL NOT SERVE THY GODS"

SERMON BY DR. J. FRANK NORRIS, SUNDAY AFTERNOON, JUNE 30, 1935, DETROIT, MICHIGAN

(Stenographically Reported)

Lenin Has Won

DR. NORRIS: There is today a worldwide propaganda, very insidious, and it is high time this country was aroused to it. The greatest brain this generation has ever witnessed was Lenin of Russia. He had the greatest scheme of ~~propaganda~~, and here are some of his emthods. I have ~~read~~ most of his writings. First, he said to his constituents, "When you go to other ~~countries deny~~ you are a Communist; never admit you are a Communist." First, win them.—"Then," he said, "we will attack the schools, then the pulpit." And that from the brain of a man who set in motion the propaganda and schemes that destroyed the pulpits ~~and churches~~ in Russia!

The first method is to honey-comb the churches, then destroy them. Now that is the method we have in this country, the same thing. You take perhaps the most outstanding Bishop known among the Methodists—I know there are people who say they don't think we ought to deal in personalities—my answer to that is then don't let them deal in things that destroy our young men and women and their personal faith—(applause)—my answer to it is that I am opposed to Bishop Francis J. McConnell being active in the American Civil Liberties Union—in this country there are forty some odd organizations of Russian Communism. The principal one is the "American Civil Liberties Union"—get the Red Net Work and read it—everybody ought to read it. You find in there a long list of prominent citizens listed as members of this "American Civil Liberties Union"—also you will find the wife of the President of the United States! You will find the President of the Chicago

University there, too, and a long list of prominent educators. It is a fulfillment of the Scriptures that while the men slept the enemies sowed tares.

During the five years of the greatest depression—and everybody wants to relieve the depression—here is what has happened over night. The various denominational organizations have ceased to preach the Gospel of blood redemption—they have even gone so far that they say, the preachers from the pulpits, that mass evangelism is a thing of the past, and that we can't have great revivals where people are born again individually—no, now they say what we need to do is to clean out the stables, clean up society—like some Baptist preachers who met up here at Lansing, and it came out in the papers that they agreed that it was their business to bring about a "social reconstruction."

When Northern Baptist Convention Went Over to Communism

In 1934, at Rochester, New York, there was a meeting of the Northern Baptist Convention and they appointed and endorsed a Committee of nine, and that Committee was to be known as the "Social Action Commission." All I say is being taken down and will be published so as to get it to you.

Now here is the exact language—I quote it to you:

"That the Northern Baptist Convention desires that the churches shall have an approach"—and the words they use are "economics," "political," and "international affairs"—and by that vote last year the Northern Baptists went into the realm of "politics," "economics" and "international questions."

Let me put before you this question: Suppose that the next day after Pentecost, where they had three thousand baptized, then the church numbered 3120—suppose the next day after that great baptizing, Simon Peter had gotten up in church and said, "Brethren, I move that we go on record—appointing a committee to see about this church going into the realm of economics, into political and international affairs of the Roman empire."

Suppose you could read that in the New Testament?

Of course you say the very statement of it is absurd. Yet, my friends, that is exactly what the Northern Baptist machine has done. They brought that report to the Convention last week in Colorado Springs, and instead of their ending the matter, putting it on ice, they did this other more subtle thing—oh, the serpent is more subtle than any other creature—they got together and said, "Here, we will put this on the churches."

So now they have placed at the door of every church of the Northern Baptist Convention, from Maine to California, this social, economic, political and international plan of preaching the gospel of "Social Justice."

"Oh," you say "the churches won't go into it." But wait a minute—this morning three Baptist pastors of Detroit spoke on it, and they are in favor of it. I have the notes taken of what these brethren said. We had just as well make up our minds to it, a lot of the churches are going to adopt the report.

That crowd met out here the other day and they discussed what they were going to do with me. I may have to decide what I am going to do with them. (Laughter). My paper has wide circulation and I am going to publish anything about anybody, even the devil himself, when I think it ought to be done.

Here is what the Pastor of Jefferson Avenue Baptist Church said this morning. I have the stenographic notes:

"It was a great report on Social Action; and it was received unanimously. I didn't hear a negative vote, neither did the President of the Convention. It was a great report— a great report of 15,000 words. The papers said that there would be terrific opposition, oh, of course there were some small eddies—it was the most forward looking expression of a mighty denomination."
Then he said further:

"This report is going far, how far we do not realize. . . . it is the only course for sanity and safety"—and he repeated that several times.

Now, he said it was received unanimously, and he said there might be some words in it that one might desire to change here and there but that the liberalists and fundamentalists with one united voice spoke to high heaven.

Incidentally, Dr. W. B. Riley will be here July 16th, and he will bring us a first hand report. I wired him yesterday to come on. And this is just a little introduction this afternoon to what we are going to have.

The shrewdest scheme of the devil is not to deny outright—what do you think they are saying now?—that Jesus was a Communist;

a great social worker. My friends, the method of Jesus was to reach the individual soul as He reached Nicodemus, and changed that individual's heart—and then the redeemed individuals change human society.

You can see at once, if the devil could put over the scheme of getting the churches to be silent on blood redemption, individual salvation, of course he would have won the church to his side. Now, you Baptists have to face that situation.

I am glad to tell you the Board of Deacons of the Temple Baptist Church unanimously adopted some resolutions, and I am going to give everybody a chance this afternoon to express themselves on them, then, so nobody can raise any question, in two weeks every member will register his or her vote by private ballot, so when it is over we will have a legal record.

I think this is the largest church thus far that has made a protest—I don't say the church is unanimous—I am not interested in that. They are unanimous in the graveyard—all heads point in the same direction. (Laughter).

Now let me get the question clearly before you. The two centers today of Communism are:

First: The universities.

Second: The denominational headquarters.

I know that is shocking, but that is true. Remember what has been their platform. It has been to deny they were Communists, but to spread their doctrine in a subtle manner. To deny the name doesn't change them any—you can change the name of the rose, and it won't change the sweet aroma. You can bring a skunk under this tent, and he will change this audience just as quickly with any other name. (Laughter).

To show that is their method, to show you I am not speaking idly, I want to call your attention to two things in this morning's paper—here—three columns wide, big headlines, "RADICAL PROPAGANDA AIMS AT MINISTERIAL 'ROUND-UP'."

Now you folks who live up here in this city don't know what a "round-up" is. I have rounded-up, and I have been rounded-up—I went out one afternoon to round up some cattle—and I made the mistake of walking out among them, the first thing I knew they were rounding me up, and the only way of escape I could see was a Chinaberry tree a quarter of a mile away. You talk about a boy running—I ran, and I ran—those steers kept me up in that tree all day, and left a standing committee to stay there that night—I know what a round-up is. (Laughter).

But the article:

"Strenuous efforts are being made by radical propagandists to swing the clergy in behind programs ostensibly 'liberal,' but which are linked in a plan to set up some sort of Socialist republic and destroy democracy as we have known it.

"The most pretentious attempt at 'rounding up' the ministry has been made by the magazine, 'The World Tomorrow,' through the circulation of a long list of questions among ministers and divinity students. This has resulted in a declaration by Kirby Page, editorial writer, that"—This paper, "The World Tomorrow," is the official organ of the Civil Liberties Union of America—and incidentally, Kirby Page, the editor, wrote the life of Jesus Christ, and he delivered the Commencement Address to Baylor University's graduates, three years ago—I took them to a cleaning for it. Now Kirby Page says:

"Among all the trades, occupations and professions in this country few can produce as high a percentage of Socialists as the ministry."

That is what was published this morning in one of your papers, and here is the result of the questionnaire sent out:

"'The World Tomorrow' questionnaire went to 100,000 persons. Replies came from about one-fifth, 20,870, and Editor Page writes:

"'Of the total number responding, 62 per cent record themselves as pacifists"—friends, there is nothing in all this "pacifism" —it is all Russian Communism. We don't want any Russian pacifism while they are arming to the teeth—We need to arm to protect our country, our homes.

"Even more encouraging"—says this official organ of Russian Sovietism in America:

"Even more encouraging are the tendencies reflected in the answers of the students in theological seminaries, 73 PER CENT OF WHOM ARE PACIFISTS, AND 48 ADVOCATES OF SOCIALISM."

Now the brood of cuckoos are hatching, they are coming out in this country and are preaching in the pulpits of this land! That is what you Baptists are supporting every time you put a dime in this machine, and every time you give, you encourage this Communistic, Socialistic, unbaptistic machine. Yes, sir. Will you continue?

Crowd: "No."

Furthermore I want to show you something else—this was published in the 27th issue of one of your papers. Listen to this:

"Red Week"

" 'Red Week' on the campus of the University of Chicago, which has just been freed by a legislative investigating committee of Communist propaganda, shows the lengths to which the subversive elements will go when there is no active, aggressive opposition.

"The students were addressed, among others, by"—I wouldn't attempt to pronounce these names—I'll just spell them to you—"Trovarish Trovanovsky, Russian ambassador, and Trovarish Boyeff, of the Amtorg Trading Corporation.

"The boys and girls are being told the advantage of swapping vodka for our capitalistic-cursed machinery.

"Is the University of Chicago an American educational institution or a branch of the Moscow department of foreign trade?"

Here is something else, I want you to get it—yesterday afternoon there came out in the Evening News an interview with Dr. H. C. Gleiss in which he says that the report on this "Social Action Commission" was "epochal"—that is what Dr. Gleiss says. Dr. Gleiss is head of the Baptist machine here in Detroit—what there is left of it. (Laughter). Now, furthermore he said, that this report was not Communistic, yet he goes on and says:

"The topics touched upon in the report include peace, international relations, economic and industrial affairs, rural life and rural churches, marriage and the home, temperance and the problems of alcoholic beverages, propaganda and education and race relations."

All these questions are the very platform today of this social gospel. Not a word is said about blood redemption in the report.

Now Dr. Gleiss said there was no Communism in his report— let me show you some things—and you Methodists and you Presbyterians and Congregationalists—it is not only the Baptists, but that is what all your machines have gone over to.

Now here is part of the report that was authorized by the Northern Convention's endorsement:

"1. That the N.B.C. institute a board for social action, which shall have adequate funds at its disposal to accomplish the work that may be assigned to it.

"2. That the N.B.C. adopt and work for the realization of a program of social change which shall embody in general such features as the following:

"(a) Society (the people acting through the state) shall assume control (which may involve actual ownership) of all the God-given natural resources of the earth; including the land surface, mineral and oil wealth and the products of lake, sea, and river, including the water power.

"(b) Society shall control or own all natural monopolies that have to do with the necessities of modern living, such as the water supply, gas, electricity, telephone, telegraph and radio.

"(c) Society shall control or own such competitive businesses as have to do with the necessities of life (milk, bread, coal, oil, gasoline, etc.) in order to eliminate the waste in production, competition and mismanagement, and to guard against the very life of the people being made the sort of financial hocus-pocus. For the immediate future the competitive profit system should be restricted to the non-essentials of life.

"(d) Society shall take over the entire control of the money and banking function and conduct it as a non-profit producing social service.

"(e) Society shall tax incomes by a scale that will help to prevent the accumulation of great money-power in the hands of individuals or groups of individuals. * * * * * *

"3. That the N.B.C. through agencies already in existence or to be created for the purpose, shall adopt a definite plan (five-year, ten-year) for the education of its clergy and other teachers, in the social, business, political and industrial implications of the Gospel."

Not one word said about blood redemption—it is a social, business, political and industrial program.

What Was the Purpose of the Northern Convention?

Ladies and gentlemen, I quote to you what was the purpose of the organization of the Northern Bautist Convention. This Convention was organized in 1907—what would be—7 from 35 would be 28 years ago—now there are those who say we cease to be Baptists if we withdraw from the Convention—we are going to answer this question if this church votes to adopt this resolution, and I think I know what this great people will do—the deacons have already unanimously adopted it—and I am going to give you the opportunity to express yourself—to the question that we cease to be Baptists—in the first place, Baptists were here 1900 years before you ever heard of the Northern Baptist Convention. The second answer is that the charter of the Northern Baptist Convention states specifically that the purpose of the Northern Convention is for the evangelization of the world, and not to go into politics, not to regulate society and the economic life; no, but to preach the Gospel. They put it in there 28 years ago. The Northern Baptist Convention was not organized for the purpose of taking over Henry Ford's plant, the Chrysler, or taking over the telephone companies or oil companies—I am not going to argue whether they ought to be taken over—the point I am making, that it is not the business of the churches to enter into business, to regulate society or enter into the field of economics. It is the scheme of the devil to sidetrack the Church of Jesus Christ from its one and only commission, yet the head of the Baptist machine of Detroit says this report is "epochal."

I think they are going to find themselves split from Maine to California.

Here is the answer—the third answer, instead of this church ceasing to be Baptist—the answer is it has remained Baptist—and the fourth answer is that the Convention crowd, this Socialistic, unbaptistic, modernistic, compromising crowd have gone off from Baptist doctrines. It is a fulfillment of the Scripture which says, "They went out from us because they were not of us."

"The Evangelization of the World"

This is the chartered purpose of the Northern Baptist Convention. It is found in Section 2, of the articles of Incorporation.

"The Evangelization of the World"; Beautiful and Scriptural. If the proponents and organizers of the Northern Baptist Convention had put it in the articles of Incorporation that it is the purpose and aim of the Northern Convention "to approach or regulate the social, political, economic and international" questions of this age and generation—the Convention would have died still-born.

Therefore, the church which refuses to endorse this socialistic scheme of the Northern Baptist Convention and remain true to the one and only mission of the church; namely, "The Evangelization of the World"—it is the Convention and not the true churches which has ceased to be Baptist. The Convention machine has departed from the true faith and gone off after false gods. It is the Convention, and not the churches, that is offering "strange fire." The Convention comes with the hands of "Baptist orthodoxy," but with the voice of Russian Sovietism.

"Well, now," somebody says, "look here, I am a deacon in a church and the pastor is a modernist, what can I do?"—Well, if you haven't sense enough to know what to do I couldn't advise you. (Laughter). Suppose I give you some Scripture on that—here is what it says, II Cor. 6:14-18, "Be ye not unequally yoked together with unbelievers: for what fellowship hath righteousness with unrighteousness? and what communion hath light with darkness? And what concord hath Christ with Belial? or what part hath he that believeth with an infidel? And what agreement hath the temple of God with idols? for ye are the temple of the living God; as God hath said, I will dwell in them, and walk in them; and I will be their God, and they shall be my people. Wherefore"— what does it say? Listen—"come out from among them, and be ye separate, saith the Lord, and touch not the unclean thing; and I will receive you."

I make bold to tell you here these preachers who masquerade under the livery of heaven—I don't care how many degrees they have after their names—LLds, DDs, Asses, they are infidels when they deny the Word of God. Yes, sir—I have more respect for Tom Paine in his grave, and Bob Ingersoll—at least they had self respect enough to stay out of the church and out of the pulpits— they were not like these little modernistic, lick-the-skillet, two-by-four aping, asinine preachers who want to be in the priest's office so they can have a piece of bread, and play kite tail to the Communists.

I am not going to say anything about them this afternoon, but I plan to do so sometime soon. (Laughter).

"Oh!" some sister will say, "I don't think that's the Christian spirit"—Honey, you wouldn't know the Christian spirit, any more than a bull would know Shakespeare. (Laughter).

I'll tell you the spirit we need in this compromising, milk-and-cider, neither-hot-nor-cold—you want to know the kind of spirit we need? We need the spirit of old John the Baptist when he told that Sanhedrin, "You are a generation of snakes."

We need again the spirit of the Apostle Peter when he stood before the Sanhedrin and said, "Is it right to obey man rather than God."

Talk about you Methodists, we need again the spirit of old John Wesley when he preached out of his father's church and stood on his father's slab and preached a sermon that shook the world! (Applause).

We Baptists need the spirit of Roger Williams when he walked out in the snows with the Naragansett Indians rather than to stultify his conscience.

We need again the spirit of those Baptist preachers in 1767 yonder on the Court House yard in old Culpepper, Virginia, when stripped to the waist with hands tied and held up, the strap was put on their bare backs and drops of blood fell—Patrick Henry rode up and said, "What crime have these men committed?"—When they answered, "They were preaching the Gospel of the Son of God without a license." He answered one word three times: "My God, my God, My God."

Hear me, friends, you Baptists especially, the scheme today is what? To Sovietize the churches of America, to honeycomb the public schools, then the red propaganda can go on unmolested. They know if they can break down the voice of the pulpit—the greatest moral force time ever witnessed, they will have this whole country—yet you Baptists will go and put your money, your time, your presence into that sort of thing. You say, "What can I do?" "Come out from among them, and be ye separate, saith the Lord."

Friends, there is going to be a separation—all present existing denominational machines are gone—you Methodists, your machine is gone, too, and it ought to be gone—the truth of Jesus Christ will survive, but we are going to have a terrible conflict in this country and we had just as well face it—that bunch of atheistic, Communists have charge of this government, and it is high time we found it out. (Applause).

Now if that be treason, make the most of it!

If the laboring classes think they will solve their problems by going Communistic—Come with me down into the mines of Russia and see the condition there—if the farmers think it will solve their problems come with me and I will show you five million Kuluks, the owners, the highest class of farmers, driven from their homes to yonder cold Siberia never to return. If you think it will solve your problems, go yonder and see the greatest country in the world for resources—it is the devil's scheme to destroy this present civilization—But I believe old America will stand! (Applause.) We will meet them at Philippi!—They snatch the new born babies from their mother's arms—They don't believe in marriage—a man may be mated a dozen times—there is no regard for sex relation. This is not hearsay. I know what I am talking about. I have seen it first hand.

What shall we do? "Wherefore come out from among them, be ye separate, saith the Lord, and touch not the unclean thing; and I will receive you."

Old Amos says, "Can two walk together, except they be agreed?"

Here is the situation we are facing—I am talking about our own upheaval—we are going to let you backslidden Methodists alone while we attend to ourselves—follow me—your machinery, your leadership, your Board, your officialdom, your Detroit Baptist Union, the head of it—they come out and say, "This is our platform"—not mine. I am not going into any social, economic, political scheme instead of blood redemption. (Applause). That is what we are facing. Now whenever we render encouragement to that bunch of modernists, when we bid them Good speed, just remember what Jehu said to Jehoshaphat when he returned from battle where he had made an unholy alliance with Ahab, "And Jehoshaphat, the king of Judah returned to his home in peace to Jerusalem, And Jehu the son of Hanani the seer went out to meet him, And said to king Jehoshaphat,"—Listen to this— "Shouldest thou help the ungodly, and love them that hate the Lord? therefore is wrath upon thee from before the Lord."

Listen again to the Word of God on what we should do—Rev. 18:-5, "And I heard another voice from heaven, saying Come out of her, my people, that ye be not partakers of her sins, and that ye receive not of her plagues: For her sins have reached unto heaven, and God hath remembered her iniquities."

Now you will be glad to hear this resolution recommended by unanimous vote of the Deacons—and this is what I am going to ask everybody here this afternoon to express themselves on:

WHEREAS, the Temple Baptist Church of Detroit, Michigan, has supported and co-operated with the Northern Baptist Convention and the Baptist Convention of Michigan, by sending money to their Boards and delegates to their annual meetings;

WHEREAS, June 24th, 1935, the Northern Baptist Convention at Colorado Springs forced on the churches of the Northern Baptist Convention for their consideration, adoption or rejection, the Communistic plan of Karl Marx, by the following action of the convention:

"1—Received the report and authorized the General Council to make it available to individual churches for study.

"2—Continued the Social Action Commission for a year with the understanding that its educational program and peace plebiscite among churches be conducted only for those churches desiring them.

"3—Stated that neither the whole 15,000-word report nor a part of it 'shall be made a test of Baptist fellowship or service.' "

Let me stop here—I want to say that I can turn to fifty places in the writing of Karl Marx and find that identical expression, "Social Action Commission"—Yes, sir, and that instead of being put on the table has been forced upon the churches—that is what they propose to put over—that isn't all:

WHEREAS, the Northern Baptist Convention officially appointed the "Social Action Commission" for the avowed purpose of binding the Convention to a political and economic program which is a violation of the most fundamental doctrine held by Baptists, namely, the separation of church and state; and further the Convention by its action in receiving, authorizing and continuing the "Social Action Commission," and forcing its communistic plan upon the churches, has thereby thrust a divisive issue among all the churches;

WHEREAS, the report of the "Social Action Commission" sums up, sets forth, and advocates essentially the revolutionary, communistic plan of Soviet Russia, which is better known by its American Brand of "New Dealism";

WHEREAS, the one and only business of the church and the ministry is not to enter into or regulate the economic or political affairs of the Government, but to follow the admonition of our Lord, "Render to Caesar the things are are Caesar's, and to

God the things that are God's," thereby maintaining the age-long and cherished Baptist faith of separation of church and state; that the one and only mission of the church of Jesus Christ is to preach the gospel of salvation to the individual, thereby carrying out the Great Commission, "Go preach the gospel to every creature";

WHEREAS, the leadership of the Northern Baptist Convention and the State Convention of Michigan, has departed from the age-long and Scriptural position held by Baptists, by substituting a so-called social or communistic gospel instead of the gospel of salvation for the individual soul;

WHEREAS, ten years ago the Northern Convention at Seattle, Washington, adopted what is known as the "inclusive policy," sending out both modernist and fundamentalist missionaries, and at which Convention the action adopting the inclusive policy repudiated a resolution offered by the late Dr. W. B. Hinson, "requesting all the missionaries of the Northern Baptist Convention to signify their belief and acceptance of the fundamental doctrines of the Virgin Birth, the Deity of Christ, the Atonement on the Cross, the Resurrection of Christ, and the New Birth of the individual soul";

My friends, you can get the Minutes and you will find where they turned down Dr. Hinson's resolution; namely, "Requesting all the missionaries of the Northern Baptist Convention to signify their belief and acceptance of the fundamental doctrines of the Virgin Birth, the New Birth of the individual soul."—My friends, I saw that crowd of Northern Baptist modernists vote that resolution down two to one. Here is what it means: It means that the missionaries don't have any longer to believe in the Atonement on the Cross, in the New Birth, in the Deity of Christ, in the Virgin Birth, or the Resurrection of Christ—no, they are going out under a social gospel that has dictation over the churches.

Readng on, the resoluton:

WHEREAS, there has rapidly developed in the Northern Baptist Convention an unscriptural and unbaptistic, ecclesiastical, centralized dictatorship over the churches, as evidenced by many definite, concrete actions through the years, the latest of which is the action of the Northern Baptist Convention at Colorado Springs when the Convention "authorized" in the report of the "General Council" to the churches what was designated by the "15,000-word report" of the "Social Action Commission";

WHEREAS, the so-called plan of designation of mission funds is a misnomer and dishonest, because when the church designates a certain amount to a mission station the Foreign Mission Board simply decreases the appropriation to that station, thereby forcing orthodox Baptists to support, in an indirect though very definite way, the unscriptural, modernistic, socialistic leadership of the Northern Baptist Convention;

WHEREAS, the Northern and Michigan Baptist Conventions belong to, and are a part of the World Baptist Alliance, which is controlled and dominated, in the main, by modernistic leadership; and

WHEREAS, the Temple Baptist Church has been on record for several years in its stand for the hitsoric faith once for all delivered to the saints;

THEREFORE BE IT RESOLVED, by the Board of Deacons of Temple Baptist Church, and the members of the entire church, in special called session at 3:00 p. m. Sunday afternoon, June 30, 1935, that we exercise, as a church, our inalienable, sovereign right as a body of believers, in recognizing Christ only as head over all things to the church, and reaffirming our faith in the fundamentals of the Christian faith as commonly held by Baptists; and further we reaffirm and declare it our purpose to have no part or lot with the unscriptural, unbaptistic, socialistic, modernistic Convention;

RESOLVED SECOND, in separating from these bodies, from these eclesiastical organizations, which have departed from the faith held by Baptists, we call upon all true orthodox Baptists throughout the Northern Baptist Convention, to join with us in contending for the faith once for all delivered, and giving the gospel of salvation to the individual soul;

RESOLVED THIRD, that we reaffirm our faith in those foundation principles—freedom of speech, freedom of press, and freedom of worship;

RESOLVED FOURTH, that Temple Baptist Church urge every individual member to make regular contribution to worldwide missions; and that we support the Association of Baptists for Evangelism in the Orient, which Association of Baptists has adopted the identical Confession of Faith held by the Temple Baptist Church;

RESOLVED FIFTH, that copies of these resolutions be given

to the denominational and secular press that the world may know of the uncompromising position and stand of the Temple Baptist Church against all the present day vagaries of modernism, socialism, communism, ecclesiasticism, and our positive stand for the faith in the whole Bible as our only rule of faith and practice.

The Dishonesty, the Duplicity, and Insincerity of These Denominational Politicians

I know that this is strong language but we are performing a major, triple operation in order to save the patient.

You have noticed how these denominational politicians are saying that the report of the Social Action Commission is not communistic.

Here they are following the advice of their patron, Lenin. I can take the writings of Karl Marx and Lenin and put them beside the identical writings of the Social Action Commission.

Now, I am going to make a charge that the Social Action Commission and Russian Communism, especially two principle American branches are identical. Let me quote from the report:

"We are convinced that the economic system as it has been operated has also created serious obstacles to Christian living. There are multitudes of Christians in high and low positions in our economic and industrial life who desire to express their Christianity in these relations but who find it impossible within the system. The church has a responsibility to them. It is futile to bring up generations of youth in Christian ideals which they are compelled to discard when they go out to make a living. Christians owe it to themselves and to their fellows to work for an economic order in which Christian motives have freer chance for expression and in which Christian ideals have larger hope of realization.

"The possibility of change for the better must be accepted as a fact by the Christian. The economic system has been man-made and it can be changed by men. Changes must begin with the individual and an improved operation of any system rests with individuals. "No gain can be achieved by society that is not supported by human wills."

"In view of these conditions, what may be done by our denomination to effect the changes which are necessary to provide more opportunity and encouragement for men and women to live as Christians in their economic and industrial relations and to secure fundamental justice for all?

"It is clear that the denomination corporately cannot prosecute particular measures for social change. It should however have a constant program of education on these matters for its constituency which will enable them to act in accordance with Christian standards in these relations.

"We therefore recommend that such a program be conducted by the denomination through the local churches with the following definite objectives:

"I—To create social attitudes based on these fundamental considerations: * * *

"II—A second definite objective of such a program of education should be to keep before our constituency certain basic issues, among them being:

"(1)—Economic security for all. This would involve general education on the need of unemployment, sickness and accident insurance and old age pensions; assembling and distributing the facts relative to specific measures for economic security; making available lists of information sources and agencies; and co-operation with other denominations and agencies for the furtherance of economic security.

"(2)—Collective bargaining in industry. This would involve a program of education for a better understanding of the relative positions and problems of employers and employees in bargaining over wages, hours and conditions of work; and further the provision for a social action committee in every church, or in co-operation with other churches, to ascertain and publish the facts in the event of conflict and to encourage the exercise of moral judgment; and finally the support of whichever party in a dispute is in the right by purchasing the products of the industry or by contributions to the needs of the workers of funds, moral encouragement and places of meeting where needed.

"(3)—More adequate representation of consumer interest in the determination of economic policies. This would involve the study of how the government may safeguard the consumer and promote his welfare and how consumers themselves may be informed so as to buy for their real needs and best interests instead of being at the mercy of the producer's and seller's advertising.

"(4)—Keep open the channels of discussion of controversial economic and industrial issues. This would involve the dissemination of information about anti-sedition legislation designed to prevent the discussion and advocacy of legitimate economic changes and the organiaztion of sentiment and effort for the defeat or repeal of any such laws as infringe upon constitutional liberties. It would also involve giving moral and financial support to those who have been the victims of discrimination.

"III—A third definite objective of such an educational program for the denomination should be to inculcate in individuals worthy economic motives and incentives that through them the basis of the economic system may be shifted from that of acquisitiveness to that of service. * * *

"IV—A fourth definite objective should be to impress upon our individual members the importance of effecting changes in the economic order by the exercise of their three-fold citizenship, political, civic and economic.

"(1)—By political citizenship support should be given to whatever political party or candidate represents, on the whole, the most favorable disposition and opportunity to effect the desired changes. Since, however, the major political parties have not come to be in any considerable measure parties of clearly avowed and continuously held social principles, political effectiveness through them in the direction of the desired economic changes must involve support of smaller interest and pressure groups whose intelligent and persistent advocacy may lead to the espousing of social principles and programs from time to time by these major parties. Such pressure groups are numerous and range in point of view in our country from the American Liberty League to the League for industrial Democracy."

"There Is Death in the Pot!"

Now we have the whole thing out. Two of the principal Russian Communistic organizations in this country are "The American Liberty League" and "The League for Industrial Democracy."

Just think of it, you Baptists, the free-est of the free people, the most patriotic! The Baptist machine authorized a committee of nine to bring in and report endorsing the two principal branches of Russian Communism!

What will you Baptists do?

What answer will you give?

So help me God, I will never bow the knee to Russian Communism in capsule form! (Applause).

Shall we sit supinely by while Lenin's Communism plays the Trojan horse act on our Baptist churches?

Northern Modernists Control Southern Leaders

Yes, Dr. A. W. Heaven runs and controls Dr. George Truett, who is sound in the faith personally, but he runs with modernists, especially when he comes North. He was eulogized to the skies by one of the modernist pastors in the city this morning. He is President of the modernist World Baptist Alliance, which is no more and no less than a small self-appointed group of modernists, pussyfooting so-called fundamentalists down South to do their bidding—there is where the trouble comes.

Now friends we have crossed the Rubicon. We have come to a great hour in this country—everybody realizes it—in the realm of politics and business as well as in the realm of religion. We are facing Kadesh-Barnea, and I make bold to declare to you who believe in a supernatural Christ, who believe He had a supernatural birth, believe He lived a supernatural life, believe He spoke supernatural words, performed supernatural miracles, died a supernatural death, had a supernatural ascension and is coming back in supernatural glory to establish a supernatural kingdom —people who believe these things are going to get together in this country of ours! (Applause).

We are in another Reformation period like they had in the 16th century—let me say something—every century has witnessed a great awakening—the 16th century witnessed the Reformation led by Martin Luther, and other great reformers; the 17th Century witnessed a great awakening led by the Puritans; the 18th Century witnessed a great awakening led by Whitfield, Wesley and others; the 19th Century witnessed what was known as the Oxford movement and the modern missionary movement; and the 20th Century is more than a third gone—Watchman what of the night?

"We Will Not Serve Thy Gods"

Here is what is coming, what is happening, God's people, the

"Seven Thousand" who have not bowed the knee to Baal are awakened and coming to light! We are coming to a time as witnessed in the third chapter of Daniel, when there went forth the decree from Nebuchadnezzar that all the people in every province when they heard the sound of the cornet, the flute, the harp, the sackbut, the psaltery, the dulcimer, and all kinds of musical instruments, that they should bow down and worship that image of gold 60 cubits high and six cubits wide, out in the plains of Dura; and every man that did not bow down and worship would be cast in the fiery furnace, and when the sound went forth, every prince, every sheriff, every secretary, every denominational leader bowed down and worshipped that statue of gold—except three that stood erect with heads up, and when the report was carried to this old king that these three Jews would not bow, he was filled with rage, and he called them before him while he sat on his throne, and said to them, "Is it true that you will not bow down as I commanded?" They said, "We are not careful to answer thee in this matter"—"We won't even bother to answer you. We will not put on your socialistic modernistic program." And they said, "If you do put us into the fiery furnace, our God whom we serve is able to deliver us from the burning fiery furnace, and he will deliver us out of thine hand"—"But if not, be it known unto thee, O king, that"—and here is my text— "We will not serve thy gods, nor worship the golden image which thou hast set up!" "We will not submit to your ecclesiastical tyranny." (Applause).

So today—America has had its Valley Forge—America has had its Gettysburg—America has had its Culpepper Court House —America has had its Concord—America has had its Alamo—and today our forefathers though they sleep in the ground, yet their spirits go marching on, and we will not bow down to the red flag, regardless of what name it comes to us under. (Prolonged Applause). We still hold our allegiance to the greatest flag that was ever unfurled to the breezes. We will still hold the Bible of our fathers and mothers. We still believe Jesus Christ was born of Mary a virgin, that He lived a sinless life, died for our sins, was buried in Joseph's new made tomb, on the first day of the week He rose, bursting asunder the bars of death, and rose in triumph and victory and glory, and that He ascended back to the right hand of the Father, leading captivity captive, and giving gifts to men, and that one day He will come down the pathless skies, surrounded by a great company of angels to put down all rule, and to establish His reign on the earth!—I still believe it friends. (Prolonged applause).

Oh, God give us a little backbone—I am praying that the preachers will wake up—here is what is going to happen among Northern Baptists, and it is true in the South.

"Oh," somebody says, "there goes Norris stirring up controversy"—Yes, and I am going to stir up some more, too. Sure. Yes, my friends, old Isaiah had some controversy. Old Jeremiah had some when he walked the streets with the ox yoke around his neck—he had some more when they put his feet in the stocks and put him up for a laughing spectacle, but it only served as a pulpit for Jeremiah, and he kept on preaching—and they put him in a pit and he spoke out of the darkness of the pit—and when Jerusalem was destroyed, Nezuchadnezzar said, "Jeremiah get in the royal chariot and go home with me." But no, Jeremiah said, "I'll stay here and preach and preach to these poor folks."

John the Baptist stirred up opposition—he had lots of it until a little old flapper dancing girl danced is head off, but he woke up in heaven. Simon Peter stirred up a lot of opposition, and was crucified head downward, and today he walks the streets of the New Jerusalem! Paul had controversy for thirty years, until his head fell from the block yonder in that old Roman prison—he said, "Henceforth there is laid up for me a crown of righteousness, which the Lord, the righteous judge, shall give me at that day: and not to me only, but unto all them also that love his appearing."

Yes, sir. Let me tell you something friends, if a preacher is not stirring up the devil he is dead—already sold out. (Applause). Pray for me folks. I need it.

Think I will tell you a little secret right here, and I want it clearly understood—some of these dear preachers got together the other morning and said, "We are not going to have any business meetings this summer, and we won't grant any more letters this summer, and the Norris show will be over by that time." Here is what they said, "We know that Temple Baptist Church won't take in any members unless they present a letter."—See their scheme? But we beat them to it—the church voted that any Baptist could come into the church without a letter—so if you want to get in a church that stands wholly upon the Word of God, just come on we will take you upon experience. And all you

Methodists who have been dry-cleaned, come on and I will put you under so deep you will know you have been buried with the Lord—and all you Presbyterians, you won't go to heaven until I bury you. (Laughter).

The announcement I am going to make is this—friends, hear me, God is moving today as never before—a certain gentleman, I am not allowed to give his name asked me the other day—he said, "Norris suppose you had a big lot on which to build a brick and concrete, fireproof tabernacle that would seat six or seven thousand on one floor, would you build it?" I said, "Give me the lot." He answered, "The lot is yours." (Applause).

We could put up a big tabernacle for about twenty or twenty-five thousand dollars—folks let's build it, what do you say? (Applause). And when the frosts and snows of winter come, and the hail comes, and the rain comes, and everything comes, the Northern Baptist Communism, and the devil himself, we will preach, and pray, and shout, and sing, "The Old Time Religion," until Jesus Christ comes! (Applause). Let's build it. Folks, it is going to be done right here. (Applause). Give that to that Baptist Hindquarters with my regards. (Laughter). Tell them we are going to run on—I haven't anything against them; no, I haven't any more against them than I have against the dead. (Laughter).

Now I think we will have a new vision, a new spirit. I used to hear—Say, many of you were raised on a farm, weren't you? I was too. Well, you know the difference between "Gee" and "Haw"—this crowd doesn't know anything about it—I am going to do my best. Oh, don't I remember when the day's work on the farm was done, the mules and horses were in the stalls eating corn, hay, and fodder, mother in the kitchen washing dishes getting ready for an early breakfast—my work was to feed the horses and milk the cows, and when I would get through, I was sleepy and tired, and I would wash my feet and crawl in bed, and I could hear my mother finishing up in the kitchen, and I could hear dear old Dad going out in the front yard with his long stem clay pipe in one hand and his "Brown Mule" in the other. After awhile he would pack that old pipe full, strike a light and lean back against a tree, out under God's stars, and as a typical Southern gentleman, he would sing with a broken voice, but a voice with music out of a soul tuned in with God—I can hear him now as it came floating out on the cool, clear summer night:

"Am I a Soldier of the Cross."

I didn't understand it then. I wondered why, but in a little way I understand it now, and the son of that old farmer today is ready to join hands with every true soldier of the cross around the world, and say, "We will go forth for our God is a Man of war, the Lord of Battle, and we are not in a losing fight, we are in a winning fight." (Applause).

Must Take Sides

Every time I go to San Antonio, Texas, and in many ways it is the most fascinating city in America—every time I go there, and I go often, I have held many meetings there—I never let the time go by that I don't go to that historic shrine, the Alamo—sometimes when my spirit is drooping I love to go there and walk through that old mission—I can stand there and hear again the rattle of musketry and hear the cannon balls hurled against those thick walls, while 183 Texans, brave men from every state in the union, were surrounded by 7000 well trained men under Santa Anna—at last when old Travis saw that soon they would be entirely surrounded, and all hope of escape would be cut off, he called that crowd, then only 175 who could stand, called them together and said, "Men we can yet escape, but if we wait longer we will die. What will be your answer?" "Now," he said, "others can do what they please, but I am going to stay here—I am going to stay here and die for the liberty of Texas," and he walked to the end and unsheathed his shining sword and began here at a wall, 187 feet from one wall to the other, and old Travis drew a line from one wall clear across to the other—"Now," he said, "gentlemen, I want to know how many want to die for the freedom of Texas? If you do, step over this line with me"—And every man leaped across that line. Old Bowie was there on a cot bleeding from a dozen wounds received in battle—Bowie raised up, looked and said, "Take my sword, take my hat, take my coat across"—and when they had taken them over the line, he tried to get up, but fell back, and he said to the men, "Take me across." And they grabbed his cot and moved him across, and when the battle was over in the room where he was dead, Mexicans were piled ten feet high around him. Not a man was left in that crowd—only one woman got away. Well it has been said "Thermopylae had a messenger of defeat, the Alamo had none."

As I stood there where more than a hundred years ago old Travis made the call that set the Lone Star State free, and made it the Lone Star in this glorious Union—I could hear him calling,

"Every man who wants to die for this liberty of Texas come on this side of the line." Friends, today I hear another voice calling —He died on Calvary—He arose from the grave; He is coming; He is calling—How many of you Baptists, you Methodists, you Presbyterians, will cross over the line? How many will cross over this afternoon? As for me, I have already crossed over; friends, I have enlisted for war!

A few hours ago when my son, a young lawyer, 29 years old, switched in so that great crowd at Fort Worth heard me, he said, "Dad, the auditorium is packed, and people standing"—and when the broadcast was over he said, "The people are weeping and shouting, they are coming and rejoicing."

Oh, my friends, I see the time when the dead in Christ shall rise, and wars will be no more—and we shall be changed in a moment in the twinkling of an eye, and we shall go sweeping through the air like Elijah in a flaming chariot surrounded by holy angels—and friends, when I look on His face, then that will be glory enough for me? (Shoutings: Amen).

Folks, I have crossed over! How many will say, "Here is my hand preacher, we will cross over today?"

I am going to ask first of all, you Baptists that believe that the only business of the church is to preach the Gospel. How many Baptists here this afternoon will say, "That is my conviction, my platform, my faith, and I will live and die on it," stand to your feet. (Hundreds leap to their feet. Now you Methodists who want to say it stand up—you Presbyterians, stand up—all the Disciples, who want to say it, stand up—now all other Protestants who wish to stand on it, get up—yes, I will give the Roman Catholics the opportunity to stand against this bunch, you can stand too—all who want to say, "I am against this socialistic, modernistic gang" stand up on your feet.

Now, how many members of Temple Baptist Church—every member of the Temple Baptist Church here this afternoon hold up your hands.

I want to say to all you Baptists, not members of the Temple Church, everytime you go down and put in your time and money into one of these modernistic churches you are guilty of giving them encouragement—(Voices, Amen). You should not be partakers of their sin.

(Invitation. Large number came).

Meeting With the Ministers and Missionaries of the French Bible Mission.

THE NEW TESTAMENT DEACONS

Sermon by Dr. J. Frank Norris, Sunday Morning, Nov. 28, 1937
(Stenographically Reported)

DR. NORRIS: I want to talk this morning as one big family. We have such a large number of new members coming in all the time that it is necessary we discuss things often.

We are many people with many ideas. The time has come for the annual election of officers. The church elects thirty deacons every year. Some churches elect them for life. They have "life-termers" in the penitentiary, but I don't believe in it for a church. If the deaconship is a burden then it ought to be borne by others, if it is an honor then it ought to be passed around. There is no Scripture for "life-termers" for deacons.

The church elects thirty deacons, then the deacons appoint three committees:

First Trustees. These are required by the laws of this state, to hold property, sign all contracts, deeds and so on and all by authority of the church. They are a necessary legal proposition.

Second: another committee is the Finance Committee. They handle the finances of the church. It is their duty to be responsible for all financial accounting to the church, sign checks, and make distribution, and make regular auditing through certified accountants. The books are audited at regular times, and everybody can have full access to all financial records at any time.

Third: the Discipline Committee. These men act on all matters of discipline, and this committee acts by the authority of the church. It is the height of folly that an unseemly piece of misconduct should be brought before a great congregation. We would make ourselves the laughing stock of the devil himself. This committee, the same as the other two, should be composed of the very highest type of men, filled with the Spirit, possessed with plenty of good common sense, and men who hold the confidence of the entire church. The Discipline Committee has performed nobly, tenderly, as well as courageously. All matters of misconduct or breaking of the covenant can be brought before this committee, and they will receive and consider the same patiently and prayerfully.

Therefore I am going to read what the Scriptures say on deacon-ship. In electing these men we want to keep this in mind. Futhermore we are going to have ballots made, and you can put your names on the ballot as has been done formerly, and in that way the entire membership can have a say so—I want everybody to have part. I have never been afraid to trust a great body of believers. Let the folks express themselves. I am never afraid for a thing to come before the congregation. I am not only not afraid for it to come, but want it to come, let all the people talk on it, and everybody pass on it, and that matter is settled. Like a fellow came to me and said, "I can't get along with my wife, what must I do?"

I said, "How long have you been married?"

He said, "twenty-two years."

"You should have come to see me the day before you married. It is to late now, brother. (Laughter.)

Some of you men know what I am talking about—some of you women too. (Laughter.)

So with the church, as long as the matter is pending, a dis-cussion is in order. That's the time for full expression, but when once a matter is settled, and then becomes the unanimous ver-dict of the whole church, it is settled forever. This must be true or there never could be any harmony and fellowship. However in case a brother could not conscientiously go along with the majority of his brethren, he can exercise the same right that he possessed when he came into the church. There are two doors to every church. The front door and the back door. And they should be like the door to the New Jerusalem, never shut.

One very happy thing about this church and the one in Fort Worth, neither church will tolerate for one hour any disgruntled individual, however good, or high, they may be or have stood, to go around trying to sow seeds of discord. I am little concerned about what they do on the outside, and the church will see to it that it does not occur on the inside.

I am just going to read this Scripture—if it means deacons—we will just accept it that it does mean deacons.

Acts 6th Chapter: "And in those days, when the number of the disciples was multiplied, there arose a murmuring of the Grecians against the Hebrews, because their widows were neglected in the daily ministraton"—I want to stop here and say this: "Now this was right after Pentecost—they had had a great baptizing, 3,000 —one Scripture says "about five thousand"—another says "a multitude"—another "multitudes." Isn't it peculiar that right in the midst of this great revival the devil got in the church. Why, in the preceding chapter two prominent members died three hours apart. They kept back some of the Lord's money, and now in the very next chapter they had a row over some Jews, Greeks, money and widows—get those four things together and you can have a row anywhere. Did they stop everything and settle the row?

No, the preachers said, "We can't afford to stop the revival to settle this row over some widows, Jews, Greeks, and money." How are they going to settle it? "Then the twelve called the multitude of the disciples unto them, and said, It is not reason that we should leave the word of God, and serve tables. Wherefore, brethren, look ye out among you seven men of honest report, full of the Holy Ghost and wisdom, whom we may appoint over this business"—

Seven men and they were to have the following qualifications:

1. "Full of the Holy Ghost."
2. "Wisdom."
3. "Men of honest report."

In other words:

1. They were to have a heart full of religion—"full of the Holy Ghost."

2. "Full of wisdom"—common sense—vision—people don't care how good they are they ought to have some sense; they need sense—good common sense. Some people think the less sense you have the better qualified you are for religious work. If there is any place in the world that needs real good sound judgment it is in the Lord's work.

3. Men that the people can trust—men that have a good reputation.

Therefore they said, select men who have got good sense, and there is no use to select men the church can't trust, and no use to select men who don't have a good case of religion.

"Appoint Over This Business

The next statement: "whom we may appoint over this business."—Mark this word—"appoint over this business." It does not say they appointed these men as a committee to meet together and whatever their findings were to come and bring to them— they said "whom we may appoint over this business." In other words, they could trust these men, who were Spirit-filled and reputable men. If they couldn't trust these men, then they couldn't trust anybody.

Let's be practical—Therefore when they appointed these men, the business was turned over to them. It was the church that delegated that power and authority. Any sovereign body has that right, any fraternal body has that right, any corporate body has got the right to delegate to any body of men to attend to certain business.

"Whom we may appoint over this business—so we can go on with the main business."

Take on the question of discipline. I remember the first little country church of which I was pastor had an awful row over a 16 year old girl dancing— they argued back and forth, and so help me, if the church wasn't torn all to pieces over this girl dancing, and the next thing two women got to pulling hair— well, that thing went on for about six months, and I made up my mind I would stop the whole business— and there were two deacons in that church who were never so happy as when they could raise a row. I just decided I would stop it.—How many of you have known churches in your existence that were torn and rent by factions just because two people got cross ways with each other? Hold up your hands. (Numbers of hands lifted.)

Now it is the business of the pastor to stop that. You can put this down, whenever there are factions in the church you blame the preacher. He should teach and administer that church so as to prevent that, and if he doesn't, fire him and get another. If the congregation goes wrong blame the preacher, if it goes right you get the credit and give God the glory.

If a man's family goes wrong he is to blame for it. He is the head of the household. I am doing a little private, quiet instruction here this morning. How many of you think I am right? (Voices: Amen) I know you think so.

I am talking here this morning about the administrative affairs that mean a great deal to the larger growth of this church. And we are beginning in a larger way. There is nothing on earth as satisfactory as a happy fine fellowship in the church of

God, but it has got to begin way back down deep, and build on the Word of God—"And the saying pleased the whole multitude: and they chose Stephen a man full of faith and of the Holy Ghost, and Philip, and Prochorus, and Nicanor, and Timon, and Parmenas, and Nicolas, a proselyte of Antioch." And the Apostles went on preaching the word.

Turning on over to Timothy, first Timothy, we have a word said about the deacons, and we will just take what the Word of God says, I Timothy 3:8, "Likewise must the deacons be grave, not doubletongued, not given to much wine, not greedy of filthy lucre."

"Must be grave"—that doesn't mean they must go around looking like sour-grapes. It means they must take their work seriously. Not that it is to be a great burden to them. It is a burden, but a happy burden. That's one of the qualifications of a deacon.

Here is another, "not doubletongued"—I used to have a deacon who would brag on me to my face and stick a knife in my back—as they do sometimes down in Texas. (Laughter)—Yes, down in Texas thirty years ago (laughter).

"Not doubletongued"—I had a deacon once—he just couldn't say too much praising me. When he would pray he would tell the Lord what he thought of me—he wasn't praying, he was telling the Lord what a wonderful young pastor they had—and no sooner than he would get out of the church he would go over the neighborhood criticising me, and I made up my mind that the next time he began like that I was going to sink his cork—so he began one day, "Oh, Lord we thank Thee for this young Timothy who has come into our midst—it is so wonderful how he is lifting us up to the gates of heaven!"—

I said, "Brother Deacon, Brother Deacon"—everybody stopped—I said, "That's not what you said to Sister McGee last Saturday"—that ended the prayer. It wasn't any prayer; it was downright lying, and I didn't want the Lord to strike him down. It it a dangerous thing to praise a man in prayer and then go around and lie on him privately.

You hear somebody say, "I don't like the way Norris does things"—well, you do it your way and I will do it mine. It is usually some preacher that I have helped who says it.

I am sure the 450 false prophets didn't like the way Elijah did things. But the Lord did.

I am sure the sanhedrin didn't like the method of John the Baptist. But he was a man sent from God!

"Not doubletongued"—not two faced. I wish that some deacons, I mean some of those who lived a way out West that I knew thirty years ago, I wish they had a monopoly on this. The meanest trait that even the devil himself would not be guilty of—"two-faced"—why, I have heard of some preachers—I knew one or two when I grew up who would get up in meetings, associations and Conventions, and just brag, and brag, and brag to the skies on a fellow pastor, then put their feet under my mother's table and criticize this same preacher behind his back

Now passing on, "not given to too much wine"—a deacon hasn't any business drinking wine. He has got to be sober.

"Not greedy of filthy lucre"—no covetous man ought to be a deacon. Just let a covetous man get on the deaconship and it will be worse than a speckled apple in a barrel of good apples. He will never tell you what his real objection is, but he will hinder the work and fear it will cost him something. Yes, a deacon has got to pay the price for being a deacon. He must be liberal with his purse.

"Holding the mystery of the faith in a pure conscience"—that doesn't mean the faith of salvation. It means the doctrine. It doesn't mean personal faith. It means the faith once for all delivered to the saints.

"And let these also first be proved; then let them use the office of a deacon, being found blameless." It doesn't mean they have to be found perfect. It means this, that their conduct and life be consistent with their profession.

Deacons' Wives

The Lord knew when a man was appointed a deacon his wife was appointed also, therefore He says, "Even so must their wives be grave, not slanderers, sober, faithful in all things." If a deacon has a slanderous wife, then he is in trouble to begin with. I am talking about some wives down in Texas thirty years ago. (Laughter).

If a man has a wife who can't control her tongue he has no business being a deacon. What is he going to do with her? That's his business not mine.

This is the one disease, a long slanderous tongue, that cannot be cured. It is not exactly the unpardonable sin, but it is next thing to it, and the funny part of it is you never saw a long tongued woman in your life that would admit it. There are two sins never confessed:

First, a preacher never confesses the sin of jealousy,

Second, a woman never confesses that she is a gossipper.

Since there is no cure, the deaconship should not be cursed with a man who has a wife who has a tongue long enough to sit in the parlor and lick the skillet in the kitchen. I have known of more church trouble to come from deacons' wives, and preachers' wives too. There are two sides to this business of a long tongued woman.

First, not only what she tells, Second, but still more, what she hears.

That has been the most glorious happy thing of my ministry. I will give a man any reward if he will find where anybody can go to my wife with any unseemly or schismatic story. I have known of more preachers that have been wrecked because their fool wives would sit on one end of the telephone and be the sewer for the whole neighborhood.

And a church can be just kept stirred up all the time. And only one or two deacons' wives are necessary to do the stirring.

Sometimes—I say sometimes—when a woman's husband is elected deacon it goes to her head and she feels that she has been appointed as a news gatherer and distributor for the whole church. We have had one or two examples here in this church—in the past—he is a good man, but with a wife with a bell collar hanging on the telephone all the time. Poor man, he ought to enjoy heaven. But he has no business in the deaconship.

"Let the deacons be the husbands of one wife"—it doesn't mean he has got to be married, but means he is to have only one wife. They had a multiciplicity of wives in those days.

"Ruling their children with their own houses well." And any man who holds the position of pastor, deacon or teacher, who can't rule his own househld has no business holding office. The saddest thing in the world is a preacher with a family not in sympathy with his work. He made a mistake when he married; somebody made a mistake.

So the Word of God says when you appoint a deacon, take into consideration the whole family connection. And we take the Word of God plus nothing and minus nothing.

The Diotrephes Spirit

It is very dangerous disease, very subtle, comes on gradually, and the victim is unconscious of its coming. But everybody else sees it. I have known several good men who had that disease, served well, were faithful, but unconsciously took themselves too seriously, and soon brother Diotrephes and his wife undertake to run and regulate the affairs of the church. They delight to create the impression that they have an inside track with the pastor. And in any growing church this condition cannot obtain long. It is like the turning of the grindstone. Did you ever turn the grindstone for your dad on a cold morning to sharpen the ax, to go down and cut a load of wood? Well, the faster you turn that grindstone the further it will throw the water off of it. The grindstone is turning here and sometimes a few muddy drops of water have been flung off.

The church is just like any other body in some important respects—imagine a champion football team being run by one of the players when within one foot of the goal line. It is the business of the quarterback to call the play; and then imagine still more that one of the 80,000 fans who are looking on should attempt to call the play—team work— that's the thing that is needed, the Bible term is "fellowship."

We are just one of many members in a big family that recognizes Christ as its only head, the Holy Spirit as its only administrator, the Bible as the only message and the salvation of souls the only purpose—there will be perfect fellowship in that church. It is the business of the pastor to see that no brother Diotrephes makes a spectacle of himself for too long a period of time. We know of churches, you do too, that are held down flat of their backs because there are two or three Diotrephes; the congregation is in fear, and the poor little preacher is scared of his life—well, we are happily through with that forever.

Reward of Deacon

I love to think of this side, "For they that have used the office of a deacon will purchase to themselves a good degree, and great boldness in the faith which is in Christ Jesus."

I talked a short time ago to an old man, 92 years young, a man who was one of Spurgeon's deacons. He told me how the deacons would pray for the great preacher. He was absolutely in the hands of the deacons, how they prayed, and how they carried the burdens! Many times when they knew his heart was crushed under the heavy load they would call a prayer meeting and not a word would be said but they would fall on their faces and pray. Knowing that, I could understand how that great preacher's messages in the printed page has girdled the globe, how thousands of hearts have been blessed, how millions of printed messages have gone everywhere. Why? Because a Godly set of men knew how to pray.

And it is with profoundest gratitude to Almighty God that only a few nights ago there was just such a prayer meeting of the deacons of this church—it was not planned. We met, the necessary business was attended to, and in a few minutes, I don't know how it started, nobody else knows, but soon all were on their knees, and what praying! How it blessed this tired preacher's heart. We stayed till near the midnight hour, and the burdened hearts of a noble body of men poured forth their supplication to God in tears. No man sought his own, no unkind whisperings, no backbiting, preferring one another in honor, holding one another in highest esteem, loving and trusting one another—I caught a train that night, there was a song all through the night time in my soul.

I give it as my testimony and to the glory of God there have been times when it would have been utterly impossible to have borne some things if it hadn't been that through the years God has been good, and always there have been faithful men and women I could depend on, and I forget the other things. The game of life is to forget the hurts and think of the blessings that come to us.

I could stand here all day and call the roll. Can I ever forget that Godly deacon who came to our country home, when I was yet in my teens, and in the old fashioned way hollered, "Hello!" Mother opened the door, and he said, he wanted to see "Brother Norris."

She went out in the back yard and called my father. My father went out to the gate and he said,

"No, I want the young Brother Norris".

My dad thought it was a huge joke and he came back around and said to me, "He wants 'young Brother Norris'."

I didn't know what he wanted. When he told me, I went into the house and said to Mother, "What do you reckon he wants? He wants me to go down to Mt. Antioch and be pastor of that little church." I said, "I am not a preacher." I had been talking around in school houses—I said, "I don't even have license to preach."

She put her hands on my shoulder and looked into my face with those beautiful eyes and said, "It is the doings of the Lord."

I didn't even have a grip, and only had one Sunday-go-to-meeting suit, and the trousers were too short. I grew so fast, couldn't keep them long enough. I put them on anyway, wrapped a pair of socks and some clean linen in a little sack, got in the buggy and went with him. Can I ever forget that old deacon? How often he would pray for the young preacher. I didn't realize then what a great man he was.

Can I ever forget good deacon, George White? Through many months I didn't have a thing in the world, not a shingle over my head, not a change of clothes—everything we had had been burned. He came to me with what I needed and said, "This is yours," and that great church yonder is due as much to his labors as to anything else.

Can I ever forget the deacon, now on the border line, and may slip away anytime? The last time I saw him he was very feeble. He is a way up in years. Through all the troubles we had, he always said, "God's blessings be upon you."

I would be compelled to, I don't care where I might be when I receive the message of his passing, catch the next airplane, cancel any appointment I might have to go and hold the last service for him. Why? Because in the darkest days that came to that church yonder, he stood with his pastor. He was president of one of the banks in Fort Worth, and he said, "All I have is back of you."

Oh, my friends, not till eternity's last cycle rolls around will we know the value of a good deacon in the Church of Jesus Christ. The deacons can create an atmosphere. They can create an atmosphere of wholesomeness, an atmosphere of fellowship, a frank atmosphere, an atmosphere of confidence. There are no factions, no backbiting where all are one and sit down together and talk things over frankly and freely. How different, and how happy not to have a deacon run out from the meeting and go around and whisper—while you are preaching your heart out, run around in the vestibule, standing on the sidewalk, button-holing people standing in the rear of the audience, even among sinners, and they hear him criticize everything and everybody— Oh, it is a glorious victory that we have passed all that. When we meet together, we talk frankly, freely, and when a matter is settled, it is agreed upon that it is both settled inside and outside, and they pronounce the verdict, the expression of every deacon in the church, and that has a happy effect on all the membership—all the whole church—all the young people—all the old people—all new members.

It is a settled policy of the deacons, the finance committee, of both churches that after a full happy discussion and a decision has been reached that becomes the voice of everybody and not for one-ten-thousandth fraction of a second would there be tolerated any man who would vote one way, talk to his brethren in the deaconship or in the church, then go down the back alley get on the telephone, or permit even his wife to get on the telephone and talk another way. That all belongs to the fleshpots of Egypt. The glory of this church and with the church in Fort Worth is summed up in the word, "Fellowship." Acts 2:42, "And they continued steadfastly in the apostles' doctrine and fellowship, and in breaking of bread, and in prayers."

When a short time ago when I was at Mount Hermon, I thought of the fellowship we enjoyed with you and the other beloved saints, "BEHOLD, how good and how pleasant it it for brethren to dwell together in unity! It is like the precious ointment upon the head, that ran down upon the beard, even Aaron's beard: that went down to the skirts of his garments; As the dew of Hermon, and as the dew that descended upon the mountains of Zion; for there the Lord commanded the blessing, even life for evermore."

How important to the unsaved is such a fellowship. Just let unsaved people come into a congregation and hear unseemly criticism, and they will never come again. What a tragedy to be a stone of stumbling!

Sometimes this is the spirit that ruins choirs, and we would not permit one such person in the choir. It will wreck a Sunday School class.

But how wonderful to a tired distressed broken hearted people, mothers and fathers, who have buried their own child yesterday, the prodigal boy away from home, gray haired men and women who have lost their grip on life, how wonderful to come into an atmosphere of brotherly love, of kindness, of tenderness.

That is what prevails in the New Testament Church, and I am very happy that we are in a New Testament Church. I speak of it very freely, I would trust you with my life. I would trust you with my name. I would trust you with my soul. I trust you with the affairs of this church. I am not afraid of anything you do. And there is a similar crowd down yonder. They get under the load together and lift.

This word, you saw in the paper where four million tons of earth, yonder in California slid down in a terrible avalanche. The word flashed that there was a little hut near by, where the keeper lived. He wasn't at home. His wife and children had no warning, and suddenly that terrible avalanche overwhelmed the little hut—thousands of people dug frantically. Why? to bring out of that terrible avanlache of death this little family.

So today here is a group of men who with your tears, prayers and love, to whom you will say, "We trust you through the terrible avalanches of terrible storms."

Oh, how our hearts were made sad, yet there was comfort, when night before last two young women and two young men, members of Temple Baptist Church, one a distant cousin of Tom Long's, met with a terrible accident through no fault of their own, and their lives were snuffed out, and their souls went into eternity. When I took the hand of that little wife, of one of the men and two little boys, I said, "How wonderful it is that amidst your tears you have hope."

This morning I got off the train from Louisville, and I was a little late for broadcast, when I walked into the studio, I didn't have time to get any thoughts together for that hour, I met a man as I went in who said to me, "I am Williams"—I said, "I have just come in and I haven't time"—but he said, "I have come down to tell you I have been saved by hearing you over the radio and reading the Fundamentalist." As quick as a flash I took him and told him to give his testimony over the raido. I asked him if he was married—he told me he had a wife and six children, and had been drinking for twenty years—I was tired from speaking every day and every night last week, but somehow or other my soul was suddenly refreshed—here was a man who had been in the grip of drink, God touched his soul through the radio messag?.

and the messages in the Fundamentalist, and he was saved! Let that be your husband, and you will know what it means. Oh, who is there that doesn't know the awful curse of drink, seeing your father come home like a beast—incidentally, I want to tell you something, one of the Baptist preachers of this city, one of the leading pulpits of this city referred to this church, stood up last Sunday referred to this church as the place where the drunkards and gamblers come—he said that criticising this church. Shame on a preacher, or anybody who would say that. I want to say to all you gamblers and drunkards, come on and we will give you the gospel of Jesus Christ. (Voices: Amen.) I am going to take the lid off over the radio and publish it in the Fundamentalist. I think if Jesus Christ were in Detroit, He would say to all the gamblers and all the drunken fathers and drunken boys, "Come unto me, and I will make you sober men." Oh, God forgive that poor preacher for his criticism!

Imagine if Jesus Christ were here and some poor stumbling drunkard should stagger in and say, "Lord, Lord, will you save me and give me back to my wife a sober, saved husband?" What would He do? That is what is going on in this church—Oh, friends that is the mission of this church.

Before we sing, I wonder how many will walk down this morning—is that man, Brother Claud Williams here, if he is will you kindly come to the front?—here he comes. He is coming to be baptized, he heard the message over WJR, read the Fundamentalist, was saved, and now coming to be baptized. That is what I am talking about.

One of the large crowds which heard Dr. Norris in Charlotte Chapel, Edinburgh, which the largest Baptist Church in Scotland. Noted for the great ministers, Dr. Joseph Kemp and Graham Scorggie.

THE PARTNERSHIP IN WITNESSING WITH THE HOLY SPIRIT

*An address of Dr. J. Frank Norris to the women
of Temple Church.*

DR. NORRIS: Indeed it is a great joy to see so large attendance at this women's meeting today. I think of what Paul said when I see you and know of your zeal and works:—Philippians 4:3:

"And I intreat thee also, true yokefellow, help those women which laboured with me in the gospel."

We have had to go through some necessary experiences in order to throw the grave clothes off and come back to the simple New Testament method, as well as the message. It was expected that a few good people would misunderstand. That was the price that had to be paid. There is nothing that is so hurtful and hindering as the average inside organizations in church work today. They are dead.

Our plan of work here is very simple. We are set to do but one thing. We read in the New Testament—Acts 8:1 of the persecution:

"And Saul was consenting unto his death. And at that time there was a great persecution against the church which was at Jerusalem; and they were all scattered abroad throughout the regions of Judea and Samaria, except the apostles."

The entire church was scattered abroad except the apostles, and they took a vacation. The 4th verse of that same chapter tells us:

"Therefore they that were scattered abroad went everywhere preaching the word."

"Preaching"—not education!

"Preaching"—not social service!

"Preaching"—not political economy!

But "Preaching the Word of God!"

The old and unscriptural conception of the pastor's office has done great mischief. I have said it repeatedly that the modern pastor's office is of the devil! (Amen!) We need to come back to a proper understanding of the scriptural pastor's office.

If the pastor is to be a hack-horse, a gad-about, a door-knob-ringer—if in short, he is to tie up all the sore toes and rub down the fur of all the disgruntled, he will have no time left to preach the Gospel and win souls. (Amen!)

Then besides there is another very important matter, viz.: the blessing that comes to the members from doing the work, is lost. So many of you have had great joy in going in New Testament fashion "from house to house."

The Two Fold Witnesses

I want today to quote some Scriptures to you that changed my whole thinking, my whole plan of work.

Are you worrying?

Are you burdened beyond your power to bear?

Are you timid and hesitant about speaking to people about their souls?

There is a whole lot of bunk going around about the work of the Holy Spirit and the people who say the most about being "baptized of the Holy Ghost" and so on, usually have the least of it. Just like when people are always talking about their prayers, they usually do very little praying.

A good fisherman doesn't have to give a discussion on fishing. Let me see his string of fish.

There is but one test of our faith, and that is the results of souls won. The one unanswerable credential of the divine character of Jesus was—Matthew 11:4:

"Go and shew John again those things which ye do hear and see."

There Are Two Equalities in the State of the Believer

We are absolutely equal with Christ in our saved state. I have the Scriptures for it:

"And you hath he quickened, who were dead in trespasses and sins." Ephesians 2:1.

Christ was dead in the grave, so we are dead in our sins.

Christ was raised from the grave, so He hath raised us up.

"And hath raised us up together, and made us sit together in heavenly places in Christ Jesus:"—Ephesians 2:6.

Not only raised us up, but made us sit together heavenly places —heavenly relationships with Him.

Not only so, but we are sons of God!

Not only so, but we are heirs of God!

Not only so, but we are joint-heirs with Christ!

Not only so, but we are equal with Him!

Not only so, but John tells us in I John 3:2:

"Beloved, now are we the sons of God, and it doth not yet appear what we shall be: but we know that, when he shall appear, we shall be like him; for we shall know him as he is."

Not only so, but we are predestinated to be conformed to His image:—Romans 8:29: "For whom he did foreknow, he also did predestinate to be conformed to the image of his Son, that he might be the firstborn among many brethren."

Not only so, but we shall sit on thrones with him!

Not only so, but we shall reign with Him!

Not only so, but in the ages to come He will shew the exceeding riches of Christ through His kindness to us in Christ Jesus.

Therefore, we are absolutely equal with Christ in our saved state!

The Second Equality of the Believer

We are absolutely equal with the Holy Spirit in giving our testimony:

Leave your Bibles closed and let me quote you these Scriptures and then we will study them.

The first Scripture I call your attention to is Luke 24:46-49:

"And said unto them, Thus it is written, and thus it behooved Christ to suffer, and to rise from the dead, the third day:

"And that repentance and remission of sins should be preached in his name among all nations, beginning at Jerusalem.

"And ye are witnesses of these things.

"And, behold, I send the promise of my Father upon you: but tarry ye in the city of Jerusalem, until ye be endued with power from on high."

Mark the words "Ye are witnesses."

Also notice carefully "upon you" and "ye be endued." The Holy Spirit comes into the person of the believer, clothes himself with the believer, and the believer is thus furnished, endued, panoplied, equipped, and the witnessing is the two-fold voice: (1) of the Holy Spirit, and (2) of the believer. They are one and equal.

The second Scripture I call your attention to is John 15:26-27:

"But when the Comforter is come, Whom I will send unto you from the Father, even the Spirit of truth, which proceedeth from the Father, He shall testify of Me. And ye also shall bear witness, because ye have been with Me from the beginning."

Mark you, there is the Triune God in the 26th verse.

(1)   The Comforter comes of His own sovereign choice.

(2)   The Comforter is sent by the Son.

(3)   He proceedeth from the Father.

All three Persons have one aim, and that is the testimony of the Holy Spirit. And of what does He testify?

What Person—"Testify of Me."—Christ.

Then the next verse begins "And ye also."

This means nothing by itself—these three words—but can be interpreted only by what precedes and what follows.

Here is what it means, that as the Holy Spirit testifies of Christ, so also and equally the believer testifies of Christ.

"He shall not speak of himself"—John 16:13 "Howbeit when he, the Spirit of truth, is come, he will guide you into all truth: for he shall not speak of himself; but whatsoever he shall hear, that shall he speak: and he will shew you things to come."

And it is exceedingly important that we bear in mind that the Holy Spirit does not glorify Himself, but that He glorifies the Son, and that is why when some over-zealous, no doubt well meaning and misled people, go around talking about their "baptism of the Holy Ghost," they are doing the utterly unscriptural thing. Let the words speak—John 16:13: "He shall not speak of Himself."

The Holy Spirit takes the things of Christ, even as Eliezer took the necklaces, pearls and bracelets from his sack of treasures and showed them to Rebekah.

Eliezer did not brag on himself and tell her how he was head of the ranch, or over his master's household, but he magnified and glorified his master.

So our Eliezer, the third Person of the Trinity, wins us, woos us and compels us to fall in love with our Isaac, our Lord and Bridegroom.

Therefore, when you go into a home to talk to that soul, you have this assurance that the Holy Spirit is also there by your side —that's what the word "Comforter" means and He is also speaking to that lost soul.

There is power in the knowledge that the same Divine Person that moved upon the face of the deep in the time of creation, is moving upon the hearts of those to whom you carry the message of salvation.

The third Scripture which I call your attention to on the two-fold witnesses is John 16:7-11:

"Nevertheless, I tell you the truth: it is expedient for you that I go away: for if I go not away, the Comforter will not come unto you; but if I depart, I will send him unto you. And when He is come, he will reprove the world of sin, and of righteousness, and of judgment; Of sin, because they believe not on me";

This means that it is profitable for us for Jesus to go away and another—mark the word—"another Comforter." That is why we do "greater works."

How overwhelming is the thought that the Comforter comes to the believer—into you—"unto you"—and through you; the believer then goes to the world.

How overwhelming and how humbling when we think that God has never reached a world, never saved a soul except through the testimony of a believer.

Then how great is that responsibility!

The world needs to know of its sin, its need of righteousness, and of judgment.

And can only know this all important message of sin and salvation through two-fold witnessing:

(1) of the Holy Spirit, and (2) of the believer.

They are one, inseparable and equal.

The fourth Scripture that I call to you is Acts 1:8: "But ye shall receive power, after that the Holy Ghost is come upon you: and ye shall be witnesses unto me both in Jerusalem, and in all Judaea, and in Samaria, and unto the uttermost parts of the earth."

Notice that this verse is a contrast of what precedes. It is not ours to speculate or to set times and seasons or to inquire into the things that even the angels are not permitted to look into. We are set to do one thing and one thing only.

Now mark the order!

"But ye shall receive power."

Now when?

Not before, but "after the Holy Ghost is come upon you."

Here is the clear statement of the coming of the Holy Ghost as the Administrator of the church. We are born of the Spirit and we know Him in addition to His administrative work. We have Him as our personal Witness. He is our Leader. He is our Guide. But in addition and over it all, He is a special Witness for salvation of the lost and tells the lost soul of Jesus Christ in, through and by a saved human witness.

Therefore, the next step is "and ye shall be witnesses."

Witnesses of what?

The answer is "unto Me."

There you have the Holy Spirit testifying.

There you have the believer also testifying.

They are one inseparable and equal and that testimony begins at Jerusalem and goes to the uttermost parts of the earth.

The fifth Scripture that I call to your attention is Acts 5:29-32:

"Then Peter and the other apostles answered and said, We ought to obey God rather than men. The God of our fathers raised up Jesus, whom ye slew and hanged on a tree. Him hath God exalted with his right hand to be a Prince and a Saviour, for to give repentance to Israel, and forgiveness of sins. And we are his witnesses of these things: and so is also the Holy Ghost, whom God hath given to them that obey him."

Here Peter is before the Sanhedrin and the authority of the Apostles is challenged.

Now note very carefully verse 32. "We are his witnesses of these things."

Mark the possessive pronoun "His."

~Mark also the two words "these things."

Now what is included in the two words "These things?"

Go back and call the roll:

(1)   The resurrection of Christ—"God of our fathers raised up Jesus."

(2)   The crucifixion of Christ—"Whom ye slew and hanged on a tree."

The resurrection was put first because the Sadducees denied the resurrection.

(3)   The exaltation of Christ—"Him hath God exalted with his right hand."

(4)   The coronation of Christ—"To be a Prince."

(5)   The salvation through Christ—"a Saviour."

(6)   Redemption through Christ—"For to give repentance to Israel, and forgiveness of sins."

Now these are included in the "These things."

And what else?

That is what the believer is to tell a lost world?

Then read on, "And so is also the Holy Ghost."

The believer tells a lost man of the resurrection of Christ, the crucifixion of Christ, the exaltation of Christ, the coronation of Christ, the salvation through Christ, and every time you go into a home, every time you talk to a man on the street car, or in the shops, or factories, you have the absolute assurance that there is another One also witnessing. And that is God Himself in the Person of the Holy Ghost!

Now how do we know that we have the Holy Ghost?

Do we know it according to our feelings?

Do we know it because we separate ourselves in some hidden place?

Don't misunderstand me, we should certainly enter into the closet and pray, but that is not what I am talking about. I am talking about the one and only condition of our having the Holy Ghost in our lives and here are the words of the Scriptures:

"Whom God hath given unto them that obey Him."

Now keep the one issue clear, viz.: Peter says "we ought to obey God rather than men" and then he says, "God gives the Holy Ghost to them that obey Him."

What is the issue of obedience?

The issue is witnessing for Jesus Christ to a lost world.

Talk about a revival. This is the way they had a revival in the New Testament.

And it is the only way to have a revival in any age.

We should quit praying for the coming of the Holy Ghost. He is already here. And yet a lot of people put in time, mistakenly praying for the coming of the Holy Spirit and the "baptism of the Holy Ghost," and so on, when instead of praying for the Holy Spirit to come to us we should pray that God will help us to give ourselves to Him.

Our prayer should be not so much for more of the Holy Spirit but that He may have more of us.

That song is thoroughly orthodox:

> "Take my life and let it be
> Consecrated, Lord, to Thee;
> Take my hands, and let them move
> At the impulse of Thy love.
>
> Take my feet, and let them be
> Swift and beautiful for Thee;
> Take my voice, and let me sing
> Always, only, for my King.
>
> Take my silver and my gold,
> Not a mite would I withhold;
> Take my moments and my days,
> Let them flow in ceaseless praise.
>
> Take my will, and make it Thine,
> It shall be no longer mine;
> Take my heart, it is Thine own;
> It shall be Thy royal throne."

The sixth Scripture that I give you is the Holy Spirit in the life of Phillip—Acts 8:26-29 and 39:

"And the angel of the Lord spake unto Philip, saying, Arise, and go toward the south unto the way that goeth down from Jerusalem unto Gaza, which is desert.

"And he arose and went: and, behold, a man of Ethiopia, an eunuch of great authority under Candace queen of the Ethiopians, who had the charge of all her treasure, and had come to Jerusalem for to worship, was returning, and sitting in his chariot read Esaias the prophet. Then the Spirit said unto Philip, Go near, and join thyself to this chariot. . . . And when they were come up out of the water, the Spirit of the Lord caught away Philip, that the eunuch saw him no more: and he went on his way rejoicing."

Here are three examples of the partnership of the Holy Spirit in the life of "Philip the evangelist." If he were a deacon, and I am not sure that those seven in the 6th chapter were deacons, but I am very glad to think they are, because what a revival would come to our churches if all the deacons would do like Philip did.

(1) The Holy Spirit sent Philip down into a desert place—a very hard field.

(2) The Holy Spirit commands Philip to get on the running board of the chariot of the Ethiopian.

(3) After winning and baptizing the Ethiopian the Holy Spirit caught away Philip and he went and held more meetings, for we read in the 40th verse of that same chapter:

"And passing through he preached in all the cities, till he came to Caesarea."

The seventh Scripture I give you is in Acts 13:1-4. What a revolution would come in our lives if we could realize for once that the Holy Spirit is our Administrator and Guide and Witness in winning souls!

"Now there were in the church that was at Antioch certain prophets and teachers; as Barnabas, and Simeon that was called Niger, and Lucius of Cyrene, and Manaen, which had been brought up with Herod the tetrarch, and Saul.

"And they ministered to the Lord, and fasted, the Holy Ghost said, Separate me Barnabas and Saul for the work whereunto I have called them.

"And when they had fasted and prayed, and laid their hands on them, they sent them away.

"So they, being sent forth by the Holy Ghost, departed unto Seleucia; and from thence they sailed to Cyprus."

Here was the church, a local church at Antioch, and the word "church" is used in this sense 112 times in the New Testament.

Just think of it here is a church that is engaged in a prayer meeting!

It was not one of these cut and dried, powerless mid-week affairs, but the world's greatest missionary enterprise started in this prayer meeting.

Mark that while they were praying, there came also another Person unto that prayer meeting—the Holy Spirit, and He said:

"Separate me Barnabas and Saul for the work whereunto I have called them."

Just think of it—here is a church where the Holy Spirit could come and be at liberty to speak to the membership and even the preachers.

What did He say?

(1) "Separate."

(2) "I have called."

No man has any business in the ministry or going as a missionary until he has, beyond all question of doubt, a definite, specific call by the Holy Spirit.

Now notice carefully the use of one word twice:

(1) "They sent them away."

(2) "So they being sent forth by the Holy Ghost."

The church sends and the Holy Spirit sends.

Equal in partnership is the testimony of the church and the Holy Spirit.

Is it any wonder then that hearts were opened and multitudes—both Jews and Greeks—were saved.

Everywhere Barnabas and Saul went the Holy Spirit was there waiting for them.

The eighth instance of equal partnership is Acts 15:28.

"For it seems good to the Holy Ghost, and to us, to lay upon you no greater burden than these necessary things";

Mark the expression "it seemed good to the Holy Ghost and to us."

At Antioch there was a great missionary fellowship and it was in the church.

Not in the "Board."

Not in the "Association."

Not in the "convention."

Not in the "council"—whether the council at Jerusalem or the Federal Council of Churches or "Baptist Council of ordination."

Here at Jerusalem was an issue of heresy—viz.: of Judaism to be tacked on to justification by faith. That is, if a man was a Jew by birth, it was then plus Christianity, and if he were a Gentile it was Christianity plus Judaism.

In other words, Judaism was either the cow-catcher or the caboose.

And that has been the issue through the ages and is the issue now, whether or not we will "plus" the Gospel of Jesus Christ.

That is why it is unscriptural to tack on all these machines and cogs. That is why the church is broken down today, because it has too many unscriptural programs on the inside.

That is why there is no room for anybody's headquarters over the churches.

God's plan is a very simple method of saving a group of believers by His grace, calling them together into the church, a group of baptized believers, recognizing Christ as the only Head, the Holy Spirit as the only Administrator, the Word their only creed, and the salvation of souls their only mission.

These churches had fellowship in New Testament times with one another.

But they had no organic connection and they belonged to no organization of any kind or character.

The ninth example of partnership and witness is Acts 16:14—

"And a certain woman named Lydia, a seller of purple, of the city of Thyatira, which worshipped God, heard us: whose heart the Lord opened, that she attended unto the things which were spoken of Paul."

The same Divine Spirit that called and separated Barnabas and Saul was by the seashore and opened the heart of Lydia while Paul witnessed to her: "The Lord opened . . . that she attended." There you have the whole thing in a nutshell.

God's side of the witnessing and man's side.

Therefore, every time you go forth on your personal visitation for Jesus Christ, to tell of His salvation, you have the absolute assurance that the Holy Spirit precedes you, goes with you, talks with you, walks with you, and opens the hearts of all you talk to. And it is a heart matter. Don't be afraid of "emotionalism" in Christianity, no salvation without it.

I repeat that this was the greatest truth that ever came into my life next to my salvation.

Do you want a holy boldness in your testimony? Then go forth and testify of Christ.

Suppose you don't feel like it. Go anyhow.

The Word does not say that God gives the Holy Spirit to them that feel like it. But He gives the Holy Spirit to them that "obey Him."

I can take the average woman or man with a small amount of faith and if they will use that faith, however small it is, obey God, tell a lost soul of Jesus Christ, they will come back with more faith.

That is how to grow in grace!

That is how to obtain Spiritual power!

That is how to have the "filling of the Holy Ghost!"

You ask, "Should we not pray for the power of the Holy Spirit?"

Most assuredly we need that power and we have it by obedience to Him, absolute surrender to Him, yielding ourselves to Him, that is why Paul says "we have this treasure in earthen vessels."

We have power in proportion as we present to Him our body, soul, mind, time, money, and all.

That is why He said we are the "temple of the Holy Ghost." I Corinthians 6:19. "What? know ye not that your body is the temple of the Holy Ghost, which is in you, which ye have of God, and ye are not your own?"

Do you want to get out of your own troubles?

Are you seeking comfort in sorrow?

There is only one way.

Quit nursing your troubles.

Quit brooding over your losses.

Get up and go and witness to a lost soul about Jesus Christ, and then you will have power and peace.

That is how we obtain the fruits of the Spirit, which are a by-product:—Galatians 5:22-23.

"But the fruit of the Spirit is love, joy, peace, longsuffering, gentleness, goodness, faith, meekness, temperance: against such there is no law."

Do you want the joy of the Lord?

Do you want Him to be the health of your countenance?

Do you want to grow young while you grow old with years?

Do you want the inner-man to be strengthened while the outward man perishes?

Here is how:

I had a deacon by the name of George White, one of the best men that ever lived. He is in glory now.

We were very closely associated and he came to me repeatedly begging me to pray for him, always telling me how weak he was and that he could not do personal work like others. And one day he came to me all down-cast, and said:

"Brother Pastor, I want you to pray for me. I am so weak."

I just shoved him in water over his head and said, "I am not going to do it!"

When he came up the third time for air, I explained to him what I meant. I said:

"If the Lord has not heard all the prayers I have prayed for you already, there is no use to pray any more."

I said, "Brother White, you need, not more praying for, but you need to get up and go after lost souls and tell them of your salvation."

But he said, "I am too weak. I can't do it!"

I said: "Everything you touch makes money, you know how to sell machinery, you can sell cattle, and I know you can tell the world of Jesus Christ, if you make up your mind to do it."

He said: "I will do more harm than good. I will drive them away."

I said: "No danger—they are already away."

I said: "There is old Dr. McMorris, you have been running around with him. Go work on him. He comes to church usually and sits on the back seat. You can go back there and try your hand on him. No danger of hurting him. The next time he is in church, go bring him up."

Deacon White said: "Suppose he won't come?"

I said: "Bring him anyhow."

The deacon said: "He will be there at the front next Sunday night."

So when I had finished the message the next Sunday night, others came, but, of course, Dr. McMorris did not come.

Deacon White was standing there at one side. I turned and looked at him and said:

"If there is anybody in this house that you are interested in, go after them."

The invitation closed, and I turned and looked, and Deacon White fairly flew down the aisle next to the wall, rushed up to his friend and said: "Come on!"

After much hesitation the deacon won, and brought him down to the front seat, and said: "Here he is."

I said: "Get down on your knees, both of you."

The deacon began to confess his sins to his friend and the friend said: "I know I need salvation. My years are few."

Then the deacon looked up at me and said: "Come and help me," and I prayed with them and the deacon prayed and Dr. McMorris prayed the one prayer, "God be merciful to me a sinner."

They both are in glory now.

What happened?

Ever afterwards Deacon White would come to me and say:

"If you have any old hard nuts that nobody else can crack, turn them over to me," and these two men brought in the largest number of hardened sinners, who were gloriously saved.

This is our plan of work, viz.: "The two-fold witnessing."

We have equal testimony with the Holy Spirit.

HOW DUAL PASTORATE WAS BROUGHT ABOUT

Rev. Louis Entzminger was called as co-pastor of the Temple Baptist Church when I announced under no circumstances would I resign the First Baptist Church at Fort Worth. The church grew but the denominational leaders and the opposition also grew in intensity, and the whole Northern Baptist Machinery moved in to take possession. It is a matter of record how the officials of the Detroit Baptist Machine, together with representatives from the East, hindered the work and undertook to block and defeat Entzminger's work and make it impossible. They carried on a guerilla warfare, and satanic whispering campaign. Their scheme was to call the Rev. Cary Thomas of Altoona, Penna. He is a reputed Fundamentalist but is with the machine.

There were several secret caucuses of the opposition and several meetings in the name of "prayer meetings."

I was in Fort Worth, going on about my duties, and had made up my mind to dismiss Detroit entirely, feeling sure that the wish of real Fundamentalists had been carried out. But on the last Tuesday in May, 1935, Entzminger called long distance and said, "If you want to save the situation you had better come up here for things are popping."

He further said, "They are going to call a meeting and have a big row the next night."

I said, "I will be there in the morning."

It was then straight up 12 o'clock and a fast plane left in twenty minutes for Chicago. I called the air port and they held the plane and I arrived at Chicago at 6:30 P. M.

There never walked on shoe leather a truer man than Louis Entzminger.

A short time after arriving in Detroit the big tent meeting started and while I had arranged for some others to help in the meeting, yet I was compelled to do the preaching for four solid months, and never did a man do finer work in personal soul winning than Bro. Entzminger, and so did a fine group of consecrated men and women. Not a single service that didn't witness salvation and additions. It was the greatest meeting I ever witnessed.

At the end of the meeting a new church was born.

If the denominational leaders had kept their hands out and not interferred with the will of an independent local church, I never would have gone to Detroit, but once I put my hand to the plow, and that meeting was launched there was no turning back.

Both churches by a silent vote unanimously agreed for me to divide my time between the two, and for two years both have enjoyed unprecedented prosperity and growth. The Fort Worth Church decreased its indebtedness over $120,000 during this time, and has had the greatest Spiritual experience of its whole history, and going today as never before, averaging twenty to thirty additions every Sunday.

The Temple Baptist Church has increased its property approximately more than a quarter of a million dollars in the two years, and increased its membership four-fold, and these two churches now have the largest membership in the South and North, respectively, and not only the membership of the church, but the two largest Sunday Schools, with combined average attendance of around 6,000.

The dual responsibility of two great churches was humanly unbearable but both churches threw themselves into the work and the experience of having to carry the responsibility has been the making of both churches.

There are two great visitation days in both churches of the men and women respectively, and there is an average of more than 2,000 personal visits made in both churches each week.

The two churches enjoy the happiest fellowship with each other, instead of there being any rivalry or jealousy they work like Bands and Beauty and are both greatly humbled and feel that they are called to the Kingdom for such a time as this. They have given a concrete demonstration of "daily" New Testament evangelism.

Both churches are sending out a large number of young ministers and missionaries.

The radio program of both churches covers both the North and South and their joint publication, the Fundamentalist, goes throughout the North American Continent, and the whole world. It has four times the circulation of the largest denominational organ.

In addition to the work of the two churches both congregations are one-hundred per cent behind the pastor in sending him forth as their missionary to the whole North American Continent and to regions beyond. He averages from one to two evangelistic and Bible Conferences every week. These conferences are attended by multitudes and large numbers of souls are saved.

The two highest mountain peaks of both churches are their annual Bible Schools for eight days and during the year 1937 practically every state in the Union and provinces in Canada were represented at the Bible Schools, and there was a total of more than 6,000 in attendance.

Both churches support for foreign missions the Fundamental Baptist Mission Fellowship and Mid-Missions. In addition another very happy missionary work is that both churches send forth the gospel in several large sound trucks, valued at more than $3,000.00 each, and these sound trucks carry the recorded sermons of the pastor, together with the best gospel music.

In addition there is running a permanent Bible School at Detroit with classes and lectures every day.

Both churches are enjoying an unusual revival and souls are being saved daily and great crowds attending the ministry of the Word, due to the fine personal work of a large number.

Therefore here are two New Testament witnesses 1300 miles apart that are giving a concrete demonstration of the truth of the Word of God plus nothing and minus nothing, giving an unanswerable credential to the power of the gospel to save multitudes of hardened sinners in this day of twentieth century materialism. Hundreds of churches and pastors all over America have taken new heart by the example of these two witnesses and are throwing off the grave clothes of ecclesiasticism and going forth witnessing for their risen and coming Lord.

Mr. G. B. Vick, Superintendent Temple Baptist Church. He was with the First Baptist Church for ten years.

THE HOW—METHODS OF ENLISTING MEMBERS

By G. B. Vick, Superintendent Temple Baptist Church

As clearly, as concisely and as unadorned as possible, I desire to set forth in this chapter, a few of the methods which have been used to build and maintain these two churches, which are said to be the largest congregations in the North and South respectively.

Having been associated with Dr. Norris at the First Baptist Church in Fort Worth for nearly nine years, and having worked with him in Detroit nearly two years, I have had the opportunity of observing the inside workings and the methods in personal work, in house-to-house visitation, in Bible study, and in finances. For those of you who have not had a like opportunity I pass this on.

The Bible Only

One of the most startling departures from the ordinary church methods was made by the First Baptist Church more than sixteen years ago, when it pioneered in discarding the International Sunday School lesson series, all quarterlies, leaflets and man-made literature, and announced that henceforth the Word of God itself would be the only text book in the Sunday School, as well as the only rule of faith and practice in the church.

Wide publicity was given to this far reaching step and soon around the world this church, which had already built the largest Sunday School in the world, now came to be known as "The Church that studies the Bible only."

There were several reasons why this step was taken:

1: Because we believed that it was better to study the Word of God than to study merely what some man had written about the Word of God.

2: Because the International Sunday School lessons, as used by churches all over the world, never covered or even touched upon three-fourths of the Bible. A survey was made of the lessons for sixteen years past, and this was found to be true.

3: The hop, skip and jump method of taking a few verses out of one chapter this Sunday and next Sunday studying an entirely different portion of the Scriptures, was not giving our teachers, much less our Sunday School pupils, a clear, coherent grasp of the Bible as a whole.

4:   Another fact that no one will deny is that the Quarterlies and literature of all denominations are written from the post-millennial viewpoint and either misapply, or, as is usually the case, omit entirely, most of the great prophetic Scriptures.

Immediately many happy results were noted. Many of our teachers who, at the first, had entered into the proposition with fear and trembling, were surprised at their own rapid growth as real Bible teachers.

Another immediate result noted was a large increase in attendance throughout the whole Sunday School. Within a few short weeks after we started teaching the "Bible only" the Sunday School attendance showed an increase of over 900 above what the attendance had been running.

Most important of all, our experience showed indisputably that more souls are saved when we teach the "Bible only" than when we used the quarterlies.

One of the by-products of our new method was the greater spirit of reverence and better deportment, particularly with Juniors and Intermediates. We found that there was a deeper spirit of reverence when every pupil opened his Bible than when they turned, in their quarterlies, to the lesson text.

Another thing, it is easier to get people to bring their Bibles when we study the "Bible only" than when we merely give them 10 per cent for bringing their Bibles, according to the old denominational "Standard of excellence."

One of the results that we did not foresee was the increased attendance at our mid-week teachers' meeting. We realized that no Sunday School could do its best work without a well-attended, regular weekly teachers meeting. That is where plans for the next Sunday are set forth by the Superintendent, where the weak places in the various classes and departments are strengthened and where due acknowledgment is made and encouragement given for extraordinary accomplishments.

We found that after discarding helps and literature that the teachers were anxious to hear the next Sunday's lesson as it would be taught by the Pastor or Superintendent on Wednesday night.

Therefore, every Wednesday night from 7:30 to 8:00 the teachers and workers of each department meet and discuss those problems and plans which are peculiar to their own age group. Then at 8 o'clock all departments come together in a general meeting where the Pastor or Superitnendent gives the lesson for the next Sunday.

We have found that it is impossible for a teacher and indeed his entire class to keep step with the rest of the Sunday School and Church if the Wednesday night teachers' meeting is neglected.

Visitation—"Daily . . . in Every House"

Besides the study of the "Bible Only," another distinguishing feature of the First Baptist Church at Fort Worth and the Temple Baptist Church at Detroit, is their constant, persistent Scriptural house-to-house visitation.

From the human standpoint the secret of the growth of these churches may be summed up in one word "Visitation." It is impossible to have a church-going people without you have first a people-going church. In other words, the average unsaved, unregenerate man of the street is not going to anybody's church if that church doesn't first go to him. Jesus knew this to be true, and therefore, said:

"Go out into the highways and hedges, and compel (constrain) them to come in, that my house may be filled." Luke 14:23.

The secret of the phenomenal growth of the First Church in Jerusalem is found in Acts 5:42:

"And daily in the temple, and in every house, they ceased not to teach and preach Jesus Christ."

That is the New Testament method, and God's method of building a great church and Sunday School. Certainly we cannot improve upon it.

In the 9th and 10th chapters of Acts, we also have two splendid examples of the far reaching results of two personal visits made in two homes.

In the ninth chapter God told Ananias (who as far as we know was not a preacher but an ordinary layman who loved the Lord) to make a personal visit. God gave him the name and address and said, "Go to the street which is called Straight, to the house of a man named Judas and there call for Saul of Tarsus. He is a good prospect and needs your visit just now."

But Ananias argued with the Lord and said: "Lord, I don't

believe it would do any good for me to call on him. I have heard a lot about that fellow. He is bitter against the church. He persecutes believers unto prison and even unto death, and besides that, he is well educated and possibly knows more about the Old Testament Scriptures than I do, and I am not gifted or qualified to make a visit to such a man. Someone else could do it much better. Besides all that, Lord, I have had a hard day at the office or shop, and I am tired, and don't have an automobile so I don't feel like making that call tonight." Or perhaps Ananias said: "We have some friends or relatives coming to our house tonight and I have a very important social engagement, and I just can't make that visit at this time, and anyway I don't believe it would do any good."

But God said: "Ananias, you do what I told you, for he is a chosen vessel to bear my name before the Gentiles and kings and the children of Israel. I am going to give the world a demonstration of what God can do with a transformed life."

Speaking from the human standpoint suppose Ananias had not made that visit. The scales would never have fallen from Paul's eyes. He could never have preached in the power of the Holy Spirit and would never have become the greatest preacher, evangelist and soul winner of all time; thousands of souls whom Paul personally won to Christ would have been lost, and we would not have thirteen books in the New Testament today, written by the great Apostle to the Gentiles.

· On the other hand because Ananias obeyed God and made that particular visit, Ananias has some part in all the souls that Paul won to Christ, and every soul that has been saved by reading any part of Paul's epistles.

If today you or I can be used of God in making one visit whereby we will win one soul that will turn many to righteousness, then let us rejoice in the opportunity and not neglect it. It is still God's plan for men and women who love Him to go into the homes daily to teach and preach Jesus Christ.

In the 10th chapter of Acts we have another wonderful example of a visit that Peter made to the home of a man called Cornelius. Here too God had to almost compel Peter to make this call. When God told Peter to go to Caesarea to the home of Simon the tanner who lived on a street near the seashore Peter also argued with the Lord. He said: "Lord, it is an unlawful thing for a man that is a Jew to keep company or come unto a man of another nation," but God said, "Peter if I can visit that home with a special visitation of my divine power, certainly you can afford to visit there."

And as a result of Peter's visit in that home Cornelius and all his household were saved, and the door of salvation was opened to the Gentiles.

Plan of Visitation

On Monday night of each week our men meet at the church at 6 o'clock, coming directly from their work. There they are served a good warm supper, which has been prepared by the good women of the church. At 6:30 the men are handed a group of cards (usually not more than five or six) and go out into the homes two by two. These cards contain the name, address, church affiliation, a word about the spiritual condition, or any other helpful information that we have concerning that individual. The cards have been copied in advance by a secretary who always retains the original card for every prospect in a permanent prospect file, which is kept in the church office. A duplicate card has been made out in advance and all of those living in different sections of the city have been grouped, so that as little time as possible will be lost in going from one house to another.

The men go into the homes and make a good Spiritual visit, not merely a polite social call. We urge them always to have prayer in every home before leaving it. The men get all the information possible concerning every member of that household, who is not a regular attendant of some church or Sunday School. They write the names and ages of every individual on the back of the card, together with a brief report or summary of what they have found in the home.

At 9 o'clck they meet back at the church to give their reports and it is a rare thing that a Monday night passes without good news of several conversions in the homes that night.

Of course, that does not mean that we win somebody to Christ in every home that we visit. Often times the workers find that the best thing to do in some homes is to tell them how God is blessing our work and merely give them a warm cordial invitation to attend our Sunday School and church the next Sunday, and if that is not sufficient, to make arrangements to go by for them and bring them to Sunday School the next Sunday morning. That usually gets results.

Whn the men's reports are concluded, they all hand in their cards with the written reports on the back. These cards are carefully gone over by the Visitation Secretary and she puts the results of each visit on the back of her permanent card in the prospect file. In that way every one who follows up that visit has the benefit of the information found by the first visitor, and each succeeding one.

The Visitation Secretary also makes out individual prospect cards for every new prospect found in that night's visitation, and distributes them to the class in whose age-group they belong.

The ladies' work is carried on in a similar manner each Thursday as they gather at the church at 9:30, receive their cards and visit in the homes until 12:30, when they meet back at the church for lunch and fellowship, which is followed by their reports and a short, practical Scriptural message by the pastor.

The ladies bring their own lunches and spread them all together.

In addition to these periods of special visitation, every class and department carries on a constant visitation of their absentees, sick members and prospects.

I have before me last week's report, which shows that there were 56 present at the men's Monday night visitation, and 73 present for the women's visitation on Thursday. The total number of visits reported for the week was 948.

The numbers of visits made and the visitors in the homes varies, of course, from week to week. Sometimes the women have as many as 125 present and the men about 75, with 1100 or more visits made some weeks.

In taking the verbal reports of visits made from the men and women Monday nights and Thursdays, we try to emphasize two things about the reports:

1st. _Be brief_, stating only the important things, and 2nd, be enthusiastic. In other words, we urge every worker to talk only about the good things and not sound a discouraging note. If the people of one particular home visited are not interested or if they are antagonistic, we tell our workers to write the report of that upon the card, but not to talk about it in the group meetings. We want them to bring back good news—"As cold waters to a thirsty soul, so is good news."

That is very important because if two men who are perhaps naturally pessimistic get up and begin to tell about all the hard times that they had and all the discouraging obstacles they met, they will soon have everybody in the meeting crying on each other's shoulder—or at least feeling like it.

The good King David once had a messenger put to death because he was the bearer of bad news. In some ways it wasn't such a bad law, at that.

God's Plan of Financing His Church

We believe that God's plan of financing His work through His church is set forth in His word.

We do not believe that it is God's plan that His work should be financed by suppers, ice cream socials, rummage sales, neither by lotteries, other gambling schemes nor dances as some of the churches here in the North put on to raise money. We are convinced as a matter of conviction and as a matter of experience that when Christian people hear what God's Word teaches as to our financial responsibility in carrying on His work, a good proportion will respond.

Here at the Temple Baptist Church for the past year we have not even asked anyone to pledge any certain amount per week. We merely ask them to sign a card, covenanting with God to obey Him and bring all their tithes and offerings into His storehouse at this church. The only pledge card that we use, reads as follows:

"The Tithe is the Lord's . . . it is holy unto the Lord."—Lev. 27:30.

In obedience to the Saviour's comand, and in gratitude for His many blessings, I will gladly bring my Tithe into the Lord's store house at the Temple Baptist Church during the year 1938.

Name ....

Address ....

Dept..   Class............................

"Bring ye all the Tithes into the store house."—Mal. 3:10.

When born-again people sign such a card in goodly numbers the church finances are solved. Thus we place upon every teacher the responsibility of properly teaching and properly enlisting the members of his class in weekly Scriptural giving.

May I say in this respect that we have a Finance Committee of seven men who O. K. every check that is given out. This Finance Committee has a weekly meeting preceding the Wednesday night services and a financial report is made to the church every Wednesday night. Every check has to be signed by two individuals selected by the deacons.

Church Architecture

Even on the matter of church architecture the First Baptist Church at Fort Worth and the Temple Baptist Church of Detroit have decided convictions. Instead of cloud-reaching spires, and churches patterned after ancient cathedrals, we believe that the church building should be a modern lighthouse, a work shop for the Lord. We believe it ought to be practical and simple.

One reason why many poor people do not go to church today is that they feel ill at ease and not at home in a church with stained glass windows, a fine carpet on the floor and mahogany pews. We want our churches to be simple but comfortable, attractive but not extravagant, inviting to people of all classes and conditions; not too shoddy for the wealthiest and not too fine for the humblest and poorest. For instance we believe it is very desirable that a church shall not have any steps on the outside. Stores, business houses and places of amusement have found that such are not conducive to getting the greatest number of people on the inside and people are what we are after. Some preachers and churches say there is nothing in numbers. But we believe that to get people saved we must get them under the sound of the Gospel.

DR. NORRIS DOES MUCH PERSONAL VISITATION

From Sermon Dec. 26, 1937

Since I was here a great soul went home to God. I shall never forget one morning—the office was right over yonder—she came in a morning ahead of time, before we were expecting her. Someone knocked on the door and I said, "Come in."

The door opened and there stood a slender girl. She said, "This is Kate Tarlton."

I rose and said, "Why Miss Kate you have come ahead of time. I was going to meet you this afternoon."

I looked at her. She looked at me. That was nearly a quarter of a century ago that happened, and not until the leaves of the judgment book unfold will this church know some of the things she and others went through. Do you know when our greatest crisis was? It was when our property was destroyed, with the depression following. Some of you wondered why we didn't tell you our real financial condition. We knew you couldn't stand it. The congregation was scattered and we had no central place in which the church could meet. We met in tabernacles on the North Side, East Side and South Side. The bookkeeper sitting over there will tell you I never got one check for salary during those three years. Business went to pieces and one insurance company after another crashed and went into receivership. We had to take what was left. Indeed, it was very dark.

There were only five persons on earth knew the actual condition of the finances. A. L. Jackson, Jane Hartwell knew it, Kate Tarlton knew it, and Harry Keeton knew it, and I knew it.

And so we decided to take all the blame. We were criticised.

When I saw the conditions, people losing their jobs, and I walked around this pile of smouldering ruins—at first in the weakness of the flesh I was tempted to give up. But I called Kate Tarlton and said, "Kate, we are facing the greatest crisis. Our flock is like a flock of sheep scattered abroad. We can't get one central place. There is no such place. Without saying a word about it I am going into the homes of these people. You get the membership list up to date and be at my command."

And morning, afternoon and night that girl and I drove and held meetings all that spring and summer and fall for the next year. And many of you can testify to it, even in the hottest days of the summer—many of you are saved today because of those visits.

I remember one night way out here in Arlington Heights. The address wasn't on the street but around at the side. They had dug a basement and had a concrete foundation. She sat in the car until I would find them and then she would get out and come in. A man says, "They live around on the back side of that lot." And so I tore out, walk pretty fast as you know, and I hit that concrete foundation. And when the undertaker lays me out he will see two chipped places on both shins. I turned forty somersaults down into that basement. I thought the judgment day had come. After while when I got up I was so disfigured and my wife never saw me until I had gone by the hospital.

We drove and drove and drove. And oftentimes at the close of the day when the battle was hard she and I would join together and we would sing together when I would come and put her out at her home on West Second. And the other day I saw Miss Jane at my daughter's home—her hair is almost white. I said, "Yes, the First Baptist Church put those hairs gray there." She will be back soon. And when my wife phoned me Kate had passed away I immediately called up the airport. There was a terrible snow storm in the West and all the planes were grounded and it was impossible for me to make it.

I wrote her mother and wired her too, and I received the most wonderful letter from Mrs. Tarlton. She said, "I am so grateful for her life. I am so grateful that that night when she called me to her bed she knew that she was crossing and said, 'Mother, hold my hand. Hold it close. Hold it tight. Hold it, mother, I am nearing the crossing.' And then she said, 'Mother, go and lie down and go to sleep. Please do, for my sake.'"

And when the nurse took her mother to the room and came back Kate had turned over on her side. She touched her and said, "It is time to take your medicine," and she did not respond. She shook her—she too had gone to sleep.

And this mother says, "It is worth everything in the world that

I was permitted at the last moment to hold my child's hand when she crossed over."

At the funeral she says, "The whole earth was covered with snow and the sun shining so bright. It is all a beautiful picture of her white life. We buried her body in the cold earth, but her great soul has gone to be with God, and it won't be long until I too will hold that hand again."

Baptizing an Erab El Nemens in the River Jordan Sunday morning, August 8, 1937, at the traditional place where John baptized Jesus.

Dr. Norris with his eminence the Grand Mufti at Jerusalem, who by unanimous vote of all the Muftis of the Mohammedan world, was made their head. This picture was taken in the private office of the Grand Mufti, who is charged with the British government as the instigator of the present uprising in Palestine. He claims to be the true lineal descendant of the Prophet Mohammed. There are 250,000,000 Mohammedans, and the Grand Mufti holds the peace of the world is his hands. It is difficult to interview him.

"BUT GOD"—THE GREATEST SERVICE IN THE HISTORY OF THE FIRST BAPTIST CHURCH

*Sermon by Dr. J. Frank Norris, First Baptist Church,
Fort Worth, Texas*
(Stenographically Reported)

(A great crisis was on in the church. Much misunderstanding and many false rumors and reports were published in the papers. Dr. Norris was absent from the city in an evangelistic campaign. His office force called him by long distance phone when the crisis broke and newspapers headlined it. He refused to come back or to issue a statement, and a week later there was read to the congregation this telegram:

"Regarding the matters that have been widely published I will return in two weeks and give an answer."

A great crowd was present. It was a scorching hot Sunday in July. People were not only packed around the wall but standing on the outside looking in. There was intense anxiety. Dr. Norris rose and said,

"Regarding the matter that has been so widely published I did it. I assume the entire responsibility. I did it for you. My text this morning is just two words, 'But God.'"

That was the only explanation he gave and the whole incident that had caused so much discussion immediately became past history. His method through the years of meeting great crises is to leave the whole thing in the hands of the great God of the universe.)

DR. NORRIS: I invite your attention to four Scriptures:

The first is found in Ephesians second chapter, fourth verse, "But God, who is rich in mercy, for his great love wherewith he loved us."

The second is found in the last chapter of Genesis—the words of Joseph to his eleven brethren, Genesis 50:20, "But as for you, ye thought evil against me; but God meant it unto good, to bring to pass, as it is this day, to save much people alive. Now therefore fear ye not."

The third Scripture is found in I Cor. 15th chapter and 38th verse, "But God giveth it a body as it hath pleased him, and to every seed his own body."

The fourth Scripture is found in the book of Daniel on the momentous occasion when Daniel stood before Nebuchadnezzar and interpreted his dream, that the wise men of Babylon could neither tell nor understand, "But there is a God in heaven that revealeth secrets, and maketh known to the king Nebuchadnezzar what shall be in the latter days."

A very interesting thing happened last week, two of the best women in this church. neither knowing what the other said, said to me, "You preached a sermon many years ago on two words that linger in my soul, I wish you would preach that sermon on those two words again." Unfortunately I did not make any notes on the sermon, and when I had the sermon looked up—it was gone—I guess it's all right.

Those two words—I counted them at one time—and they occur 252 times in the whole Bible—there may be more than that number.

The two words are found in the four Scriptures which I read to you.

First, found in Ephesians 2:4.
Second, found in Gen. 50:20.
Third, found in I Cor. 15:38.
Fourth, found in Daniel 2:28.

Around these four statements can be summed up all the destiny of the soul of man.

There are four things that a man needs:

1. He needs salvation.
2. He needs comfort and grace in the struggles of life.
3. He needs to have an answer to the question of what is beyond this life.
4. He needs to understand what is going on in this present turbulent world.

If you answer those four questions you will have a true philosophy of life.

I repeat them.

1st. A man must know that he is saved—saved from something to something. Saved from sin to righteousness. Saved from hell to heaven. Saved from death to life; and

2nd. After he is saved he must have the answer to the problems of suffering in this world; in other words, a daily supply for his needs as he journeys through this pilgrimage here below; and

3rd. When he looks into the open grave he must have an answer to, "Is there a life beyond this life?"

4th. When he sees that all civilization is going down, governments crashing right and left, he must understand that there is the Hand that guides it all.

The first of these expressions is found in Ephesians 2:4, "But God"—as I said before I counted them once, and they occur 252 times, I marked them in my Bible, but it was lost in the fire.

There is our salvation—as I said to a dearly beloved friend a while ago, when we walk through the pearly gates wondering angels will say, "How did you get here, you so great a sinner?", our answer will be "By the grace of God"—"By grace are ye saved through faith; and that not of yourselves: it is the gift of God."—and in a world that shall never see the setting sun, we will join the innumerable throng in singing,

> "When we've been there ten thousand years,
>   Bright shining as the sun,
> We've no less time to sing His praise,
>   Than when we first begun."

Then we will know the breadth and length, the height and the depth of the exceeding riches of His grace, and the meaning of the language of Paul when he said, "That in the ages to come he might shew the exceeding riches of his grace in his kindness toward us through Christ Jesus."

Then this glorious sunlit text of Scripture, after it describes the darkness of death, "Wherein in time past ye walked according to the course of this world, according to the prince of the power of the air, the spirit that now worketh in the children of disobedience; Among whom also we all had our conversation in times past in the lusts of our flesh, fulfilling the desires of the flesh and of the mind; and were by nature the children of wrath, even as others"—born in sin, doomed to die—helpless—then like an over arching rainbow on the bosom of the storm, these words: "But God."

"But God"!

Over the guiltiest sinner that ever stumbled and fell arches the word of grace:

"But God"!

"But God", in contrast, not the work our puny hands can do, not the rivers of briny tears that might come unbidden from our anxious souls, "But God," the Man, the Omnipotent, the Everlasting One has a listening ear, a forgiving heart, He who is rich in mercy, forgives and makes us His.

That is the first thing we need—Our salvation.

> "With broken heart and contrite sigh,
> A trembling sinner, Lord, I cry:
> Thy pardoning grace is rich and free:
> O God, be merciful to me.
>
> I smite upon my troubled breast,
> With deep and conscious guilt oppressed;
> Christ and His cross my only plea:
> O God, be merciful to me.
>
> Far off I stand with tearful eyes,
> Nor dare uplift them to the skies;
> But Thou doest all my anguish see:
> O God, be merciful to me.
>
> Nor alms, nor deeds that I have done,
> Can for a single sin atone;
> To Calvary alone I flee:
> O God, be merciful to me.
>
> And when, redeemed from sin and hell,
> With all the ransomed throng I dwell,
> My raptured song shall ever be,
> God has been merciful to me."

Second: Having been saved we are on our wilderness journey—with many troubles we do not understand—the problems of suffering never will be understood.

Some sorrows come because of our own misdeeds. Only a few minutes ago I saw the quivering, trembling, broken, weeping form of a little wife and mother. The worst thing that could happen to a wife is to have a drunken husband; he not only breaks her heart, but he takes the stars out of her sky. This particular case, like millions of others, has been of long standing through the years. Tell me not her sufferings are for any wrong she has done; it is because of another. Therefore, we have to come and plant our feet on the Rock in the midst of the storms of life.

Here is a most outstanding case: Joseph, loved of his father, envied, and hated by his brothers—and that is a sure way to earn the hate of some of the people (and preachers)—if you are especially blessed or have a little more success, there are some people who will never forgive you for it. You recall the tragic story of how they took him and put him in the pit; how they brought him down to the Egyptian slave market; how Potiphar's wife conspired and schemed to wreck and ruin him, and preferred false indictment against him for which he was put behind prison bars for two years, "But God!"—

"But God" was with him when the hour came for him to interpret Pharaoh's dream of seven years of plenty followed by seven years of famine—Oh, to God that somebody in Washington had as much sense as Joseph! Now some of you are not going to like that, but if you knew how little I care what somebody says —well, you wouldn't say them—you just say what you please and I will say what I please, that is the way to get along—Oh, that somebody instead of destroying the crops of America had had the sense of Joseph, we would have plenty during this time of drought! (Applause.)

I will show you tonight how the judgment of God is on America because of it.

At last when the famine drove the brothers of Joseph to his throne and old Jacob died—the brothers came together and they said—their guilty conscience was at work—"he will kill us now that our father is dead," and when they came and stood before him, and asked forgiveness, Joseph said, "But as for you, ye thought evil against me; but God!"—"Ye meant to do me evil when you put me in that pit—I cried all night; and when those iron bars clanked behind me and left me alone—ye meant to do me evil. 'But God!' You didn't reckon with God, but I did. Let me tell you something, brothers, God was with me that first night in the old dark pit—He whispered, 'Don't be uneasy Joseph.' When you told me, God said, 'Don't be afraid'—Oh, brothers, God and

I have a special understanding you didn't know anything about. Ye meant to do me harm, but I am the head of the empire now; I forgive you—ye meant to do me evil, but God."

I am going to give you a very interesting story that happened since I was last here—the next time I come to the pulpit I am going to bring me a towel. (mopping perspiration.) Last year when I went to Detroit—there are three great daily papers there, either one of which has a larger circulation than all the daily papers here put together. The church editor of one of these papers went to see the other two and said, "Let's put a boycott on Frank Norris. He stirs up trouble everywhere he goes, and the only way to stop him is to put a boycott on him. Boycott him and he won't be here long. He won't get any crowds and he will have to leave, but let him get loose here, give him publicity, and he will stir up trouble."

One of the papers, instead of putting on a boycott went back and published a lot of things that had happened here, for the past 25 years—well I didn't say anything about it—then there came out another story about me—well I went to see the head of that paper who is a Roman Catholic, but he is very big hearted. I said, "Now if you are making anything by that, all right."

He said, "I pay very little attention to the news department, but I think you are right about it."

And the next Sunday morning there came out, in double column, a very flattering write up about me. From then on up to last Saturday there were fine reports made in the Detroit Times, and soon the other papers began to do likewise. The Detroit Free Press, one of the great dailies, is owned by one man, Mr. Ed Stair. He and I had a very happy visit afterward. About a month ago our annual report was carried to the Free Press and they didn't publish it. I said, "Well that's funny."—and two or three things like that happened—so Mr. Entzminger carried my address down to the paper. He thought it would be a good piece of news, and the reporter lit in and said some severe things about me. Mr. Entzminger told me what he said.

I said, "That accounts for some things."

The next morning I went into Mr. Ed Stair's office on the 13th floor of the Free Press Building—a newspaper that has 300,000 circulation.

I said, "I have come here to take up a matter with you, that

I don't believe you know about. There has been a certain amount of prejudice."

He said, "I know all about it, and I am not going to stand for it. Anything you send down here, mark it personal to me."

And now the three papers come out with news and headlines— "Ye meant it for evil, but God!"

That's what happened; nothing to boast of, but the God of Joseph lives today as of old! That is just a commentary on Romans 8:28 "And we know that all things work together for good to them that love God, to them who are the called according to his purpose."—Sometimes we may not understand, but just await God's purpose.

Third, after we have been saved, after we have gone through this life, we hear the breakers roar, and we wonder about the crossing ahead—we would like to know—I Cor. 15:38, "But God giveth it a body as it hath pleased him, and to every seed his own body."

Two illustrations are sufficient. Years ago when crossing the old Coosa River in Alabama, as a boy only eleven years old,— another boy and I were driving two mule teams. As we went down on the old ferry boat I was afraid I would drive off of it—I was scared of the water. When we were on, the old ferryman unhitched a chain from a big tree on the bank, threw it on the flat bottom ferry and out we started—First thing I knew the old boat began to move and soon began to turn around. I was scared. The mules were scared—you know a mule gets scared when he gets out of place—the first thing I knew instead of crossing the river as I thought we should, we were going down the river—down and down we went, the trees were passing on either side—I said to myself, now that old ferryman has taken a drink, and he doesn't know where we are going—I could hear the roar of the falls a short distance below—I thought, I can't swim, but I will unhitch one of the mules and hold on to him—I was scared. That old ferryman let the boat drift—and after a while he put out an oar and began to paddle, first on one side, then stroke on the other side—and the first thing I knew we came right up to the bank on the other side where there was a graveled road, and the ferryman walked off and threw that chain around a big tree, and we drove off, safe and sound.

Oh, I have seen that a million times—sometimes I wonder

whether or not my little boat will make the landing—sometimes it begins to whirl around and drift down, and sometimes there is a dreadful load—sometimes I begin to cry—sometimes I feel God himself has forsaken—sometimes I can't see the ferryman—sometimes darkness overtakes. "But God!" is on board, and my little ferry boat will land safe on the other side! (Shoutings.)

> "Children of the heav'nly King,
> As ye journey, sweetly sing;
> Sing your Savior's worthy praise,
> Glorious in His works and ways.
>
> We are trav'ling home to God,
> In the way the fathers trod:
> They are happy now, and see
> Soon their happiness shall see.
>
> Fear not, brethren, joyful stand
> On the borders of your land;
> Jesus Christ, your Father's son,
> Bids you undismayed go on.
>
> Lord, obediently we go,
> Gladly leaving all below;
> Only Thou our Leader be,
> And we still will follow Thee."

A few days ago a very great tragedy happened—a four year old boy was on the Boulevard where there are two streets, with a strip of grass and trees which separate them—this little boy was playing with some children and they would run up and down and across—this four year old child ran behind one of the cars, just in time to be crushed to death by a powerful truck. His little body was so mangled they could not open the casket. He was the only child of this father and mother. The mother was a devout Christian, the father an unbeliever.

He said, "It's a new world, what shall I do?—When I go home in the evening and he doesn't stand on the porch to meet me, what shall I do?—When I leave in the morning and don't feel his embrace, tell me will I ever see him again?"

Thanks be unto God, Jesus will raise him up in the morning of the resurrection!

"But There Is a God"

This last word—There was a terrible condition, all the world was going to pieces, the king was in distress, Babylon was in confusion, all the wise men couldn't tell what was going on. Daniel was in bed, but God revealed the secret to Daniel and when he stood before that old Pagan king here is the word, "But there is a God in heaven that reveals the secrets, and maketh known to the king Nebuchadnezzar what shall be in the latter days."

So today beloved, I tell you there is a God—I don't understand the things that come, none of us can, but I believe profoundly that God, the God of our Lord Jesus Christ, has called me to do a specific work.

I stood the other day, yonder in upper New York state, when the thermometer was 104 degrees, and spoke to a great crowd of preachers who came from a long distance—when the afternoon session was over every thread on my body was wringing wet—a preacher whose hair was white—looked like he was past sixty, but he was just a little past forty, came to me and said, "I know you are tired, but I would like to have five minutes with you."

I said, "You can have more." I was rooming in Mrs. Miller's home next to the church, and I said to him, "Come on and go with me to my room while I bathe and change clothes and we can talk."

He did, and when he sat down in that room he bowed his head in his hands and poured out his soul, and said, "Oh God! Oh, God! I wish I had heard that message ten years ago."

What had happened? He had come into a great tragedy, the devil had defeated him, and (as is the trouble so often) the deacons who ought to have stood by him stabbed him in the back. He was a heart broken man. His wife's health was gone; his children had lost their faith in God because of what the church had done to him. I crossed over, put my arm around him and said, "God still lives."

He said, "I know He does, but He has turned His face forever from me."

I said, "He has not turned His face from you—He never did turn from one of His, when he gets down in the depths and cries out 'Lord help, help, help!'—That is what He has been wanting to hear." And we had a season of prayer.

I received a letter from him and a good church he never thought of called him to be the pastor. He is one of the happiest men in the country. He says, "Come on and help me celebrate."

God has called me to do that kind of thing. I want you to understand I am not going to forsake you. No. But God has prepared me to do that kind of thing.

I believe one of two things is going to happen—we are going to have a great revival, or Jesus Christ is soon coming again. There isn't any doubt about it.

That thing in Spain may be the spark that will set off the conflagration—You read in the papers where France is ready to go to the help of the Communists. If they do Italy and Germany will go to the help of the other crowd.

I sent George, who as you know is aboard the Battleship Oklahoma which has been ordered to the rescue of American citizens in Spain—I sent a cablegram out of an anxious father's heart, and asked him to cable at my expense—the answer was that I couldn't send him a cablegram and he couldn't send me one.

The condition, my friends, is terrible, but there is a God in heaven, and God knows what is going on, and God is going to take care of George. (Voices: Amen.)

Four things we need to know.

1. "But God," reaches down and saves us.

2. "But God" overrules everything to His glory and for our good.

3. "But God," in the morning of the resurrection gives us a new body, robs death of its sting, and the grave of its victory.

4. "But God" even knows the workings of evil men and will bring their counsel to naught.

Oh, to God we knew how to sing those words our fathers and mothers used to sing, that martyrs inscribed on prison cells, and indelibly traced with their rich red blood:

> "God moves in a mysterious way
>   His wonders to perform;
> He plants his footsteps in the sea,
>   And rides upon the storm.
>
> Deep in unfathomable mines
>   Of never-failing skills,
> He treasures up his bright designs,
>   And works his sovereign will.

Ye fearful saints, fresh courage take;
The clouds ye so much dread
Are big with mercy, and shall break
In blessings on your head.

Judge not the Lord by feeble sense,
But trust him for his grace;
Behind a frowning providence
He hides a smiling face.

His purposes will ripen fast,
Unfolding every hour;
The bud may have a bitter taste,
But sweet will be the flower.

Blind unbelief is sure to err,
And scan his work in vain:
God is his own interpreter,
And he will make it plain."

Speaking of George, I would rather have this reward than anything I know. I had a letter from George the other day, and he said:

"I am on the other side, but I want you to know that I believe in the Bible I learned at home, and in the First Baptist Church, and when I come back I want to tell them that I have still that faith, and I want you to know, although far away, every night when I read the Bible and kneel and pray, my last word is "Oh God, bless dear old Dad as he works so hard, give him strength, and may I—when he is broken down—may I be a joy and a comfort to him'."

But God lives!

Let us stand.

(Large numbers were saved and came into the church. The whole congregation broke and came to the platform and there were shoutings and rejoicings and streaming tears. Mr. John Hope stepped to the microphone and reported to the outside world what was going on. It was one o'clock when that scene, the greatest ever witnessed in the First Baptist Church, was over.)

THE 14 MEMBERS OF THE NORRIS FAMILY

The above photograph was taken at Dr. Norris' residence in Fort Worth on Christmas day, 1937. Left to right they are, Dr. J. Frank Norris, Jim Gaddy Norris, Jr., Mr. J. Frank Norris, Jr., Mr. George Norris, Jr., Mr. Charles B. Weaver, Mrs. Charles B. Weaver, Mr. George Norris, Mrs. Jim Gaddy Norris, Mr. Jim Gaddy Norris, and Mrs. J. Frank Norris. Center, Mrs. George Norris, Mrs. J. Frank Norris, Jr. Front, Julia Weaver, Lillian Weaver, and Mary Weaver.

"NOW WE SEE THROUGH A GLASS DARKLY; BUT THEN FACE TO FACE"

Twenty-eighth Anniversary Sermon by Dr. J. Frank Norris,
Sunday Morning, September 20, 1936

(Stenographically Reported)

———

DR NORRIS: I am going to ask this entire audience to stand and after we stand I want to ask all the members who were here when I came to Fort Worth to come to the front and occupy these seats here to my left.

While we stand everybody sing this great old hymn, "When the Battle's Over We shall Wear a Crown"—Listen folks, I want the choir to sing it down to the chorus, you listen to it, and then go back and everybody sing it.

(Congregation sings.)

> And when the battle's over we shall wear a crown!
> Yes, we shall wear a crown!
> Yes, we shall wear a crown!
> And when the battle's over we shall wear a crown
> In the new Jerusalem
>
> Wear a crown, wear a crown,
> Wear a bright and shining crown,
> And when the battle's over we shall wear a crown
> In the new Jerusalem.

Let us remain standing, every head bowed while Brother Gilbert Wilson leads us in prayer.

(prayer)

Now I realize how crowded we are: many of you no doubt are uncomfortable. First of all I want to ask that nobody applaud, it wastes your time and mine. I want everybody who is from outside the city, whether you are members here or not, I want you to raise your right hand. (Hundreds of hands raised) Now I want everybody who raised his hand to stand. (A big crowd stand)

Now let's give them a good old Texas hand—(Applause)

At the close of the service I want to shake hands with everyone. You may be seated. I am very happy to have you here with us today. After the services we will have lunch for you who are from out of the city, not homefolks. We have services here right after lunch. Meet in the hall at the entrance—We are going to have services all day and tonight—Mr. Morris, who has been with us twelve happy years, will have some special music with the choir, and I will bring a message.

Now I am going to risk chances of having a family row, but I will take chances. How many of you would like to see one of the happiest families on earth? (Applause) Would you? (Again applause)

Before I present them I want my friends Mr. and Mrs.. Wadsworth of Missouri, who have come eight-hundred miles for the purpose of being here today. They went up to Detroit last summer to be at the revival, and we are glad that they are here this morning (Mr. and Mrs. Wadsworth come to the platform)

Now I want you to see one of my Detroit friends who said she had heard so much about us down here that she wanted to come and see for herself. Miss Edith Swadling, will you please come to the front. (Miss Swadling goes to the front)

This is Mr. and Mrs. Elmer Wadsworth from Moberly, Missouri, and this is Miss Edith Swadling from Detroit. They all say that they came all the way from Missouri and Detroit to be here at this Anniversary. I will ask all three, "Was it worth it?"

(The three answer in unison) More!

(Voice: Dr. Norris, I walked four miles to be here)

DR. NORRIS: All right, you may be seated.

I have a ballot here—

Voice interrupts—But where is the family? (Applause)

DR. NORRIS: All right I will ask the family if they will—I know I am going to get into it, but I have been wanting to get even with these boys a long, long time—I will ask them to stand. (Family stands.) We want to see the new baby—Come up here, Jim Gaddy and call the roll. (Jim Gaddy Norris walks to the platform)

JIM GADDY: First I will call the grandchildren. Come up here Julia—This is Julia Weaver—the other two little girls come up here—This is Mary and Lillian.

Next I will call George Louis, the youngest of the family. (George walks to platform)

Next, J. Frank Norris, Jr., (Walks to platform)

Next, I will call his better half, Rita, (Walks to platform)

Next, Mrs. Lillian Weaver, (Walks to the platform)

Next, Mrs. Jim Gaddy Norris, (Walks to the platform)

Next, the best and sweetest of all Mrs. Norris—In her arms is ten pounds of Jim Gaddy II. (Mrs. Norris stands, with little Jim Gaddy II in her arms, while the audience loudly applaud)

DR. NORRIS: You may be seated, thank you.

I am very happy to tell you every member of my family believes in the same gospel their father preaches.

I am happy to tell you this magnificent auditorium and this three-quarters of a block that's half a quarter of a million dollars— the church went through it all last Wednesday night—and we are glad to tell you that this three-quarters block is safe as long as time shall last. It hasn't been without tears, struggles and trials. Now I realize I am going to do a very risky dangerous thing, but there is one man I want you to see—I know when I begin to talk about faithful men and women, I can't call the roll of the thousands, but some of you were not in the position and did not have the opportunity as may others—Here is a man who has suffered— You have heard people say, "It costs something to belong to the First Baptist Church." I am ashamed of anybody that ever says that. But I am going to introduce to you a man that it really cost him something—It cost him a whole lot of friends and money —He denies it, and says it did not cost him anything. But I know differently. He is a man who was in a position to render this church and pastor the most valuable service. Absolutely without him, I don't know where we would have been today. When the leaves of the Judgment book unfold and the record on high is made known and the events of the earth are revealed, then God's recording angel will show you one quiet man, whose life now is mostly behind him—He was a long ways from here. I called him—He had gone to the funeral of a loved one. I said to him, "I want you here as the honor guest of the church and pastor tomorrow—He is a man that has never dipped his colors—I am going to refer to it again, tell you the inside story. I have the high honor of introducing to you the best friend this little family ever had. J. T. Pemberton. He wouldn't make a speech, or I would call on him. (Applause)

Have we taken the offering?

All right. My text this morning—I Corinthians 13th chapter, 12th verse, "Now we see through a glass, darkly; but then face to face."—Words of contrast.

Ten thousand texts rush to my mind on this very happy occasion, for indeed it is a great family in Christ Jesus, we can say with Samuel at Mizpeh," Here we will raise our Ebenezer"— "Hither hath the Lord helped us."

We can say like Israel, "Out of bondage into the promised land."

We can say like Moses when he stood on Nebo's Heights, "Farewell to forty years of wilderness journey, and look over into the land of Promise."

We can say like the Apostle Paul as he looked back over the most memorable thirty years that any human being ever experienced on earth, and say, "I have fought a good fight, henceforth there is laid up for me a crown."

I do not know of any text that sums up or more adequately expresses it—the thoughts that revolve in our hearts today, "Now we see through a glass, darkly; but then face to face."

The two words of contrast in that text are these:

1. "Now," and
2. "Then"

The word "now" sums up all there is of this brief fleeting time that will soon know us no more.

The word "then" sums up all the glory that bursts on the soul of the redeemed when they put foot on Immanuel's shores, and say "Farewell to earth and time."

I shall dwell but briefly on the first half. Now first, "We see through a glass darkly."

Last night I was in a sad home, sadder than a funeral could make it, for the unfortunate father and husband is behind state prison bars, while three little children tug at the skirts of the heart broken mother and wife. For "Now we see through a glass, darkly."

I met an old man the other day, past 80, no home, no friends, no money, "Now we see through a glass darkly."

I was in a hospital a few days ago while life was fast slipping away, the shadows were gathering around that couch, "Now we see through a glass, darkly."

I saw a young wife, all hopes of a happy married life dashed to smithereens, and the bride of yesterday, her joy has turned to weeping and sorrow today. "Now we see through a glass, darkly."

Not long ago I was in a home where millions once were at their command, today two old people live in one room. "Now we see through a glass, darkly."

I had a friend in the prime of health a few years ago, today he is a nervous wreck, with pain racking his body, "Now we see through a glass, darkly."

As I look on the maps of the world—turn where you will, millions of people under every flag, on every hand, every continent war torn, in sorrow, poverty—they, "See through a glass, darkly."

When we go to yonder city of the dead, and see that casket slowly go down, and then tomorrow we reach down with trembling hands and brush away the withered flowers, placed there by loving hands, "Now we see through a glass, darkly."

Sometimes when God calls us and we are compelled to go through the fiery furnace made seven times hot, or, by hell's conspiracy we are forced into the den of hungry lions, "Now we see through a glass, darkly."

But I want to turn to the other side of the text. Let sickness come, let poverty come, let old age come, let sorrows come, let storms come, let all hell move, "but then face to face"!

That's the message I want to leave.

"All things work together for good"—it is easy to say before the trials come.

When we are well, it is easy to say, "All things work together for good."

When things are going our way, it is easy to say, "All things work together for good."

But wait till the shadows lengthen.
Wait till the night comes.
Wait till the cupboard is empty.
Wait till the little feet are on the bare ground.
Wait till you haven't got a friend in the world.

Wait till all the firey darts of hell are hurled at you.

Wait till ten thousand criticisms are hissed at you.

Wait till the poisoned dagger is stuck in your back.

Then is the time to answer, "Do you believe, 'All things work together for good?'"

My Highest Honor

I want to say this, at this hour—just some things out of my heart—I feel it today as never before. I don't care where I go, what crowds I preach to, what state I am in, whether North, East, West or South—and my friends here from the North are hearing this, I don't care—you can go to the other side of the Atlantic, what position whether Mussolini, Hitler, or Roosevelt, I say the highest honor that could come to any mortal man I have received at your hands. You honor me greatly. Somehow I have come to feel it very deeply. I have it with a feeling of gratitude. As I shook hands with friends a while ago—they were here when I came —all the members in this church here when I came to the First Baptist Church, I wish you would kindly stand. Please remain standing. You stayed from choice. You are here because you want to be here. "Plunk," wish you would come up here—just remain standing, I want the new folks to hear this—Oh, I know some folks will say, "I wouldn't refer to those things." The men in the Bible, went back and referred to things—deliverances. If you cut out the references to the past, you would cut out the most of the Old Testament.

(Andrew Plunkett walked to the platform)

Back yonder—to be exact 1913—I want you to get an answer to prayer, what God did when the powers of darkness sought to destroy this church. The final act of certain business interests was to call every employee, who were members of the First Baptist Church, before them, and put the cold unAmerican proposition up to each of them, "You take your choice beween your job and that church."

Now that's unpardonable that it should happen in America. Ask Miss Maud who had been so faithful for years at that place of business, when they told her to take her choice between her job and her church—she was cashier—she didn't wait to unbutton the apron she had on, she just broke the string and hurled it at the man's feet and said, "Here's your job!"

Mrs. J. D. Garrett, who is now in glory, when her boss called her and said to her, "We are going to stop Frank Norris, we have tried every way, and now you can take your choice between your job and that church" she said, "The job is yours."

And John Hope who has had a serious operation but will be here next Sunday, when his boss called him in and said, "Take your choice," I am glad to say that John stood like old John of old, by the Cross.

Now Andrew Plunkett here— when they called him and told him, he didn't wait till they got started, he said, "I am just a poor young fellow with a family, and you mean to say I have got to take my choice between my church or my job? You can have the job."

I want this great audience to know this man—and there are others that said it—My Friends that's the stuff that has made this church what it is. Have I told it right Plunk?

MR. PLUNKETT: You have told the truth.

DR. NORRIS: You may be seated.

When this man (putting his hand on Mr. Pemberton's shoulder) was president of the Farmers and Mechanics National Bank—and it was a great institution of Fort Worth, now part of the Fort Worth National Bank—a fine lot are running it, no finer set of men can be found on earth.—When certain big interests went into J. T. Pemberton's bank and said to him, "Pemberton you have got to stop that preacher of yours"—and they used some very unparlimentary language. "If you don't break with him, we are going to break your bank."

This man rose and walked to the little gate and said,

"Go and get your money, I will stay with my church and preacher."

Is that so Mr. Pemberton?

MR. PEMBERTON: Yes.

(Voices from extreme rear of house) Dr. Norris, may I interrupt?

DR. NORRIS: Yes.

VOICE: I was holding a position then, and the man told me "Give up your job or quit going to that church."

I told him to take his job and go to hell with it. I wasn't fired either, I held my position. (Applause)

Choir of First Baptist Church, directed by Mr. Brooks Morris, and Baptistry of First Baptist Church, Fort Worth. Everybody in great auditorium has full view of the baptising.

DR. NORRIS: Come up here on the platform—I want to show you the kind of stuff God used in making this church, and I could just call the roll down the line if I had time.

(A fine looking man comes to the platform)

DR. NORRIS: Tell where you are from and—

THE MAN: (Oscar Hanson) I was born right here close by, have been here 34 years. I have had several fights,

DR. NORRIS: No, don't tell that—(laughter)

THE MAN: My boss told me if I wanted to work for him I had to give up my church. I said to him,

"You take your job and go to hell." I wasn't fired either. (Lauhter and Applause)—Later he was converted."

DR. NORRIS: I must say that's a new way to make converts. (Laughter)

We have a twentieth century interpretation of "Not knowing the things that befall me . . . But none of these things move me, neither count I my life dear unto myself, so that I might finish my course with joy, and the ministry, which I have received of the Lord Jesus, to testify the gospel of grace of God."

The First Baptist Church is the greatest missionary church I know of on earth. Yonder in that great industrial center with its two million population, not only the world's greatest automobile industry but now the greatest steel market in the world;— have added 60,000 people to the population in twelve months,— Godless, Christless as every great American city is today—there will be a congregation like this one. They have more than doubled and almost tripled their membership in the past year and half. They have something like five hundred young men and women who have banded themselves together and are going afield throughout that great city, following the example of this once despised church in Fort Worth.

I receive invitations around the world—no boasting, but they want men and women who still believe in this gospel, the same gospel that you and I believe in, and that is what I want you to pass on this morning—it is stated on the ballot passed to you a while ago—as to whether you, with your prayers, and your tears, and your money, and your blood, and your souls, you will stand by this poor preacher as he goes from state to state, preaching the unsearchable riches of Jesus Christ, born of the Virgin Mary, living a sinless life, speaking as never man spake, performing miracles as only God could perform, dying the just for the unjust to bring us to God, buried in Joseph's new made tomb, rising the third day victorious over sin and the grave, ascending to the right hand of the Father, where he ever liveth, interceding for us, coming again in fulfillment of promise, to put down all rule, chaining the old Devil, raising the dead, and establishing His Kingdom on the earth!

I believe it as I have never believed it!

How One Man Won Notable Victory

I have made many mistakes—because I run with you. (laughter)

I am going to talk about Pemberton again. One day down here in a little board tabernacle—you talk about being broke, we didn't have anything to get broke over—24 men, bankers and other members of this church, all met to send my wife's husband to a well known place C. O. D. Mr. Pemberton was there; I was there. When he walked in he said to me, "Now listen, don't you say anything. I will answer them when they get through." They frothed at the mouth and said an awful lot of mean things about this preacher—I never had known anybody to do that—up to that time. When they got through—I can see him now, Mr. Pemberton, just began to unbutton his left cuff, and rolled up his sleeve, clear up above his elbow. I thought, "Well, he is a mighty brave man to get into a fight with all this crowd"—he walked out there, and in a few words said:

"I fought against this man coming here. I knew something was going to happen if he came. You fellows brought him here against my vote, but by the grace of God you are not going to run him off and ruin an innocent man. Before I would allow you to do that I would cut this left arm, and let every drop of my blood fall from my body on this ground."

The meeting adjourned right then, and not another word was said. Do you blame me for loving him? (Applause)

Another thing happened, my health was gone—I was in a pretty bad fix—the old devil meant to break me by taking my health— one day I was badly worn, was bankrupt—they said I was bankrupt, but I was twice as bankrupt, as they said—they didn't know how much I did owe. I went to Mr. Pemberton, and I said,

"I am going to leave here, there is no use talking, I am going crazy—everybody is saying mean things"—you remember how the papers used to come out with big headlines, and the boys would stand on the streets and holler.

"Read all about Frank Norris"—and they would sell their papers—

"Well," I said to Pemberton, "I can't stand it any longer. I want to borrow some money and take my wife and children and leave—I want to get $500.00."

He said, "That won't be enough."

I said, "Well, I need more, I'd like to get $750—I am going to Southern California, get on a ranch and regain my health."

"Well," he said, "let it be a thousand."

"You never expect to get it back, do you?"

As I started to go he said, "I don't blame you, but I want to say a word. I was down at the tabernacle yesterday morning, and I saw a lot of people, 25 or more accept Christ and were baptized, and I went back that night and saw another crowd join, and they too were baptized. Now I don't know how to advise you but just as long as that takes place you needn't care what the newspapers say."

Man, I just climbed up on top of Jacob's ladder, I leaned way over and looked the old devil in the face and said, "You go to hell, where you belong." (Applause)

And I took that note signed by me and tore it up—I didn't borrow the thousand dollars, and I know he has been glad of it, for he would have had to pay. (Laughter)

Pemberton's Reply To Seven Baptist Preachers

Let me tell you something else, seven Baptist preachers called on Mr. Pemberton,—not a one of them are in Fort Worth now— some of them have gone on, peace to their ashes, the rest of them have departed. They said,

"Mr. Pemberton how in the world do you stand what he does? Do you know what he says? Do you endorse it?"

Mr. Pemberton said, "You just go ahead and say all you have to say."

One of them said, "He said this and he said that—do you endorse that?" "Oh," they said, "Mr. Pemberton you just don't know."

Mr. Pemberton said, "Are you through?"

"Well," they said, "isn't that enough?"

Then Mr. Pemberton replied, "Let me tell you something gentlemen, now, you have told me a whole lot—"

"Oh," they said, "we can tell you a whole lot more. Why Mr. Pemberton we don't see how you can put up with a man like that."

"Well," said Mr. Pemberton, "I found out a long time ago that Frank Norris and the Lord had a private understanding and they haven't taken me in on it, and I made up my mind, any man that the Lord could get along with as well as he does Frank Norris, J. T. Pemberton is going to get along with him, too."

Dear Wayne Alliston—you four Mississippi boys sitting there know him—old Wayne got nervous and he said, "Brethren, I feel like we are doing something wrong, and I hope you will forgive me—I think we ought to get on God's side with Frank Norris," and he came running out and came up to the office and told me all that happened.

"Now we see through a glass, darkly; then face to face."

A Mother's Prayers Answered

The other day some people joined the church at Detroit from Columbiana, Alabama. They knew everybody I knew there, were raised together with some of my people—I want to tell you a story —you mothers, let me tell you something, do you ever get tired and discouraged? I want to tell you a little story that goes back into the past. I was about eight years old, one day I was standing on the porch of the public school in Columbiana, two boys came up, one was 12 and one 14, each one of them had on a nice suit of clothes, a nice overcoat. I had on a little cotton suit, no overcoat, and the coat was tight around me—these boys, sons of a banker— they came up, looked at me, and they said, "Your coat is too little" —well I knew it. Then one of them pointed his finger at me while all the boys gathered around and said, "Your daddy is a drunkard and mine is a banker." I turned went into the school room, buried my face in my hands. The dear school teacher came up to me put her arm around my shoulders and said, "Frank what is the matter?"

I couldn't say a word.

She said, "You must be sick I am going to send you home."

I fairly flew home—when I got home, mother said, "Frank, are you sick?"

I said, "Yes."

She said, "I'll give you some medicine."

"No, no, no, I am not sick."

"Well," she said, "what are you crying about?"

"I can't tell you."

I wouldn't tell her what had happened. But that night after I had gone to my room she came in and said, "Tell mother what is the matter?"

I begged hard not to tell her, "But," she said, "I must know, so we may cry together."

I said, "Mother I couldn't help it." And I told her what had happened, how those two finely dressed banker's sons had come up, pointed their finger at me and said, "Your daddy is a drunkard"— poor daddy was in a room drunk then—thank God he was saved before he went home to heaven.

Mother said, as she put her tender arms around me, and brushed away my tears, "Son, it is all right, some day you are going to wear good clothes—some day you will make a man—some day God will use you."

I said, "Mother, please don't make me go back to school."

She said, "You don't have to go back; mother will teach you."

And it was a great blessing to me—I read all the histories, memorized whole chapters in the Bible—Now wasn't it a great blessing to me?

Thirty years rolled around, one day I stood in the same little town, on the court house square—I had on a brand new suit, the best hat money could buy, a fine overcoat, and a fine pair of shoes— the whole outfit cost about $250.00 and B. W. Owens paid every dollar of it. I was standing on the court house square talking to one of my cousins—I saw an old bedraggled looking fellow coming down the street, his white hair sticking out through a hole in his hat—his face was covered with an unkept beard. My cousin said, "Do you know who that is?"

I said, "No."

He says, "That is Sam ....; he has drunk himself to death."

He called to him and said, "Sam come up here and meet one of your old school mates. He came up, I said, "Hello Sam." I

Annual Meeting of the French Bible Mission.

Congregation of the Calombes Evangelical Baptist Church, Paris, France, Which Heard Dr. Norris.

shook his palsied hand, the result of sin, and I looked into his dissipated face—he raised his eyes and looked at me and said, "Frank, you are looking mighty fine. Fortune has been better to you than it has been to me. My father left us a fortune, but it's gone now."

Thank God for a mother that said, "It is all right son, some day you will wear good clothes. Some day God will bless you." Thank God for a great mother!

(Somebody hands Dr. Norris a towel)

That's what I want, a towel—these handkerchiefs get wet the first time you use one. I am so hot.

"Now we see through a glass darkly; but then face to face."

This word briefly. This happened on the T. and P. forty years ago. An old railroad engineer had a boy, and that boy loved to go on the engine with his father—he wanted to be an engineer and sit in his father's seat. The old father would say to his son, "When you get to be an engineer just do one thing always, don't leave the engine; stay with the engine, even if it means death."

After a while he got to be engineer. It was in the days before they had automatic air brakes. One day he was on his engine climbing over a divide with fifty or sixty loaded box cars behind him, as he got over and started down he saw the river bridge was under water. He signaled the brakes to be put on, but the momentum was too great the brakes slipped and wouldn't hold. When the fireman saw death and destruction were ahead he leaped out of the engine and struck out through the woods, but that young engineer stayed with the engine. When that old engine crashed into that flooded river the fifty or sixty cars and caboose piled on top. "Oh," said everybody, "the fireman escaped, and the engineer escaped too." Somebody said they saw him running through the woods. The old white haired mother standing by said,

"You say the fireman escaped? Well the fireman may have run, but my boy didn't run, when they get down there they will find him in the engine."

Up and up they lifted the cars until they got to the bed of the river and found the old engine bottom side up; they dug down and found the mangled form of the engineer with his hand tight on the throttle.

She said, "I told you, you would find him."

Oh, friends, thank God you, and you, and you, and I have had the joy—we stayed with the old engine, and we didn't have a wreck, (Shoutings) and we will some day pull into the Union Station above! We have got orders from on high, Jesus Christ is the General Superintendent; we will throw in the best fuel, our blood, tears and money, pull wide open the throttle of divine power, ring the joy bells of glory, (Shouting) turn on the headlight of hope, and go across the bridges, through the dark tunnels, until at last we win the race and receive the crown, then we will know what it all means. One look on His dear face will be glory enough for me!

> "Trials dark on every hand, and we cannot understand
> All the ways that God will lead us to that blessed promised
>   land;
> But He'll guide us with His eye, and we'll follow till we die,
> We will understand it better by and by.
>
> We are often destitute of the things that life demands,
> Want of shelter and of food, thirsty hills and barren land,
> But we're trusting in the Lord, and according to His word,
> We will understand it better by and by.
>
> Temptations, hidden snares, often take us unawares,
> And our hearts are made to bleed for each thoughtless word
>   or deed,
> And we wonder why the test, when we try to do our best,
> We will understand it better by and by.
>
> By and by, when the morning comes, All the saints of God
>   are gathering home,
> We will tell the story how we've overcome,
> We will understand it better by and by."

My friends, there is no question of the outcome.

I leave this word with you. I never read the 23rd Psalm till last week. I thought I knew it.

I never read the eighth chapter of Romans until I had been preaching for years. I woke up the other night while the world was wrapped in slumber, there flashed into my mind like the light of the stars—Orion—Pleiades—Arcturas—and all the constellation of heaven:—"And we know that all things work together for good to them that love God, to them who are called according to His purpose. For whom he did foreknow, he also did predestinate to be conformed to the image of his Son, that he might be the first born among many brethren. Morever whom he did predestinate, them he also called: and whom he called, them he also justified, and whom he justified, them he also glorified. What shall we then say to these things? If God be for us, who can be against us?" —The Omnipotent God who created the worlds, holds them in the hollow of His hand—if He, the Almighty God, that can do this, be for us who on earth, or in hell can be against us?—"Who shall lay anything to the charge of God's elect? It is God that justifieth. Who is he that condemneth? It is Christ that died, yea rather, that is risen again, who is even at the right hand of God, who also maketh intercession for us. Now, what shall we then say to these things? "Who shall separate us from the love of Christ? Shall tribulation, or distress, or persecution, or famine, or nakedness, or peril, or sword?" What else Paul? "Nay, in all these things we are more than conquerors through him that loved us For I am persuaded, that neither death, nor life, nor angels, nor principalities, nor powers, nor things present, nor things to come, nor height, nor depth." What else Paul? He is calling the roll—he said, "I will be sure"—"nor any other creature, shall be able to separate us from the love of God which is in Christ Jesus our Lord."

David, bring your harp with you from yonder world and sing your greatest song. David looks back to the time he was a shepherd lad—he sees himself going after Goliath, and coming back with his head—He sees himself as an old man—He strikes that harp—angels bend listening ears to hear—"The Lord"— Jehovah "is my shepherd"—not "a" shepherd, or "the" shepherd but "my shepherd"—Jesus said, "My sheep hear my voice, and I know them, and they follow me."

What else David? "He leadeth me by the still waters."

What else David? "Out in pastures of tender grass."

What else? "Oh, I am tired, distressed, I am storm tossed. I do not know what to do, and 'He restoreth my soul'—But wait a minute there is sorrow coming. "Though I walk deep down into the valley of the shadow"—it's just a shadow "of death"—what is the result? "I will fear no evil." Why? "Thy rod and thy staff they comfort me."

(Voices: Amen and shoutings)

I love to talk to you because you talk back.

What else? Look at my enemies, look at them—David strikes another key. What shall he say? He sings to the Lord Himself and says "Thou preparest a table before me in the presence of mine enemies: "—And old David says, "I am going to have breakfast, dinner, and supper, and eat between meals, while all the Sanballats and Tobiahs stand on the outside and look at me while Jesus serves His tired servant." (Shoutings)

What else David? He says, "Thou anointest my head with oil; my cup runneth over."

What else David? "Oh, I was about to give up once. I thought I was having a hard time, but God said this, and I believe it is so, "Surely goodness and mercy shall follow me all the days of my life."

What else David? "I take a look down into the unknown future, 'And I shall dwell in the house of the Lord forever'"—That word means "home." David says, "I am going home, for in my Father's home there are many mansions, and we know that if this earthly house of this tabernacle, were dissolved, we have a house—a home—not built with hands." And they are going to have shade trees there, Bill. I love the trees; they tell me of God.

A professor out here at the Seminary says what the Bible says about heaven is not to be taken literally. Friends I believe there will be a lot of trees there—the Bible says so. It tells of the tree of life, and I am going to sit down under its shade and eat of the fruits of that tree! (Voices, Amen.)

I love to tell you about that river—I have seen beautiful rivers in America and Europe, but I have seen the beautiful river of life—and it is going to run right in front of my house—and there is no Paradise this side of Eden like the beautiful flowers in my yard in heaven.

I love to tell about the orchestra up there.

They have every musical instrument in heaven. Talk about a choir, they have a hundred million in that choir, and the angels too—

I'll tell you another thing, they will never foreclose on our homes up there (Voices: Amen.); no sir. And we will never have to pay taxes there. They will never tie crepe on the front door; no sir. Everybody will be satisfied.

I love to tell you about my servants—the angels of heaven are going to wait on me.

I have a lot of people waiting for me up there; yes Bill.

Down here you don't know your next door neighbor, but we will know them up there—you will be living right across the street from me.   There won't be any gossipers up there either, and no lying men or women around—they will all be in hell.   We won't have anything up there but good neighbors—nobody will steal—we won't have automobiles, we will ride in a flaming chariot like Elijah went to heaven in.   (Voices, Amen.)   Let me tell you something else, we will meet, and the congregation never will break up. Do you want me to tell you who will be some of our neighbors, right next door?—Enoch, Noah, Abraham, Moses—we will go over and spend the day with Job—and we will cross over yonder a million miles and take supper with old Samuel, and after everybody gets through David will pick up his harp, and Brooks will be there to lead the singing, and we will all sing the songs of Moses and the Lamb.   (Shoutings)

And then the best of all in heaven, Jesus Christ Himself will appear, and we shall look on His face, and when He shows us those nail scarred hands, then all heaven will fall down at His feet and worship Him!

"FOREVER"

I see something new in this marvelous Psalm of David each time I repeat it.   At two o'clock the other morning while I was repeating it, for the first time I saw the fullness of the meaning of the word, "forever."

I wish I knew how to quote that last verse:

"Surely — goodness — and — mercy — shall — follow — me — all — the — days — of — my — life; — and — I — will — dwell — in — the — house — of — the — Lord — for — ever."

Here is what he means to say as he looks back over a life of trials and triumphs of lights and shadows:

It is "My Shepherd"—"Green Pastures"—"Still Waters"—Deliverances—table loaded with good things—a running over cup of joy!

And then as he looks out into the unknown future, as the shadows lengthen, his steps slow and feeble, his shoulders bending with the weight of years, his eyes growing dim—these two twin graces like the shining angels from the skies on Mount Olivet—

they whisper in the ears of the old soldier, "Fear Not"—"Fear not to touch Jordan's brim, for when you get there 'Goodness' and 'Mercy' will be there. They will go with you. And when they have carried you over into Canaan's fair and happy land"—What else?—"I will dwell in the house of the Lord forever!"

Now the word that I never saw until the other morning—"Forever"—"Forever"—"Forever"—"Forever"—long after the heavens have been folded together as a garment that is old and moth-eaten —long after this old wicked world has been burned up and war drums will be heard no more. When crime,—murder,—prisons,— asylums,—graveyards,—tears,—pain—out beyond it all—"Forever" —"Forever"—"Forever."

Here for the first time all twelve members of my dear family, together with the youngest, the grandson of a few months—will we ever be together again? We know not. But there is a time coming when we will be together—"Forever"—"Forever"—"Forever."

We will have an anniversary then where the sun will never go down, and no shadows ever fall.

Oh, what a reunion!

> "Our friends will be down at the river
> When death shall call us away
> To enter the glories of heaven,
> O what a wonderful day!
>
> The music of heaven will greet us
> As we shall near the bright home,
> And millions of glorified angels
> From God's own city will come.
>
> We'll enter the city with Jesus,
> And kneel at His blessed feet;
> Our songs of His praises will echo
> Thru all eternity sweet.
>
> We'll rest by the beautiful river,
> Beneath the wide-spreading tree:
> We'll dwell in the light of His presence,
> How sweet, how sweet, it will be."

A Part of the Large Number Who Helped to Prepare and Serve Meals in the Fort Worth Bible School, Nov., 1937.

Where Large Numbers Were Given Three Meals a Day at the Bible School, First Baptist Church, Fort Worth.

Our friends will be down by the river!

Bill thought he was going to cross over not long ago—Bill sent for me, and he said,

"Frank, I may cross over before you come back, but when I get up there"—Bill—Some of you visitors may not know Bill, he was the head of the Retail Liquor Association in Texas—Now, Bill, aren't you glad you didn't run me out of town?

BILL: I sure am.

DR. NORRIS: Aren't you glad when you met with the crowd, down at the Metropolitan Hotel and drank to my demise—you know something happened?

MR. BLEVINS: It sure happened.

DR. NORRIS: God was around in this country about that time!

But Bill said, when he thought he was going to cross over, "Frank, I may cross over before you come back—when I get up there I am going to look up the Superintendent of that country, the General Official, and ask Him for two favors, I am going to ask him to please let me know the day when Frank is coming home."

Then he said, "I am going to ask Him for another favor. I am going to ask him for a holiday that day, I want to get off and be down there at the gate when you come home. I want to be the first to put my arms around you."

I don't know Bill, you probably will go on first, now you be sure to remember your words and look up the Superintendent——say folks there are going to be lots of us there—I know more there already than I do here.

Thank God, while now "We see through a glass. darkly; then face to face."

> "There's no disappointment in heaven,
>   No weariness, sorrow or pain;
> No hearts that are bleeding and broken,
>   No songs with a minor refrain.
> The clouds of our earthly horizon
>   Will never appear in the sky.
> For all will be sunshine and gladness,
>   With never a sob nor a sigh.
>
> We'll never pay rent for our mansion,
>   The taxes will never come due;

Our garments will never grow threadbare,
  But always be fadeless and new;
We'll never be hungry or thirsty,
  Nor languish in poverty there,
For all the rich bounties of heaven
  His sanctified children will share.

There'll never be crepe on the door-knob,
  No funeral train in the sky;
No grave on the hillsides of glory,
  For there we shall never more die;
The old will be young there forever
  Transformed in a moment of time;
Immortal we'll stand in His likeness,
  The stars and the sun to outshine.

I'm bound for that beautiful city
  My Lord has prepared for His own,
Where all the redeemed of all ages
  Sing 'Glory' around the white throne.
Sometimes I grow homesick for heaven
  And the glories I soon shall behold,
What a joy that will be when my Savior I see,
  In that beautiful city of gold!"

Some of these nights or days the papers will have headlines, "J. Frank Norris Died Last Night." It won't be true. I won't be dead. This little engine may stop and this old body may fall to the ground, but Bill, you be up there waiting for me! (shouting).

Let everybody be quiet for a few minutes—Friends this is the greatest church on the face of the God's footstool, not only great in numbers, but great in faith—and there is another great church up yonder. Who wants to come and on this Anniversary Day and join the church, by faith and baptism, letter or experience? I wonder if anybody will rise where you are, and come right now, without a song—here they come, amen. Come on now—who wants to come and take fellowship in the greatest church on the face of the earth?—I am going to give you a chance.

(A great number came, while people shouted, and crowded to the front to shake hands with Dr. Norris. The services continued for over another hour after the sermon was finished).

WHAT FUNDAMENTAL BAPTIST CHURCHES BELIEVE

(1) We believe the whole Bible from Genesis 1:1 to Revelation 22:21, as the verbally inspired and infallible Word of God.

(2) We believe Jesus Christ was born of Mary the Virgin. and is the Son of God and God the Son.

(3) We believe that Christ died for our sins according to the Scriptures, the just for the unjust that He might bring us to God.

(4) We believe that He rose from the grave the third day according to the Scriptures.

(5) We believe that He only is our great High Priest, and we need not the intercession of any man, but that Christ ever liveth to make intercession for us.

(6) We believe that Christ will come in person, bodily, visibly, to establish His Kingdom on the earth.

(7) We believe in the resurrection of both the just and the unjust, and that the righteous will be raised at the Return of Christ.

(8) We believe in the New Birth of the soul; that regeneration is a new creation of the soul dead in trespasses and sins.

(9) We believe that the church is a body of baptized believers, whose only mission is not to "reform the world," but to preach the gospel to every creature.

(10) We believe that Christ only is the head over all things to the church which is His body.

(11) We believe that the Holy Spirit is the only Administrator of the church, and that it is unscriptural for any hierarchy to Lord it over the Church of Jesus Crist.

(12) We believe that all true believers should be baptized as the Lord has commanded—"Go ye therefore, and teach all nations, baptizing them in the name of the Father, and of the Son, and of the Holy Ghost."

(13) We believe that baptism is the immersion in water of a believer, a new born soul—"Then they that gladly received his word were baptized."

Acts 8:36-38, "And as they went on their way, they came unto a certain water: and the eunuch said, See, here is water; what doth hinder me to be baptized? And Philip said, If thou believest with all thine heart, thou mayest. And he answered and said, I believe that Jesus Christ is the Son of God. And he commanded the chariot to stand still: and they went down both into the water, both Philip and the eunuch; and he baptized Him."

(14) We believe that the Great Commission was given by the Head of the Church, to the Church, and the one and only mission of the Church, and of every believer is set forth in this Great Commission: Mat. 28:18-20, "An Jesus came and spake unto them, saying, All power is given unto me in heaven and in earth. Go ye therefore, and teach all nations, baptizing them in the name of the Father, and of the Son, and of the Holy Ghost."

"GIVE ME THIS MOUNTAIN"

Excerpt from New Year's sermon, Jan. 2, 1938.

(Before the great crowd that overflowed the huge auditorium, Dr. Norris delivered his New Year's message on Caleb's request, "Give me this mountain." It was one of the greatest days in the history of the church, more than seventy people were saved and received into the membership.)

In order to encourage, I believe we should give testimony continually of the marvelous deliverances, the abounding mercy of our God. David said, "Forget not all thy benefits."

We are now for the first time where we can say we are out of the woods and the morning has come. When they were telling I was broke, the only thing about that, was I was broke twice as bad as they said I was. I will just tell you how broke I was—I hesitate to give it but I give it to the glory of God.

I went down to Waxahachie in 1914, Luther, in that meeting and got $1240 for two weeks. I didn't have but one suit of clothes and it was like a looking glass. I said, "Well, I am going to buy me some clothes, and I couldn't pay all of my debts, but I could pay a little of them." We had a lot of bills my wife said had to be paid.

As soon as I got back everybody in the church began to tell me what a bad fix we were in. Mr. W. C. Pool, chairman of the Finance Committee at that time, told me how bad off the church was. And I decided I was rich. So help me if I didn't endorse that whole check over to the church. Mr. Pool remembers it.

When I got home my wife said, "Here are the bills. We will go over them."

I said, "Well, we will just go over them." And we went over them and I said, "We will just keep going over them."

Wife said, "But I told all these people when you got back we were going to pay them."

I said, "We will do it the next time I get back."

I wasn't very strong physically, but I tore out up here to Mangum, Oklahoma, and stayed ten days, got $720. And when I got home I found something else. I was having big crowds and large numbers saved; the more the devil fought the more the Lord blessed.

Wife said, "What are we going to do?"

I said, "Wait until I get home from the next meeting."

And so I held seven meetings that year and every dollar went into this church. I wasn't obligated; I was glad to do it—had to. Don't anybody feel sorry for me. I am having a perfectly good time. I am enjoying good health and the blessings of the Lord. Don't be afraid to make a little investment. Stand up and take your losses. But you can't lose.

And then I went out to Midland, Texas. And you know what happened? We had a great meeting. And they got together, six cattlemen, and met at the First National Bank and said, "Let's help this preacher out. He is a hard fighter." And they gave me a cashier's check for $4,434. And bless your life, when I got back here the creditors was about to foreclose on this property. Well, I had that $4,434—and, Luther, what did I do? (Turning to L. L. Cooper who was sitting on the platform.)

MR. COOPER: You put it in the church.

DR. NORRIS: Did I ever get it back?

MR. COOPER: No, sir.

DR. NORRIS: And I can't get it back. Any man that can get $4,434 after he puts it in here is smarter than I am. (Laughter.) And so I got my expenses and a $100. That is what I got. I think it was a good investment.

And when we saw this place covered with ashes and wreck and ruin and the clouds were dark, and it looked like we couldn't go any further. Jane Hartwell worked and walked and pulled and went and got $1.00 here and $5.00 there, and $10.00 there, and $25.00 there. And she came in one day and said, "Here is a big bill for steel, what in the world are we going to do? We can't go another step; the work has stopped."

I got on the train—just had a few minutes to catch the train. I told one of my boys, "Tell Mother I am gone to St. Louis." I didn't take time to change clothes, get a grip or anything. I went in to the offices of the insurance company and said, "What is the cash value of my insurance policy?"

And I will ask Mrs. Ruby Woodruff, the bookkeeper, what was the amount of cash of that insurance policy?

MRS. WOODRUFF: $7,000 and some odd dollars.

DR. NORRIS: And they gave me the cashier's check for $7,000 plus.

I came in and Miss Jane said, "What will your wife say about it?" I said, "I didn't tell her about it."

And so I have $7,000 in this church building you are now sitting in, and I never got seven cents of it back. Isn't that so, Ruby?

MRS. WOODRUFF: Yes, sir.

So we got along pretty well and I went down here to a friend of mine and said, "Say, I want to borrow $10,000."

He said, "What?"

I said, "I want to borrow $10,000."

He said, "I heard you the first time."

He said, "What security can you give."

I said, "My name and the Lord."

"Well," he said, "I know the Lord is all right." Well, I don't mind telling you his name, A. P. Barrett. And I said, "You have got to loan me $10,000 and don't argue about it." And so he loaned me the money. And every cent of that $10,000 went into this church.

Isn't that so?

MRS. WOODRUFF: Yes, sir.

DR. NORRIS: I ask you as bookkeeper to state whether I ever got any of this $10,000 back.

MRS. WOODRUFF: No, sir.

DR. NORRIS: But the bank was paid a long time ago. How did I pay it? I sweat blood and tears and went up and down the land and as the financial result of my meetings and lectures I paid it out in installments, and I consider the investment here the greatest that I ever made.

All enemies were doing their worst. All hell had conspired to destroy. The Sanballats, the Tobiahs, the Gashmus were circulating all kinds of evil reports. Many of the members were discouraged and the weaker ones fell by the wayside. But thanks be unto God for a great army that fought on—and fought on—and fought on.

And to the glory of the Head of the Church, this same body that I am now speaking to, this church, is as glorious as the sun, as fair as the moon, and as terrible as an army with banners.

The light and influence of this church, its work, its example, its New Testament plan have girdled the globe and going today as never before.

All the meetings that I hold, Bible conferences, evangelistic services, churches made over, including the Detroit church, all the meetings on this side and the other side of the seas—all are products of your work. And I repeat to you the words of the Apostle Paul concerning you. Rom. 1:8, "First I thank my God through Jesus Christ for you all, that your faith is spoken of throughout the whole world."

And again when he says concerning the church at Philippi, I say to you, "Ye are my joy and crown."

Such loyalty! Such sacrificial labors! Oh, not till the last wave of time reaches the farthest shore of eternity will you know, will I know, will the angels know the loyalty, the heroism, the fellowship, the glory of it all.

And we worked and paid for it and were happy to do it.

Now, why am I saying all this? I am saying it because those things happened while we were in the wilderness and we were glad to do it. Some day—listen to me—when the leaves of the eternal records unfold in the glory land on the other side, and we will have plenty of time then, and as dear Kate Tarlton used to say when a day's work was done after we had visited twenty-five or thirty homes—she would strike up the song:

"Trials dark on every hand, and we cannot understand
All the ways that God would lead us to that blessed Promised Land:
But He'll guide us with His eye, and we'll follow till we die,
For we'll understand it better bye and bye."

Don't be sorry for me. I have already got me one good country church over in Arkansas in the Ozark mountains. There is a beautiful little church and close by are some big oak trees. Some day you will get out here on the corner—some of you I baptized—and you will say, "The old man's clutch is slipping and he doesn't know it"—don't be sorry for me! But by the grace of God I am stronger today than ever before.

Yes, some day I know the outward man will fail.

Some day I know these eyes will grow dim.

Some day the hearing will grow dull.

Some day I know I can't drive at the same rate and energy I am now going.

Oftentimes I know not what it is to sleep more than three or four hours a night. My wife and I, just us two, when we have passed the four score years, ninety if the Lord tarries—some day you may pick up the newspaper—"Extra! Extra!"—They issued ten "Extras" in ten days once—some day you may get one, "J. Frank Norris is dead." You say, "That is another lie; he is not dead.

He just moved out of the old house and he is living on high"—
(shouting) don't be sorry for me. There's lots of joy in it. And
as we go upon this enlistment campaign our purpose is to have
joy. I would rather have one thousand people give a dollar than
to have one man give one thousand dollars. For that would mean
we would have a thousand people praying where we would have
only one. I would rather have ten thousand people bringing their
gifts backed by their tears and prayers than one man bringing ten
thousand dollars.

You will enjoy this, the folks up yonder at Detroit enjoyed it
one day. Many years ago when the Northern Convention and the
Southern Convention met at Washington, D. C., just a day between
we saw two old white haired men. And these two old men threw
their arms around each other and wept. When one of them spoke,
Dr. J. B. Gambrell, he referred to an incident that took place in
the hardest fought battle of the war. He said the earth was covered with the dying and the midnight hour was rent with shrieks
of the wounded and the suffering. The one word that went up from
every wounded boy whether North or South—"Water!"—"Water!"
—"Water!"—"Water!" And he said, "I with others. My life was
fast ebbing away. My lips were burning and parched. I was fast
lapsing down into deep unconsciousness, and I felt an arm. He
lifted me, and then I felt his canteen as he touched my fevered
lips, and I drank. And I said, 'What is your company, your division? He said he was not from the South, but he was a boy
from the North. I said, 'Thank you, I hope we will meet sometime when the war is over. If not, I hope we will meet on high'."

And when he told that story, he didn't know that in the audience
was another old white haired man. He arose and walked to the
platform and said, "I am the boy that gave you the water." And
that is the last word they said. What a happy reunion!

I said it is a picture of the hour when on Canaan's fair and
happy shores, when war will be no more—no more funerals, no
more tears, no more heartaches, no more sad farewells, but together—together—in the presence of the Lamb that sitteth upon
the throne, from the East and the West, from the North and the
South, from far off islands, they shall come and sit down together
with Abraham and Isaac and Jacob and Enoch and Noah, Joseph
and Moses and Joshua, Isaiah and Paul, Peter and James, and my
mother and my father and your father and your mother—and that
will be glory enough! Then we shall rejoice. What a wonderful
privilege to bear the cross, to wear the crown of thornes, to suffer

just a little bit—not much. Then when we come into His presence we will do like a painting I saw when all the field martials of Napoleon went to Fontainbleau Palace and stood outside with their battle-tattered flags of every division and folded them and presented them to him, their Emperor, and he with the golden scepter in his hand lifted and blessed them—he is gone. His empire is gone.

But I will tell you of Another who holds the scepter of Judah in his hands! His empire is spreading from shore to shore, from sea to sea, and he will reign till suns and moons rise and set to shine no more—long after yonder stars have been faded out of existence forever, and the heavens have passed away with a great noise, and all earth is only a pile of ruins, and nations shall know war no more—thanks be unto God we shall stand before Him and He will give us a crown incorruptible, undefiled, that fadeth not away!

Won't it be wonderful that we can all be there? You will be there. I will be there. And we will never say good-bye. We will never have a heart ache or a hurt, but a song that we will sing with Moses and the Lamb to the end of an endless eternity.

> "There's a land that is fairer than day,
> And by faith we can see it afar.
> For the Father waits over the way
> To prepare us a dwelling place there."

(The whole audience was tremendously moved. People broke and wept and shoutings were heard throughout the audience. Large numbers of penitents came rushing to the front. Several seats were filled. The services lasted long beyond the usual closing time, and it was past one o'clock when the people left.)

STATEMENT OF MR. W. J. BAILEY BEFORE GREAT CROWD THAT PACKED THE AUDITORIUM SUNDAY NIGHT, JANUARY 2, 1938

Mr. W. J. Bailey is one of the best known citizens in Fort Worth and in Texas who has stood in the highest ranks in the political and business world came to the front during the invitation with a large number of others and in making his confession of his faith in Christ stated as follows:

"I have heard tonight the greatest sermon of my life and from he greatest evangelist in North America. He has been through the fires of persecution and they have made him. Dr. George W. Truett spoke recently at the Kiwanis Club where I am a member, and forty years ago he happened to the great tragedy when he killed his friend, the chief of police, in Dallas accidentally. This sorrow broke his heart and he never smiles, but it made him one of the greatest preachers in Texas.

"I joined the Baptist Church when I was a boy in Mulberry, Tennessee. I have lived in this city for forty-five years. I want us to pray that God will bless Dr. Norris' labors as he goes up and down the land preaching the old time gospel. And I want us to make it possible for the whole world to hear this greatest of all evangelists."

There were 104 additions, breaking the previous New Year's record for additions of 99.

The testimony of this book is summed up in

Matt. 7:16, "Do men gather grapes of thorns, or figs of thistles?"

Matt. 11:4, "Go and show John again those things which ye do hear and see: The blind receive their sight, and the lame walk, the lepers are cleansed, and the deaf hear, the dead are raised up, and the poor have the gospel preached to them."

I Pet. 2:15, "For so is the will of God, that with well doing ye may put to silence the ignorance of foolish men."

Gen. 50:20, "But as for you, ye thought evil against me; but God meant it unto good, to bring to pass, as it is this day, to save much people alive."

TITLES IN THIS SERIES

The Evangelical Matrix
1875-1900

The Formation of
A Fundamentalist Agenda
1900-1920

Fundamentalism Versus Modernism
1920-1935

Sectarian Fundamentalism
1930-1950

■ 30. Charles G. Trumball
Prophecy's Light on Today
New York, 1937

■ 31. Joel A. Carpenter, ed.
Biblical Prophecy in an Apocalyptic Age:
Selected Writings of Louis S. Bauman
New York, 1988

■ 32. Joel A. Carpenter, ed.
Fighting Fundamentalism:
Polemical Thrusts of the 1930s and 1940s
New York, 1988

■ 33. *Inside History of First Baptist Church, Fort*
Worth, and Temple Baptist Church, Detroit:
Life Story of Dr. J. Frank Norris
Fort Worth, 1938

■ 34. John R. Rice
The Home — Courtship, Marriage, and Children: A
Biblical Manual of Twenty -Two Chapters
on the Christian Home.
Wheaton, 1945

■ 35. Joel A. Carpenter, ed.
Good Books and the Good Book: Reading Lists by
Wilbur M. Smith, Fundamentalist Bibliophile
New York, 1988

■ 36. H. A. Ironside
Random Reminiscences from Fifty Years of Ministry
New York, 1939

■ 37 Joel A. Carpenter,ed.
*Sacrificial Lives: Young Martyrs
and Fundamentalist Idealism*
New York, 1988.

Rebuilding, Regrouping, & Revival
1930-1950

■ 38. J. Elwin Wright
*The Old Fashioned Revival Hour
and the Broadcasters*
Boston, 1940

■ 39. Joel A. Carpenter, ed.
*Enterprising Fundamentalism:
Two Second-Generation Leaders*
New York, 1988

■ 40. Joel A. Carpenter, ed.
Missionary Innovation and Expansion
New York, 1988

■ 41. Joel A. Carpenter, ed.
*A New Evangelical Coalition: Early Documents
of the National Association of Evangelicals*
New York, 1988

■ 42. Carl McIntire
Twentieth Century Reformation
Collingswood, N. J., 1944

DATE DUE

HIGHSMITH   #LO-45220